MYSTERIES OF THE MESSIAH

UNVEILING DIVINE CONNECTIONS FROM GENESIS TO TODAY

RABBI JASON SOBEL

W PUBLISHING GROUP

AN IMPRINT OF THOMAS NELSON

Published in Nashville, Tennessee, by W Publishing Group, an imprint of Thomas Nelson.

Thomas Nelson titles may be purchased in bulk for educational, business, fundraising, or sales promotional use. For information, please e-mail SpecialMarkets@ThomasNelson.com.

Unless otherwise noted, Scripture quotations are taken from the Holy Scriptures, Tree of Life Version. © 2014, 2016 by the Tree of Life Bible Society. Used by permission of the Tree of Life Bible Society.

Scripture quotations marked AMPC are taken from the Amplified® Bible (AMPC), © 1954, 1958, 1962, 1964, 1965, 1987 by The Lockman Foundation. Used by permission.

Scripture quotations marked CJB are taken from the Complete Jewish Bible by David H. Stern. © 1998. All rights reserved. Used by permission of Messianic Jewish Publishers, 6120 Day Long Lane, Clarksville, MD 21029.

Scripture quotations marked CSB are taken from the Christian Standard Bible®. © 2017 by Holman Bible Publishers. Used by permission. Christian Standard Bible® and CSB® are federally registered trademarks of Holman Bible Publishers, all rights reserved.

Scripture quotations marked JPS are taken from the JPS TANAKH: The Holy Scriptures According to the Masoretic Text. © 1917 by the Jewish Publication Society of America. All rights reserved.

Scripture quotations marked KJV are taken from the King James Version of the Bible. Public domain.

Scripture quotations marked NASB are taken from the New American Standard Bible®, © 1960, 1962, 1963, 1968, 1971, 1972, 1973, 1975, 1977, 1995 by The Lockman Foundation. Used by permission. All rights reserved.

Scripture quotations marked NIV are taken from the Holy Bible, New International Version®, NIV®. © 1973, 1978, 1984, 2011 by Biblica, Inc.® Used by permission of Zondervan. All rights reserved worldwide.

Scripture quotations marked NKJV are taken from the New King James Version®. © 1982 by Thomas Nelson. Used by permission. All rights reserved.

Scripture quotations marked NLT are taken from the Holy Bible, New Living Translation, © 1996, 2004, 2015 by Tyndale House Foundation. Used by permission of Tyndale House Publishers, a Division of Tyndale House Ministries, Carol Stream, Illinois 60188. All rights reserved.

Scripture quotations marked NRSV are taken from the New Revised Standard Version Bible, © 1989 National Council of the Churches of Christ in the United States of America. Used by permission. All rights reserved worldwide.

Scripture quotations marked TPT are taken from The Passion Translation®. © 2017, 2018 by Passion & Fire Ministries, Inc. Used by permission. All rights reserved. ThePassionTranslation.com.

Boldface added to Scripture quotations are the author's emphasis.

Any internet addresses, phone numbers, or company or product information printed in this book are offered as a resource and are not intended in any way to be or to imply an endorsement by Thomas Nelson, nor does Thomas Nelson vouch for the existence, content, or services of these sites, phone numbers, companies, or products beyond the life of this book.

ISBN 978-0-7852-4006-8 (TP)

ISBN 978-0-7852-4588-9 (IE)

Library of Congress Cataloging-in-Publication Data:

Names: Sobel, Jason, author.
Title: Mysteries of the Messiah : unveiling divine connections from Genesis to today / Rabbi Jason Sobel.
Description: Nashville, Tennessee : W Publishing Group, an imprint of Thomas Nelson, [2021] | Includes bibliographical references. | Summary: "Highlighting connections that have been hidden from non-Jewish eyes, Rabbi Jason Sobel pulls back the curtain to shed God's light on the holy scriptures. Most people do not understand how the Bible fits together—even people of faith. Too many Christians accept half an inheritance in that they are content to embrace merely the New Testament. On the flip side, Jews often experience this by embracing only the Old Testament. But God has an intricate plan and purpose for both"— Provided by publisher.
Identifiers: LCCN 2020043903 (print) | LCCN 2020043904 (ebook) | ISBN 9780785240051 (hc) | ISBN 9780785240075 (ebook)
Subjects: LCSH: Messiah—Biblical teaching. | Jesus Christ—Messiahship. | Bible—Criticism, interpretation, etc.
Classification: LCC BS680.M4 S63 2021 (print) | LCC BS680.M4 (ebook) | DDC 232/.1—dc23
LC record available at https://lccn.loc.gov/2020043903
LC ebook record available at https://lccn.loc.gov/2020043904

Printed in the United States of America

22 23 24 25 26 27 LSC 10 9 8 7 6 5 4 3 2 1

To the most important people in my life:

Yeshua, my Messiah, who pursued me and
transformed me by His love and grace

My *eishet hayil* / woman of valor, Miriam, the one in
whom my heart delights. You have been such an incredible
source of encouragement, love, and support. I am eternally
thankful for you and will love you till my last breath!

And my whole family, Mom, Dad, Avi, Judah, Aunt
Carol, and Aunt Wendy, Mama, and Pop whom I miss
greatly. You have been the wind that has caused me to
rise above every situation and circumstance. I love you
all so much and can't imagine life without you!

CONTENTS

FOREWORD

I met Rabbi Jason Sobel in 2016 in New York during the frantic, hectic Christmas season. Hoda and I were exhausted from our schedule at the *Today* show, taping two, sometimes three shows a day so we finally would be able to take a two-week holiday. All I wanted to do was finish and hightail it down to the Florida Keys with my family and forget about everything that Rockefeller Center had come to represent to me at that time of year: chaos.

For six weeks every year, it became almost impossible to navigate the busy Manhattan streets. The crowds of tourists were festive and frenzied, yet to me it felt as though the season had nothing to do with the true meaning of Christmas—the celebration of the birth of Christ, the Messiah. Every year I felt a profound sadness that the message of God's love was seemingly nowhere to be found.

Then I met Rabbi Jason. That singular day changed my whole perspective and ultimately changed my life and the way I understood the Scriptures. In the course of a three-hour lunch at my favorite restaurant, Neary's Pub, I sat across from this stranger, basically, who literally and very patiently explained to me what actually happened in the Bible story more than two thousand years ago. What the Rabbi taught me lit a fire in my soul to study the word of God in its original source, the Hebrew and Greek languages. One year later Rabbi Jason and I wrote *The Rock, The Road, and the Rabbi*, which became a surprise bestselling book that is currently in its nineteenth printing.

There is a deep, innate, and, I believe, profound yearning in every human soul to know God intimately—not just to visit Him once a week or on Christmas Eve and Easter morning. How are we supposed to live every other nanosecond of our existence? What does God have to say about that? This is the eternal God of the Bible that Jason will introduce you to, perhaps for the first time.

Or maybe you are already a believer in Jesus (Yeshua), but you long to grow your faith and know His peace. In *Mysteries of the Messiah*, Rabbi Jason brilliantly explains the perfection and beauty of God's redemptive plan for all of humankind. It is truly a masterpiece of insight and illumination. Feast on it. Ponder it. And rejoice over it, for in Yeshua alone "we live and move and have our being" (Acts 17:28).

Shalom, shalom! And to Him be honor and praise forevermore.

Kathie Lee Gifford
December 2020

THE ADVENTURE BEGINS

Who doesn't love a mystery? Whether we're binge-watching a series on Netflix or turning book pages late into the night, we are driven by the desire to uncover clues and figure things out. Many of these stories revolve around a central figure, the protagonist, who works to solve the mystery and save the day.

The Bible is one of my favorite mystery books. From the opening words of Genesis to the final chapter of Revelation, God's Word is filled with tantalizing clues, fascinating revelations, and an extraordinary plot. Many of the Bible's mysteries have nagged at our imaginations for centuries. There are odd characters, dysfunctional families, bloody battles, and courageous heroes yet incredible wisdom within the writings. And readers ask, Who is this mystifying protagonist called the Messiah, the Redeemer who will come to save the world?

Mysteries of the Messiah will help you unlock some of these mysteries. You will learn not only about the Messiah but also how the Bible reveals Him and unveils His intense love for you and His relentless pursuit of redemption for all.

Connecting the Old Testament with the New Testament is essential to this book's investigation into the mysteries of the Bible. The catalyst is Matthew 13:52: "Every *Torah* scholar discipled for the kingdom of heaven is like the master of a household who brings out of his treasure **both new things and old.**"

Unfortunately, many people don't appreciate how the Old Testament and the New Testament fit together. Too many Christians accept half an inheritance by being content to embrace merely the "new." On the flip side, Jews have an incomplete picture when they embrace only the "old." We must not settle for either when *both* are essential to experience our full inheritance in the Kingdom and fully understand the Messiah.

In Matthew 13:52, Jesus referred to "old" and "new" treasures to draw an analogy between not only the two Testaments but also the Jews and Gentiles. Both are God's priceless possessions, neither more nor less valuable than the other. However, *together*, their value increases dramatically. Who would neglect old treasures just because new treasures exist?

Each chapter of *Mysteries of the Messiah* will spark connections between the old and new. As this happens, you will begin to see Scripture in high definition, gaining a clearer understanding of the Messiah and a new perspective on how His story flows through all the Bible. Like the disciples on the road to Emmaus (Luke 24:13–31), throughout this book you will learn these connections and will experience an unraveling revelation that will cause your heart to burn with increased hope and blessing. This revelation will cause a fiery yearning for Yeshua the Messiah.* It will give you a passion for the Torah† and a desire for the *Brit Chadashah* (New Testament)—a combination that ignites transformation and renewal within followers of Yeshua.

BEFORE YOU START YOUR ADVENTURE

Before you begin untangling the *Mysteries of the Messiah*, there are a few things you need to know that will help you on your journey.

---

* I use Jesus' Hebrew name, Yeshua, frequently in this book. It clearly reflects and reminds us of His Jewish roots.

† In Jewish tradition, "Torah" is most frequently used to designate the text of the first five books of the Bible, also called the Pentateuch.

Hebrew and Greek by the Numbers: The Code of Creation

Since English translations can dilute or lose some of the intended message, it's essential that we study the Bible based on its original languages of Hebrew and Greek. These two primary languages are genuinely beautiful and unique.

Most of the world's languages separate numbers from letters, but not Hebrew and Greek. Both languages use letters—their respective alphabets—for numbers. Each letter in the Hebrew and Greek alphabets has a numeric value.[1] Because of this, numbers can spell words, and words add up to numeric values. So both words and numbers are significant as we study the mysteries of the Messiah in the Bible. Let me share some common questions people have about biblical letters and numbers.

Why is it important to study the numbers? The Bible often uses numbers in patterns, and there is significance to many of these patterns. For example, the first word of Genesis 1:1 is *bereisheet*, "in the beginning." The first letter of *bereisheet* is *bet*, which has a numeric value of 2. Why is it significant that the first letter in the Bible has a numeric value of 2? Because God created the world in twos. He created heaven and earth. He created light and dark. He created day and night. He created the sun and the moon. He created the sea and the dry ground. He created man and woman. The letter *bet* also represents blessing. Only when these two opposites come together is God's blessing fully released.

How can I study the Bible using numbers? Here's an example of studying the significance of numbers in the Bible. The Lord told Moses to consecrate the tabernacle for eight days. On each of the previous seven days, Moses erected the tabernacle and took it down. But on the eighth day, the glory of God filled the tabernacle after Moses and Aaron blessed the people (Lev. 9).

Why did the Lord choose the eighth day?

- 8 = the number of vestments worn by the high priest (Ex. 28)
- 8 = sprinklings of blood on Yom Kippur for atonement (Lev. 16:14–15)

- 8 = spices used in the tabernacle, including the anointing oil and incense (Ex. 30:23–24, 34)
- 8 = instruments used by Levites, seven plus the voice of the choir[2]
- 8 = poles for carrying the holy vessels: the ark, the table, the golden altar, and the copper or brass altar (Ex. 25, 27, 39)

This repeated use of the number eight created a consistency and pointed to the person and work of the Messiah. For example, Yeshua died and rose from the dead on a Sunday, which is both the first day and the eighth day. The Messiah died on Friday, which is the sixth day. Like the Father, He rested on the seventh day after finishing the work of redemption. Then He rose on the eighth day. Can you see how studying words and numbers can help you connect the Testaments and go deeper in your Bible study?

How do numbers in the Bible work? The alphabet in Hebrew is called the *Aleph-Bet*. It derives its name from the first two letters of the Hebrew alphabet. When put together, the first letter, *aleph*, and the second letter, *bet*, spell the Hebrew word for father (*Ab*, as in *Abba*, "God the Father"). This communicates that the Hebrew alphabet derives from God the Father.

If added together, the letters in the name *Aleph-Bet* have the same value as "*aleph* and *tav*," the first and last letters of the Hebrew alphabet. Both phrases have a numeric value of 523, which underscores the intentional alphanumeric structure of Hebrew. But that's not all! *Aleph* and *tav* are the Hebrew equivalent of "the Alpha and Omega" (the first and last letters of the Greek alphabet), an expression Jesus used to describe Himself in Revelation 22:13: "I am the Alpha [*Aleph* in Hebrew] and the Omega [*Tav* in Hebrew], the First and the Last, the Beginning and the End." This is significant because 523 is also the full numeric value of

"Those who know Your Name trust You"	Psalm 9:11
"Immanuel"	Isaiah 7:14
"The virgin"	Matthew 1:23 in biblical Greek

The mathematical connection between these three key concepts shows how the entire *Aleph-Bet* (523) points to the Messiah.

What's more, since each letter in the Hebrew (or Greek) alphabet corresponds to a number, it is easy to determine the given value of any word from the Bible and use it to better understand the Scriptures. For example,

- The Hebrew word for "leper" (*metzora*) has a numeric value of 400 when the individual letters are added together. The number 400 is assigned to the Hebrew letter *tav*. This connection is significant because the ancient version of the letter *tav* was the shape of a cross. The cross (400) is the reason they scorned the Messiah and treated Him like a leper (*metzora*).
- In Greek, the word for "grain" (*kokkos*) has a numeric value of 400. Jesus said, "Amen, amen I tell you, unless a **grain** of wheat falls to the earth and dies, it remains alone. But if it dies, it produces much fruit" (John 12:24). *Katzir,* the Hebrew word for "harvest," also adds up to 400.
- Jesus died like a "grain" (*kokkos,* 400) on the "cross" (*tav,* 400), ultimately fulfilling His role as the "messianic leper" (*metzora,* 400) and bringing about a great spiritual "harvest" (*katzir,* 400)!
- The number 400 is also associated with God's pouring out of judgment (Ps. 69:25). Jesus became a "leper" (*metzora,* 400) and died like a piece of "grain" (*kokkos,* 400) on a "cross" (*tav,* 400) so that God would not "pour out" (*shofek,* 400) His judgment on us. Instead, we can personally experience that "the LORD is gracious and full of compassion" (Ps. 145:8 NKJV), which also equals 400 in Hebrew. What greater demonstration of grace, compassion, and love could there be?

Connections such as these make the study of the Bible's original words and their associated numbers fascinating and life-changing.

How far back does an alphanumeric understanding of Hebrew go? Coins from 78 BC provide the earliest archaeological evidence for the use of

Hebrew letters to represent numeric values.[3] They were issued by King Yannai, a Jewish Hasmonean king related to the Maccabees. The coins' inscription shows two Hebrew letters, *caf-heh*, representing the twenty-fifth year of Yannai's reign. It is likely that this alphanumeric understanding of Hebrew dates even further back in biblical times.

The first biblical use of letters in place of numbers can probably be found in 1 Samuel 13:1. Scholars have difficulty translating this verse because the Hebrew literally says, "A son of one year was Saul when he began to rule." The majority of translations either add a number or leave Saul's age blank, such as "Saul was ____ years old when he began to reign" (JPS). The issue is solved, however, when the first word of this verse, *ben*—which means "son"—is read alphanumerically as 52. This reading provides a logical solution and makes perfect sense when interpreted as "Saul was fifty-two years old when he began to reign over Israel." It also explains the apparent issue of how Saul's son Jonathan was an experienced warrior if Saul began to reign at age thirty, as many translations suggest.

During the time of the second temple, when Jesus lived, there is clear evidence that Hebrew and Greek alphanumeric values were used to reveal deeper insights. For example, the book of Revelation says, "Here is wisdom: let the one who has understanding calculate the number of the beast, for it is a number of a man, and his number is 666" (13:18). Six is the number for man in Hebrew. When something is repeated three times it means the maximum, which in this case is pointing to the biological aspect of man apart from the spiritual. It is indisputable that Hebrew and Greek alphanumeric structures provide deeper insight into the Scripture and corroborate theological truths, such as the virgin birth. But these numeric values should never be used to create novel interpretations that are unsupported by Scripture or that contradict its intended meaning.

Scientists and scholars often argue that we live in a mathematical world, and they think there isn't any way God spoke the world into existence. These scientists see a contradiction between the biblical and scientific accounts of origins. There is, however, no contradiction if we understand that letters and numbers are interchangeable. The words God spoke, their letters and the numbers associated with them, are not only the physical structure of our world but also the spiritual structure.

Underlying the physical reality of Creation itself is the number behind God's Word and the very mathematical structure of Creation. God is the original programmer. He spoke the world into existence, and each spoken word represented a number. In doing that, God created the "code of Creation."

How do I apply numbers to my daily life? Earlier, you learned the significance of the number eight and where it can be found throughout Scripture. However, the more important lesson is not where it's located but what it means and what it means to you. Remember, Jesus rose on the eighth day. His resurrection redeemed you; it released you from the bondage of sin. How do you apply the Hebrew value of eight? You can declare freedom from the slavery of sin and walk in His ways. You can apply the numbers by realizing what they mean and gaining a deeper understanding of what God is telling you in His Word. You can declare, as the church fathers would say, "Every Sunday is a mini Easter"—or, in this case, another eighth day.

The Rabbis and Jewish Tradition

The Bible was written in a Jewish context. Jesus Himself was a Jew and a popular teacher of the Torah who was called "Rabbi" by the disciples and the crowds (Matt. 26:49; Mark 9:5, 10:51, 11:21; John 1:49, 20:16). Yet many Christians are unfamiliar with the Jewish interpretative tradition that forms part of the background for the New Testament. A better appreciation of this can lead to a richer understanding of both the Old and New Testaments.

The primary text of Judaism is the Old Testament (*Tanakh*), or the Hebrew Bible. The *Tanakh* has the same number of books as the Christian Bible's Old Testament, only they are arranged a bit differently. Much of the Hebrew Bible was handed down orally from generation to generation.

Jewish thought and Bible commentary are not a single or continuous tradition but rather a mixture of works from centuries of study. For several of the sources, the dating is even a mix of times. The writers reflect specific theological thoughts and historical positions. Also, many of the works were oral teachings that were later written.

What makes these works important is they represent Jewish thinking about the Bible and help us see things from different perspectives. These diverse perspectives are critical as you learn to connect the Old Testament with the New Testament. As Lois Tverberg pointed out, the insights of sages and rabbis from long ago help us understand that "Jesus was taking part in a tradition known for generations before his time. This makes all the difference in the world in terms of painting the Jewish reality around him."[4]

In this book I reference several sources from many centuries of Jewish thought. These sources help us open up the Jewish meaning of many passages and their connection to the Messiah and New Testament. Just as Christian pastors and teachers use multiple sources to explain Scripture, we are bringing together essential sources to study the Messiah.

Around AD 200, Jewish scholars compiled the *Mishnah*—written text describing and explaining the Jewish law code that was mostly oral before that time.

Later, the Talmud, a collection of teachings and commentaries on Jewish law, was created. The Talmud contains the *Mishnah* and other texts, plus biblical interpretations from thousands of rabbis. They finalized the first Talmud around the third century AD. The rabbis completed a second edition in the fifth century AD.

Midrash is a Jewish method of interpreting Scripture as well as a compilation of such interpretations, which were composed between AD 400 and 1200. The Hebrew term *Midrash* comes from the biblical verb *darash*, which means "to seek out" or "to inquire." The rabbis were sensitive to the details in Scripture and therefore found meaning in every nuance of the text. For example, *Midrash* finds profound meaning and unique new insights in words, letters, unusual spellings, phrases, missing letters, and so on. The rabbis, like good detectives, often questioned the text in pursuit of greater wisdom and truth. Midrashic insights never replace the literal meaning of the text but are intended to stand alongside it as an additional layer that clarifies a question, solves an issue in the text, or makes a practical application to the reader's life.

Judaism embraces many other texts and commentaries written by rabbis over the centuries. *Mysteries of the Messiah* uses these to help connect the Old Testament to the New Testament. Since many manuscripts were compilations, we don't know who the scholars were. For that reason, this book includes references to "the rabbis" or "Jewish tradition" without specific citations or notes. Extensive research has gone into this book, and these rabbinical resources are invaluable for us to understand the connections and mysteries of our Messiah.

The Tree of Life Version of the Bible

Most of the Scripture references in this book are from the Tree of Life Version of the Bible. The Tree of Life Version speaks with a decidedly Jewish-friendly voice—a voice like the Bible authors themselves—to recover the authentic context of the Scriptures and biblical faith. It was produced by Messianic Jewish and Christian scholars who sought to highlight the rich Hebrew roots of the Christian faith. Since this translation restores the Jewish order and numbering of the books of the Old Testament, you may find that certain verse citations are one number off.

A FINAL THOUGHT

In essence this book is about the Messiah and unveiling the factual story that He is not merely a New Testament, end-times persona. Instead, the Messiah and the mysteries wrapped around Him are found throughout the entire Bible, starting in Genesis and ending in Revelation.

I hope *Mysteries of the Messiah* will bring you insights about the Redeemer and how He can be discovered in the many connections throughout the Old and New Testaments. It's my earnest prayer that the uncovering of these mysteries will give you eye-opening moments and new ways to reflect on your life and the Messiah who came to die for you, live again for you, and give you incredible hope for a future with Him.

Baruch HaShem! Praise God!

chapter
ONE

THE JOB DESCRIPTION
OF THE MESSIAH

As a young Jewish boy growing up on the streets of New Jersey, I encountered many things that influenced me. My parents and their faith were my heritage, but my friends and their ways were different. It was a little challenging to reconcile everything. But while I became fluent in the culture, even learning how to "rap with my homies," I remained faithful to our Jewish tradition. Not just because I had to but because I wanted to. Yet I often felt there was something more.

At the age of eighteen I found myself one day in a state of meditation. This was something I did regularly as I attempted to figure out things in the midst of a world that was constantly pulling me away from spiritual things. It was an ordinary day but a truly extraordinary experience in that I had a personal encounter with Yeshua. This was the first time I'd ever felt as though the Lord was speaking directly to me. It was so unbelievable and yet so real, and I will never forget His words. He said, "Many are called, but few are chosen."

In my innermost being I knew exactly what he was saying, but I needed to ask, "Lord, am I chosen?"

He sweetly smiled and replied, "Yes."

I was overcome by the peace and presence of God—energized and in awe of the experience. I felt as if I were in a state of euphoria. This filling, which was much like an indwelling, kept me in a state of deep contentment. I ran down the steps and into my front yard. Not caring who was watching, I jumped up and down, screaming at the top of my lungs, "I am called to serve Him! I am called to serve Him!"

At this same moment my mom pulled into the driveway and saw her good little Jewish son running around in circles like a crazy man for all the neighbors to gawk at. Surely she thought I was *mashugana* (a Yiddish term describing a person who is nonsensical or silly). I didn't care; I was so elated by the fact that God, the God who created the universe, wanted to use me.

Although she did not understand what was happening to me, my mother did not want to rain on my parade. There was only one problem. I wondered, *What does it look like for a nice Jewish boy to begin serving Yeshua?* I had no clue.

My best friend was John. I met him as part of a wannabe Filipino gang. We became close, practicing martial arts together and discussing spiritual things. By this time, John had become a believer in Yeshua and talked about it with me as often as possible. One day he called and asked, "You went to Hebrew school as a child, right? Do you think you could tell the difference between the Old and New Testaments if I read you some passages?"

I said, "Sure."

He read me a passage about this guy dying on a cross and asked if it was from the Old or New Testament.

I said, "Obviously it's from the New Testament because it's talking about Jesus."

He read another passage: "He was pierced for our transgressions, He was crushed for our iniquities. . . . He was led like a lamb to the slaughter." Then he asked, "Is this from the Old or New Testament?"

I said, "It must be from the New Testament because it sounds like it's talking about Jesus."

John paused, then said, "It's from the Old Testament, from Isaiah 53 [vv. 5, 7 NIV]. Isaiah was a Jewish prophet who lived seven hundred years before the Messiah was born."

That got my attention.

After our conversation I agreed to go with John to the messianic synagogue led by Rabbi Jonathan Cahn, who would later write the highly acclaimed and bestselling novel *The Harbinger*.

During the service, Rabbi Cahn talked about being "born anew," but I didn't think a good Jewish boy should ever do that. However, when he gave the invitation, I stood up. Rabbi Cahn led me in a prayer to receive Yeshua. My friend had prayed to lead one Jewish person to faith in Messiah Jesus, but he never thought it would be me.

After the service I was given the first New Testament I had ever seen. I took it home, not quite sure what had just happened, and hid it in my room—God forbid my parents should find it. Of course, Mom did find it and confronted me: "What is this? Don't tell me you're a Jew thinking about believing in Jesus!"

By then, I had read the New Testament and believed that Jesus was the One that Moses and the prophets had foretold. He was the One who spoke the words of eternal life.

My mom was concerned and called our rabbi to meet with me. I knew I needed to verify for myself that Yeshua was the Messiah of the Hebrew Bible. As I studied in preparation for my meeting with the rabbi, I made a list of all the messianic promises and prophecies in the Hebrew Scriptures that I could find. I wanted to make sure I clearly understood and could articulate what I believed about the Messiah based on the Hebrew Bible and Jewish sources.

The rabbi asked me how I had come to believe in Yeshua as the Messiah, and I read all the passages that had impacted me. This chapter is a fuller version of what I shared in our meeting.

There are five major areas that reveal key clues about the Messiah: (1) His humanity, (2) His ethnicity and tribal identity, (3) His royalty, (4) His virgin birth and divinity, and (5) His suffering and rejection. All of these create a powerful, prophetic portrait of the person and work of Yeshua, the Messiah.

THE MESSIAH'S HUMANITY

The LORD God said to the woman, "What is this you have done?"

The woman said, "The serpent deceived me, and I ate."

So the LORD God said to the serpent, "Because you have done this,

"Cursed are you above all livestock
　　and all wild animals!
You will crawl on your belly
　　and you will eat dust
　　all the days of your life.
And I will put enmity
　　between you and the woman,
　　and between your offspring and hers;
he will crush your head,
　　and you will strike his heel."

—Genesis 3:13–15 NIV

In the aftermath of the Fall, the Lord appeared in the garden, offering a ray of hope. God promised Adam and Eve, the parents of humanity, that in the future a seed ("offspring") would be born who would defeat the serpent. This first prophecy about the coming Messiah is the root from which all other messianic prophecies sprout.

The Creation and fall of humanity are connected to the number six. Man was created on the sixth day, and in Jewish thought the Fall occurred on the sixth day. In order to understand this, we must explore the meaning of the number six from a Hebraic perspective. As I explained in the introduction, the Hebrew language is alphanumeric: each letter has a numeric value, and numbers are written with letters. The number six is written with the letter *vav*. *Vav* is the sixth letter of the Hebrew alphabet and appears for the first time in the Bible at the beginning of the sixth Hebrew word of Genesis 1:1, where it functions as the conjunction "and." "In the beginning God created the heavens **and [*vav*]** the earth." In this verse, *vav* literally connects "heavens" and "earth." When Adam and Eve sinned, they broke the *vav*, the connection between heaven and earth, which, again, according to Jewish tradition, happened on the sixth day (a Friday). We revisit another significant biblical use of the letter *vav* in the last chapter of this book.

The "mark of the beast" (Rev. 16:2), which, as I also mentioned in the introduction is 666 (Rev. 13:18), connects to the letter *vav*. There are six dimensions of the physical world, as seen in the six factors that make up the basic units of measurement—**length**, comprised of (1) left and (2) right sides; **breadth**, which is (3) front and (4) back; and **depth**, which is (5) top and (6) bottom. The numeric value of *vav* also corresponds to the six directions of the physical universe: (1) north, (2) south, (3) east, (4) west, (5) above/up, and (6) below/down. Since Adam and Eve were created on the sixth day, this also makes the number six the number of mankind.

How does this tie to 666, Satan the serpent, and the mark of the beast? In Hebrew, anything said or written three times expresses the highest degree or quality. The reason the angels cry out, "Holy, holy, holy" is because they are declaring that the Lord is the One who exhibits maximum, complete, and ultimate holiness (Isa. 6:3). Since six represents the number of the physical world, 666 (the number six expressed to the highest degree) represents total materialism. It is complete physicality, earth apart from heaven.

In the beginning, God created heaven and earth, and He created mankind to embody the ideal union between heaven and earth. We find this ideal union in the name of the first man, Adam. In Hebrew, Adam's name means "man," and it is comprised of three letters: *aleph*, *dalet*, and *mem*. Man, who is a microcosm of Creation, has both a physical body and spiritual soul. Likewise, Adam's name can be broken into these two parts. The Hebrew letter *aleph* represents the spiritual aspect of man: his soul. The name of God used in the Creation account, *Elohim*, also begins with the letter *aleph*, which underscores the connection between *aleph* and the spiritual part of mankind. The other two letters of Adam's name, *dalet* and *mem*, spell "blood" in Hebrew, which points to the physical aspect of humanity. The image of God can only be fully expressed when the physical and spiritual aspects of humans, represented by the three letters of Adam's name, are completely connected.

Satan's goal is for humanity to focus on our physical needs at the expense of our souls, so that we become no better than animals, no longer bearing God's image in the world but instead bearing the mark of the beast (666).

The Fall can be summarized by one word: "exile" (Hebrew, *golah*). The antidote to exile is redemption (*geulah*). In Hebrew, there is only a one-letter difference between the words "exile" and "redemption"—the letter *aleph*, the letter of God's name. When the Lord is removed from our lives—from our families, from our nation, and from the world—we are left in a state of chaos and exile. The promise of Genesis 3:15, commonly referred to as the protoevangelium (literally, "first Gospel"), is that the Seed of the woman, the Messiah, would come and reverse the effects of sin and death caused by Adam and Eve's disobedience. The promised messianic Seed of the woman died on a Friday, the sixth day of the Hebrew week, to restore the *vav*, the connection between heaven and earth.

THE MESSIAH'S ETHNICITY AND TRIBAL IDENTITY

Now the LORD had said to Abram:

"Get out of your country,
From your family
And from your father's house,
To a land that I will show you.
I will make you a great nation;
I will bless you
And make your name great;
And you shall be a blessing.
I will bless those who bless you,
And I will curse him who curses you;
And in you all the families of the earth shall
be blessed."

—*Genesis 12:1–3* NKJV

"I will richly bless you and bountifully multiply your seed like the stars of heaven, and like the sand that is on the seashore, and your seed will possess the gate of his enemies."

—*Genesis 22:17*

The Lord made a promise to Abraham that through him and his descendants the blessings that were lost in Eden would be restored. From this point on, the identification of Abraham's offspring, his seed, becomes one of the chief themes of the Torah. This is seen in the supernatural births of Abraham's son Isaac and his grandson Jacob. Furthermore, the Lord was at work in the births of Isaac's twin sons and chose Jacob over Esau.

The next puzzle piece of the Messiah's identity is found in the Shiloh prophecy: "The scepter shall not depart from Judah, nor a lawgiver from between his feet, until **Shiloh** comes; and to Him shall be the obedience of the people" (Gen. 49:10 NKJV). Many Bible versions translate "Shiloh" as "he to whom it belongs." The Shiloh prophecy provides the critical detail that the Seed of the woman would not only be a descendant of Abraham, Isaac, and Jacob but, more specifically, a descendant of the tribe of Judah.

The numeric value of "Shiloh," which is understood to be one of the names of the Messiah, alludes to another key aspect of the mystery of the Messiah: His divine identity. Its value of 345 is the same as "God Almighty" (*El Shaddai*). Today, traditional Jews don't pronounce the divine name, *YHVH* (*YAHWEH)*, but rather use the term *HaShem*, which means "The Name." *HaShem* equals 345 as well. The Messiah, who is known as Shiloh (345), will be the incarnation of *El Shaddai* (345) and *HaShem* (345), as in His name is the "name that is above every name" (Phil. 2:9). This prophecy also tells us that the Messiah would be a King from the tribe of Judah who would rule over Israel and the nations. It even provides answers to the mystery of the time of the Messiah's coming. We will talk more about this in chapter 4.

THE MESSIAH'S ROYALTY

> Now therefore, thus shall you say to My servant David, "Thus says the LORD of hosts,
> 'I took you from the sheepfold, from following the sheep, to be ruler over My people,
> over Israel. And I . . . have made you a great name, like the name of the great men
> who are on the earth. . . . Also the LORD tells you that He will make you a house.
>
> 'When your days are fulfilled and you rest with your fathers, I will set up your seed
> after you, who will come from your body, and I will establish his kingdom. He shall
> build a house for My name, and **I will establish the throne of his kingdom forever.**'"
>
> *—2 Samuel 7:8–9, 11–13 NKJV*

Based on 2 Samuel 7, the identity of the Messiah narrows even further. He would be from the tribe of Judah and also a direct descendant of David—thus, the Messiah is called the "Son of David." The Hebrew prophets also gave Him the name of "the Branch" (Hebrew, *Tzemach*). "In those days and at that time, I will cause a **Branch** of Righteousness to spring up for David, and He will execute justice and righteousness in the land" (Jer. 33:15; see also Zech. 3:8, 6:12). Isaiah speaks of the promised Branch (Messiah) who will restore glory to Zion in the end times (Isa. 4:2). Speaking on the messianic nature of this passage, the rabbis wrote, "What is the name of King Messiah? R. Abba bar Kahana said: 'Lord [*ADONAI*] is his name, for it is written, I will raise unto David a righteous **branch** (shoot) . . . In his days Judah shall be saved.'"[1]

The Hebrew letters of *Tzemach* ("Branch") total 138, which ties to two other key messianic prophecies in the book of Isaiah. Speaking of the birth of the Messiah, Isaiah 9:6 says, "To us a son is given" (NIV). The Hebrew phrase "to us a son" equals 138, along with "the LORD shall prosper [*yitzlach*]" in Isaiah 53:10 (NKJV). What's even more amazing is that 138 is the mathematical value of "Son of God" (*Ben Elohim*). This alludes to the son, spoken of in Isaiah 9:6, who is also the Branch (138) and the divine "Son of God" (138), who will cause the will of the Lord to "prosper" (138). The Messiah is also "the vine" (*hagefen*) who causes us to bear much fruit (John 15:5).

One of the results of the curse of the Fall is that from the ground "thorns and thistles will sprout" (Gen. 3:18). The word "sprout" in Hebrew is *tatzmiach*, which is the verb form of *Tzemach* (Branch). This is a sign of the physical curse that was brought on Creation as a result of Adam and Eve's sin. This curse was reversed as the Messiah hung on the cross. Jesus took the physical curse of Creation—with a crown of thorns on His head—and paid the price to reverse it.

The Branch prophecies are key to understanding the name of Jesus. There is a specific prophecy regarding the name Yeshua, found in two passages from Zechariah and one from Ezra, which contains the word "Branch." It starts with Zechariah 3:8:

> Listen well, Joshua [**Yeshoshua**] *kohen gadol* [high priest], both you and your companions seated before you, because they are men who are **a sign**—behold, I will bring forth **My servant the Branch**.

The high priest Yehoshua played a key role in building the second temple. He became a symbol of the Messiah.

Zechariah 6:12 elaborates further on the mystery of the One who is called the Branch:

> Then speak to him saying, "Thus says *ADONAI-Tzva'ot* [the LORD of Hosts]: Behold, a man whose Name is the **Branch will branch out** from his place and build the Temple of *ADONAI*.

The Branch is associated with Yehoshua the priest, but he is not the Branch. Yet the Branch will have the same name. Therefore, the prophet Zechariah revealed the hidden name of the Messiah to be *Yehoshua*.[2]

How then do we get Yeshua? It became a common practice to shorten Hebrew names like *Yehoshua*, which started with the root *Yehovah* (Jehovah). Yeshua is a shortened form of *Yehoshua*, as seen in Ezra 5:2. The Messiah being named Yeshua (Matt. 1:21, 25) was a fulfillment of prophecy. To meet one of the critical requirements of the Messiah's lineage, the promised

Redeemer would need to be a descendant of Abraham, Isaac, and Jacob and come from the tribe of Judah, from the family of David.

THE MESSIAH'S VIRGIN BIRTH AND DIVINITY

Therefore *ADONAI* Himself will give you a sign:

> Behold, the virgin will conceive.
> When she is giving birth to a son,
> she will call his name Immanuel.

—Isaiah 7:14

What is the spiritual significance of a virgin birth? Why is this a sign for the Messiah?

Genesis 3:15, the first messianic prophecy we studied, says the Seed of the woman would crush the head of the serpent. This is an interesting phrase, since seed ("offspring" or "descendant") is usually associated with men. For example, the "descendant of Abraham" (Isa. 41:8), "Jacob's descendants" (Ps. 22:24), and the "offspring of David" (Jer. 33:22). Isaiah 7:14 sheds further light on this by revealing that the promised Seed would be born of a virgin. Since the Messiah would not have a biological human father, it makes perfect sense that the Messiah is associated with the woman in Genesis 3:15.

The virgin birth is spiritually significant, for the Messiah's unique birth points to His identity as Immanuel, "God with us." The Messiah, the One "born of a woman" (Gal. 4:4), would be different than any other king in the history of Israel. By looking at Isaiah 7:14 in the greater context of Isaiah 9:5–6, this becomes even more evident:

> For to us a child is born,
> a son will be given to us,
> and the government will be upon His shoulder.
> His Name will be called

> Wonderful Counselor [*Pele Yoetz*],
> Mighty God [*El Gibbor*]
> My Father of Eternity [*Aviad*],
> Prince of Peace [*Sar Shalom*].
> Of the increase of His government
>> and *shalom* there will be no end—
> on the throne of David and over His kingdom.

For centuries Christians have applied this well-known passage from Isaiah 9 to Jesus. Jewish tradition also affirms this understanding: "The Messiah will be called by eight names: *Yinnon* (He shall flourish), *Tzemach* (Branch), *Pele* (Miracle/Wonderful), *Yo'etz* (Counselor), *Mashiah* (Messiah), *El* (G-d), *Gibbor* (Hero), and *Avi 'Ad Shalom* (Eternal Father of Peace)."[3]

The majority of Jews, however, do not see the names mentioned in Isaiah 9:5–6 as prophesying a divine Messiah. The divinity of the Messiah has historically been a major point of contention between followers of Jesus and the rabbis. There are, however, many clues seemingly hidden in Scripture that do point to the Messiah as being divine.

Isaiah 9:6 states, "Of the increase of His government and *shalom* there will be no end." The Hebrew letter *mem* in the phrase "of the increase" (לסרבה) is grammatically incorrect. In Hebrew, there are two ways to write the letter *mem*, open (מ) and closed (ם). The open *mem* gets its name from its shape—there is an opening on its left side. The open *mem* can be used anywhere in a Hebrew word except as the last letter. The closed letter *mem*, also known as the final *mem*, is used exclusively when the letter comes at the end of a word. Why, then, is the closed—final—*mem* used in the expression "of the increase" (*leMarbeh* / לסרבה)?

The rabbis teach that the letter *mem* can represent a woman's womb. In Hebrew, which is read from right to left, one of the biblical terms for "womb"—*me'eh* (מֶעָה) begins with the open *mem* (Ruth 1:11). The open *mem* represents an open womb—the ability for a woman to conceive in a normal way. The use of the closed *mem* in Isaiah 9:6 alludes to the fact that the Messiah would be conceived miraculously through a woman with a closed womb, one who should not naturally be able to bear a child. This refers to the virgin spoken of in Isaiah 7:14.

The two letter *mems* in Jewish tradition also point to the two great redeemers. The open *mem* points to Moses, who came as the first redeemer and who is a type of the Messiah (Deut. 18:18). The closed, or final, *mem* is symbolic of the second Redeemer, the Messiah, who will come at the end of history and bring final redemption. Another reason the final *mem* is used in the middle of the phrase in Isaiah 9:6 in the word "increase" (*leMarbeh* / למרבה) is because the Messiah, the One born of a virgin, will complete the work of salvation as the second Redeemer at the end of time.

The name of the young virgin who bore Yeshua is Mary—*Miriam* in Hebrew, which also begins with the letter *mem*. Thus, the letter *mem* also hints at the name of the virgin who would bear the Messiah, whose Hebrew title, *Mashiach*, likewise begins with the letter *mem*.

The numbers, too, allude to the identity of the Messiah as being divine. The phrase "his name Immanuel" (Isa. 7:14) in Hebrew (*shemo Imanu El*) has the numeric value of 545. This is the same numeric value of "the Name of *ADONAI*, the Everlasting God [*Shem YHVH El Olam*]" (Gen. 21:33) and "I AM WHO I AM [*Eyeh Asher Eyeh*]" (Ex. 3:14). The number 545 is also the numeric value of "my God, You are very great" (Ps. 104:1) and "the kingdom belongs to *ADONAI*, and He rules over the nations" (Ps. 22:29). The Messiah—Immanuel, the "Name of *ADONAI*, the Everlasting God," the "I AM"—became incarnate in the person of Yeshua.

The Messiah would be a King who would usher in a time of peace and prosperity for the entire world. The Messiah would be both human and divine. His divine nature is clearly seen in the names ascribed to Him in these passages.

THE MESSIAH'S SUFFERING AND REJECTION

He was despised and rejected by men,
a man of sorrows, acquainted with grief,

One from whom people hide their faces.

He was despised, and we did not esteem Him.

Surely He has borne our griefs

and carried our pains.

Yet we esteemed Him stricken,

struck by God, and afflicted.

But He was pierced because of our transgressions,

crushed because of our iniquities.

The chastisement for our *shalom* was upon Him,

and by His stripes we are healed.

—Isaiah 53:3–5

When my Christian friend John witnessed to me by reading Isaiah 53, I was absolutely intrigued and wanted to know more. It seemed clear from those verses that the Messiah was going to be rejected, suffer, and die as an atonement for sin. Growing up in the synagogue, I had heard many passages from the book of Isaiah as part of the weekly Torah reading but never Isaiah 53. So when my mom made me meet with my rabbi, I thought this passage would surely help him understand why I came to believe that Yeshua was the promised Messiah spoken of in the Torah and the prophets.

He tried to refute my claim by asserting that the suffering servant spoken of in Isaiah 53 was referring to the Jewish people, who have suffered throughout the centuries for their faith. Many rabbis and scholars hold this view, but their view is not the historic Jewish interpretation of Isaiah 53. Here's one ancient rabbinical interpretation: "Behold my servant Messiah shall prosper; he shall be high, and increase, and be exceeding strong."[4]

Medieval Rabbi Mosheh Kohen Ibn Crispin wrote:

This prophecy was delivered by Isaiah at the divine command for the purpose of making known to us something about the nature of the future Messiah, who is to come and deliver Israel, and his life from the day when he arrives at discretion until his advent as a redeemer, in order that if anyone should arise claiming to be himself the Messiah, we may reflect, and look to see whether we can observe in him any resemblance to the traits described here; if there is any such resemblance, then we may believe that he is the Messiah our righteousness; but if not, we cannot do so.[5]

The view of a suffering Messiah is also supported by many other texts, including Zechariah 12:10, Psalm 22, and the interesting numeric connection found in Isaiah 9:5. The numeric value of the four names mentioned in this verse from Isaiah—"Wonderful Counselor" (287), "Mighty God" (242), "My Father of Eternity" (87), and "Prince of Peace" (876)—add up to 1492. Two expressions in Isaiah 53 add up to this same amount: "He was afflicted yet He did not open His mouth. Like a lamb led to the slaughter, like a sheep" (v. 7) and "in His death, though He had done no violence, nor was there any deceit in His mouth" (v. 9). The phrases "[The LORD] declares to my Lord: 'Sit at My right hand until I make your enemies a footstool'" (Ps. 110:1) and "God created the heavens and the earth" (Gen 1:1) also add up to 1492.* The shared numeric value of these words connects them together and points out that the suffering servant is not Israel but the Messiah, who would have both a divine and human nature.

A critical part of the Messiah's job description required Him to be rejected by His people, Israel. He would suffer, die, and be resurrected in atonement for the transgressions of Israel and the nations. Ultimately the people of Israel will recognize the error of their ways and return to their Messiah, who suffered in order to bring them abundant life in this age and eternal life in the world to come. This national realization will occur in the end of days, according to Hosea 3:4–5:

> For the sons of Israel will live for many days without a king or leader, without sacrifice or memorial stone, and without ephod or household idols. Afterward the sons of Israel will return and seek the LORD their

---

* To make the spiritual connection, the word "earth" is not included in the numeric value.

God and David their king; and they will come trembling to the LORD and to His goodness in **the last days**. (NASB)

More than any other passage of Scripture, the Lord has used Isaiah 53 to open the eyes and hearts of Jewish people like myself to the truth that Yeshua is the promised Messiah.

WHAT THESE DIVINE CONNECTIONS MEAN FOR YOU AND ME

My rabbi and I had several discussions after our initial talk. But, in the end, we agreed to disagree about Yeshua being the Messiah. Preparing for those discussions and others like them strengthened my faith and gave me a deeper passion for Messiah Yeshua.

As a result of my newfound faith, my Jewish identity increased tremendously. Suddenly the Jewish traditions I had grown up with took on deeper spiritual significance. I had a deeper connection with and understanding of who the Messiah was and what He came to do. All the prophets foretold that the Messiah would bring the Jewish people back to covenantal faithfulness and strengthen their commitment to Jewish life and their calling to be a blessing to the people of Israel and to all nations.

I believe that by discovering the connections between the Old Testament and New Testament, your life can be transformed like mine. I liken it to experiencing your faith in high definition. Many years ago, when I bought a high-definition TV, I couldn't wait to watch the Super Bowl, but I was a bit disappointed by the experience. After the game ended, I groaned as I discovered that there were standard definition and high definition options for the same channel—and I hadn't watched the game in HD. If I had, it would have been a different game—with richness, detail, and vivid color. I fully realized my loss when I changed channels and had a comparison.

Similarly, by understanding and reading the Scripture in a way that connects the Old and New Testaments, we introduce ourselves to the Jewish roots of our faith and gain a heightened perspective. We begin to see Jesus' life and ministry from a different viewpoint, through Jewish eyes. When you "see" Jesus and the Bible in HD, you enjoy greater richness, sharpness, and clarity of details that you would have otherwise missed.

Another crucial reason to study both Testaments is that when the Jewish *roots* and Gentile *shoots* connect, spiritual revelation, renewal, and transformation occur. A notable example of this is found in Luke 24. Two grieving disciples were on the road to the town of Emmaus after the death of Yeshua. The risen Jesus encountered them, but they didn't recognize Him. He questioned their sadness, and they recounted the horror and disappointment of recent days. Jesus spoke from the Scriptures to these men. He tracked through the Old Testament prophecies about the Messiah. He taught them the cohesive message of both Testaments, and then **"their eyes were opened and they knew Him**; and He vanished from their sight" (Luke 24:31 NKJV).

Like these men, my life has been radically transformed by delving into the divine connections that reveal the mysteries of the Messiah. And I have seen numerous other lives changed completely when people learn how the Old and the New Testaments connect. Many, like myself, wondered if there was more to the Bible—and when they found it, a new love for Jesus and a passion for the Word ignited within them. I believe that our continued exploration of the mysteries of the Messiah will bring greater hope and transformation in your life too.

chapter
TWO

THE MESSIAH OF CREATION
Adam and Eve

At some point in most every situation we encounter, we find ourselves asking, "I wonder where this all began? What started things going in this direction?" Not only is it helpful to know the backstory, it's important to be aware of the foundation upon which the thing is built.

The Creation account is where it began for all of us and the world we live in today. It was not written to provide a deeply scientific or detailed history of how the universe came into being. Rather, it sets the foundation for the much larger story of Scripture, which focuses on relationship, redemption, and restoration.

Within the story of Creation are beautiful and essential insights into the person and work of the Messiah as well as profound wisdom on who God is and how we can walk with Him. This chapter explores these transformational truths.

FROM THE BEGINNING TO THE END, IT ALL POINTS TO THE MESSIAH

"In the beginning God created the heavens and the earth" (Gen. 1:1). The very first letter of the Bible is *bet*, the second letter of the Hebrew alphabet.

The rabbis have questioned why the Torah doesn't begin with the letter *aleph* since most of the names of God begin with this letter—*Elohim* (God), *ADONAI* (Lord), *Adon Olam* (Master of the Universe), *El Shaddai* (God Almighty), to name a few. The letter *aleph* is the first letter of *Abba*, "God the Father," and has the numeric value of 1, which points to the cardinal tenet of Judaism: "the LORD is one" (Deut. 6:4). Why, then, would the Torah start with the letter *bet* and not *aleph*?

One of the main reasons given by the rabbis is because *bet* is the first letter of the word for "blessing": *beracha*. God created the world to be a blessing, and only through His blessing would the world endure. The letter *aleph*, however, is the first letter of the word for "curse": *arirah*.[1] God created the world for blessing and not for cursing.

The letter *bet*, with a numeric value of 2, also alludes to the fact that there are two worlds—this world and the world to come.* This world prepares us for the place of ultimate blessing. The *bet* is a reminder that we are not living for this world but for the sake of the next. God created the world in twos—heavens and earth, spiritual and material. These are meant to work in harmony.

While both of the above explanations are true, they miss the primary point. The last word in Revelation, the Hebrew word *amen*, ends with the letter *nun*. And when you put the first letter (*bet*) of Scripture together with the last letter (*nun*), it spells *BeN*, which, as previously stated, is Hebrew for "son."† From the first letter to the last letter, Scripture points to the Son—the second person of the Godhead, through whom blessing in this world and the world to come ultimately arises.

Bet (2) is also the first letter of the Hebrew words meaning "to bless" (*barak*) and "firstborn" (*bechor*), which both have a value of 222. The Son, *Ben* (2) is the second person of the Godhead, and this word begins with the second letter of the Hebrew alphabet. The Son (*Ben*) and God's Firstborn, *Bechor* (222), are both central to experiencing blessing, *barak* (222), and crucial to

---

* Besides heaven and earth, the significance of *bet*, the second Hebrew letter, also can be seen in the two great commandments, two good spies, two houses of Israel, and more.

† The Hebrew alphabet does not have vowels.

the Word—"His words," *Davriu* (Dan. 10:6—also 222). Everything points to Jesus.

MESSIAH, THE FIRSTBORN

When *bet* is placed at the beginning of a word, it functions as the preposition "in" or "on account of." Therefore, Genesis 1:1 can be read, "**On account of** the First [*Reisheet*] the Lord created the heavens and the earth." Who or what is the First (*Reisheet*)?

"The First" could plausibly refer to Israel, but it is better understood as referring to the Messiah. Rabbi Johanan in the Babylonian Talmud stated that the world was created "for the sake of the Messiah."[2]

The Lord knows the end from the beginning. He knew that Adam and Eve would sin and that humanity's end would be physical and spiritual death. God, who is good and who wanted to create the world as a place of good, decided that before the world could come into existence, the cure would have to precede the sickness caused by sin. The only possible cure would have to come through the *Reisheet,* the Firstborn of God, the Messiah.

God predestined the Messiah's suffering. The New Testament confirms this idea by referring to Jesus as "the Lamb slain from the foundation of the world" (Rev. 13:8 NKJV). The Messiah, out of His deep love for us, committed to be slain as the antidote to sin and death even before the world's Creation. Yeshua is the *Reisheet* (the First), associated with the firstborn, as Colossians states:

> He is the **beginning** [**Reisheet**‡], **the firstborn** from the dead—
>   so that He might come to have first place in all things.
> For God was pleased to have all His fullness dwell in Him
>   and through Him to reconcile all things to Himself,
>   making peace through the **blood** of His cross—
>   whether **things on earth or things in heaven**! (1:18–20)

---

‡ From the Hebrew New Testament.

This verse connects everything mentioned above by linking the "beginning" with the Messiah being the "firstborn" to His death for the sake of redeeming and reconciling all things in heaven and on earth. God created the world on account of the *Reisheet*, Yeshua the Messiah, who is the second Adam and Firstfruits of the new creation.

Bereisheet, the first word of Genesis 1:1, has the numeric value of 913. This numeric value is the same as "[Messiah] the firstborn of all creation [*Mashiach bechor lechol nivra*]" (Col. 1:15). The number 913 also connects to the Messiah's death and resurrection through the Greek word *egeiro* (913), meaning "raise." This word is used in John 2:19: "And in three days I will raise it [this temple] up" (913). The phrase "*ADONAI* has made His salvation known" (Ps. 98:2) also equals 913, which points back numerically to God creating the world due to the salvation of His Firstborn.

Jesus was God's plan even before the foundation of the world, knowing He would become the sacrifice for all that was to come in man's disobedience.

MESSIAH, THE AGENT OF CREATION

There is still another way *Bereisheet* ("in the beginning," Gen. 1:1) can be read. The letter *bet* that is attached as a prefix to the word *reisheet* can mean "through," as in "**Through** the First, God created the heavens and the earth." This reading makes *Reisheet* the agent of Creation, which fits perfectly with John 1:1–3: "In the beginning was the Word. The Word was with God, and the Word was God. He was with God in the beginning. All things were made through Him, and apart from Him nothing was made that has come into being."

In Judaism, when the letter *bet* is interpreted as "through," it's associated with God creating the world with wisdom and understanding. In Hebrew, the word for "understanding" is *binah*, which begins with the letter *bet*. The prophet Jeremiah connects understanding (*binah*), wisdom (*chochmah*), and Creation: "He **made the earth** by His power, established the world by **His wisdom**, and stretched out heaven by **His understanding**" (Jer. 10:12).

In Jewish mystical thought, wisdom consists of an upper and lower aspect. The upper aspect looks to God the Father, whom we need to commune with in solitude to increase and perfect our wisdom. All true wisdom comes from above, so even Yeshua would spend much time in solitude with the Father. As a result, He "kept increasing in wisdom and stature, and in favor with God and men" (Luke 2:52). Like Jesus, we need to make spending quiet time with the Lord a priority so that we can spiritually mature and grow in understanding and favor.

Lower wisdom looks down on the faces of men. We need to share the wisdom of God's Word so that others can be blessed. This is a key part of what it means to make disciples. Sharing wisdom is a great act of kindness because wisdom and understanding give and sustain life (Eccl. 7:12). In 2 Corinthians 4:6, the apostle Paul said that God gives us the "light of the knowledge of the glory of God in the face of Messiah." By sharing wisdom, we share not only life but the Source of life: Jesus, the light of Creation.

We find a practical and life-changing truth here. The psalmist wrote, "Adonai, how countless are Your works! In wisdom You made them all" (Ps. 104:24). We were made with wisdom. This is important because most of us are critical of ourselves and others. How many times has someone made you feel worthless, stupid, or ugly? The world, the flesh, and the Enemy will try to speak these lies over you until you believe them. But if you believe these lies, you empower them and the father of lies who is the source of them. **You are not a mistake or ugly or worthless, for God created you with wisdom**. Let the light of God's wisdom and understanding dispel the dark lies that deceive you and lead you into emotional, relational, and spiritual bondage.

Knowledge and understanding rooted in Yeshua and the Word will illuminate your eyes to see the incalculable worth and value in you and other people. The Messiah would not have created the world and died for you if you didn't matter. No one pays such a high price for something that's worthless. The question is, will you believe this, receive it, keep meditating on it, and declare it over yourself?

OVERCOMING CHAOS

Every day of Creation reveals mysteries about the Messiah and His Kingdom. The details of Creation point to the person and work of Yeshua: "Now the earth was chaos and waste, darkness was on the surface of the deep, and the *Ruach Elohim* [Spirit of God] was hovering upon the surface of the water" (Gen. 1:2).

On the first day of Creation, the earth was in an uninhabitable state of darkness and chaos. Biblically, chaos and darkness represent evil, exile, and death. God's goodness and abundant blessing can't be fully manifested as long as chaos is on the earth; He must bring order out of chaos so that life can flourish. This is true for creation, our lives, and for the church: "For God is not a God of disorder" (1 Cor. 14:33 NIV).

The good news is that God has the power to bring order out of chaos and light out of darkness. God created order in the world so humanity could experience abundant blessing and life. When Adam and Eve sinned, disorder and chaos were no longer fully restrained but became an ever-present reality that increased in strength over time as humanity, due to its fallen state, continued to reject the Lord and His ways. God will ultimately conquer chaos and vanquish evil and darkness, but how will this be accomplished? How can we restrain chaos in our lives today?

Overcoming Chaos by the Word

Chaos will only be defeated when God's Kingdom is established on earth as it is in heaven. God has provided wisdom and resources to bring greater order out of chaos as we eagerly await that day.

God used His Word to call forth light at the beginning of Creation. The first key to overcoming chaos and restoring order is God's Word, which is a lamp for our feet and a light for our path (Ps. 119:105). We need the wisdom, power, and light of God's Word to restrain and overcome the potentially damaging spiritual, emotional, and relational harm caused by chaos in our lives.

The numeric value of "chaos and waste" in Genesis 1:2 (*tohu vavohu*) is 430. Generally, chaos and waste describe the state of being in exile.

Specifically, Israel dwelled under the Egyptian exile 430 years, but "at the end of the 430 years, to the very day, all the LORD's divisions left Egypt" (Ex. 12:41 NIV). God released the Israelites at a specific time—"to the very day"—from the state of chaos created by Egyptian control. Interestingly, the phrase "all the Egyptians [kol Mitzrayim]" (Ex. 12:30) equals 430 as well.

God released the children of Israel after 430 years, but to fully reverse their state of exile they needed His Word. Thus, in the same year the Lord gave them the Torah, the Law, at Mount Sinai. The Greek word for "Law" used in the New Testament is nomos, and it has the value of 430. God gave the Israelites the Torah/Law (430)—after they were subjugated for 430 years to the power of "all the Egyptians" (430)—so that Israel could be freed from the "chaos and waste" (430) of exile. From the first day of Creation to the Israelites' liberation from Egypt, God's Word overcame the forces of chaos in their lives. His Word will do the same for us.

The Hebrew word for "soul" (nefesh) and the Greek word for "perfect" (teleioi)—as in "Therefore be perfect, just as your Father in heaven is perfect" (Matt. 5:48)—both have the numeric value of 430. This underscores the truth that the Bible not only combats chaos in our lives but also transforms and spiritually perfects (430) our souls (430). The voice of God, through the Word of God, brings order, life, and blessing out of chaos when it is received and lived out by faith.

Overcoming Chaos Through the Messiah

As foundational as God's Word is to overcoming chaos, there is someone that is even more important. The number 430 is also connected to the Messiah. "But you, Bethlehem . . . from you will come out to Me One to be ruler in Israel, One whose goings forth are from of old, from days of eternity" (Mic. 5:1). The numeric value in Hebrew of the phrase "from of old, from days of eternity" (mikedem mimei olam) is 430. This number alludes to the divinity of Yeshua, since God alone is eternal, and it shows that the Messiah is the primary goal of the Torah (430). Only the One who existed from eternity, the Messiah, the eternal, living Word of God, can overcome chaos and restore order, for His existence precedes it and His power supersedes it.

When Yeshua was on the cross, darkness occurred from the sixth hour (Mark 15:33) to the ninth hour. This happened because He had to return to the start of Creation—to a time before light, when everything was formless and void—to undo the chaos that was released as a result of the Fall. Through the cross, He conquered the chaos caused by our sin and overcame the forces of darkness. As Paul wrote, "After disarming the principalities and powers, He made a public spectacle of them, triumphing over them in the cross" (Col. 2:15).

ADAM AND EVE

God's preamble to the creation of Adam and Eve communicates that mankind is the crown of Creation: "Let Us make man in Our image, after Our likeness!" (Gen. 1:26). Every other aspect of Creation is the result of God commanding and verbally calling things forth. But **the Lord is personally involved in fashioning human beings in a way not seen with any of His other creations**. The words "Let Us make" express God's intentionality, deliberation, and personal engagement in making the first man and woman.

Because mankind is made in God's image, every human being has immeasurable value and is worthy of respect and honor. When we disrespect or harm a person, we are actually dishonoring God. By honoring the image of God in humanity, we honor the Creator.

The Trinity's Role in Creation

Jewish and Christian scholars have debated for centuries concerning the identity of "Us" in Genesis 1:26. A common answer given by traditional Jewish rabbis, who do not believe in the triune nature of God, is that God was speaking to the serving angels who were created on the second day. Many other interpretations vehemently argue that "Us" can in no way be read as an allusion to the triune God. While these arguments are logical, I believe they are wrong in light of the full revelation of Scripture.

There is ample biblical and rabbinic evidence that the Messiah was consulted and involved in Creation. "God **created** humankind in His image, in the image of God He **created** him, male and female He **created** them" (Gen. 1:27). The verb used here is *bara*, which is composed of three letters: *bet, resh,* and *aleph.* These three letters are the first letters of each of the Hebrew names of the Trinity. *Bet* alludes to the *Ben* (the Son), *resh* to the *Ruach* (the Holy Spirit), and *aleph* to the *Av/Abba* (the Father). The three letters connect to the Trinity's involvement in Creation. The primary Hebrew word for "Father," *Av,* has a numeric value of 3, which alludes to the triune nature of God.

Each member of the Trinity had a role in Creation. The Father decreed and commissioned it, the Son designed and oversaw it, and the Holy Spirit did the work of constructing. This collaborative partnership of the Godhead is also mirrored in the work of salvation: the Father selects, the Son saves by His death and resurrection, and the Spirit seals by indwelling the believer (Eph. 1:3–14).

HUMANITY'S MISSION AND PURPOSE

What was man's role in Creation? According to most English versions of the Bible, God placed Adam in the Garden of Eden "to cultivate and watch over it [*le-avdah u'leshomrah*]" (Gen. 2:15). But cultivating the ground is work that resulted from the Fall (Gen. 3:23). A better and more accurate rendering of the Hebrew expression in Genesis 2:15 is "to worship and to obey."[3] Man and woman were created not to be gardeners but to be priests who served the Lord through worshiping Him and obeying His commandments.

The Lord created us to be worshipers. We were made by God to be image bearers with a priestly calling. The Garden of Eden was our tabernacle, but due to the Fall, work replaced worship as our primary focus. In Hebrew, *avodah* is the word for both "work" and "worship." The context of who or what *avodah* is being done for determines its meaning. Work, a result of the Fall, does not need to be a tedious task but can become elevated to the level of worship when we choose to approach it as a way to serve and glorify God.

Work is a part of life, but being worshipers is our primary calling. Work apart from God has no eternal benefit and lacks true meaning. But when we work from a place of worship and prioritize it in our lives, we fulfill our role as image bearers walking in our priestly calling.

Man's original call to be priests, which was gradually lost as a result of the Fall, was restored when God gave Israel the Torah at Sinai and called His people to be "a kingdom of priests and a holy nation" (Ex. 19:6 NIV). This was emphasized with the coming of Jesus and the establishment of the New Covenant. The apostle Peter wrote that we are "a chosen people, a royal priesthood, a holy nation" (1 Pet. 2:9).

THE TEMPTATION

Eden was a paradise created especially for the enjoyment of humanity. The garden was designed to be a place where Adam and Eve could fellowship with the Lord and flourish. But their time in paradise was short-lived. The cunning and crafty serpent tempted Eve to eat from the prohibited Tree of Knowledge of Good and Evil. Why would the serpent want to tempt Adam and Eve?

The serpent, according to the New Testament, is Satan: "The ancient serpent, called the devil and satan, who deceives the whole world" (Rev. 12:9). In rabbinic thought, the serpent represents the incarnation of evil in Creation. A functional, purposeful unity of opposition to God exists between the serpent, Satan, and the evil inclination. Some sages go so far as to see them as "three aspects of the same essence."[4]

God is the Creator; Satan is nothing but an imitator. The Lord creates while Satan copies and corrupts. This can be seen even in Satan's deceptive and demonic tactics. He "masquerades as an angel of light" (2 Cor. 11:14) and "prowls around like a roaring lion, searching for someone to devour" (1 Pet. 5:8). In the same way that God is three yet one, Satan, the serpent, and the evil inclination are one; the world, the flesh, and the devil are one; and, according to the book of Revelation, Satan, the Antichrist, and the

False Prophet work together as one. These three form an evil and unholy trinity that seeks to rob, kill, and destroy humanity.

The serpent sought to tempt Adam and Eve out of jealousy. Satan was at the top of God's created order, but that changed with the creation of Adam and Eve:

> What is man that You take thought of him. . . .
> Yet You have made him a little lower than God,
> And You crown him with glory and majesty!
> You make him to rule over the works of Your hands.
>   (Ps. 8:4–6 NASB)

When God created man, Satan lost his lofty status. Satan knew that if he could get Adam and Eve to disobey, they would be expelled from the Garden of Eden as he was expelled from heaven.

THE FALL

Eve took Satan's bait, believing that if she ate the fruit she would not die but would become "like God, knowing good and evil" (Gen. 3:5). After eating the forbidden fruit, Eve gave it to Adam, who also ate. Immediately their eyes were opened, but not in the positive way they had hoped. They perceived for the first time that they were naked, sewed fig leaves together to cover themselves, and shamefully hid from the Lord when they heard His voice calling for them.

By eating from the tree, Adam and Eve demonstrated a lack of faith. They failed to trust the Lord to be the provider of every good thing they needed. Seeking wisdom and good apart from God was utter foolishness that led to cursing instead of blessing. The tragic irony is that the only thing that could have made Adam and Eve "like God" in a healthy way was being with God.

Four Steps to Failure

The Fall was the result of a four-stage process that began with doubt, led to denial and disbelief, and culminated in disobedience. Satan led the woman to doubt when he said, "Did God really say" (Gen. 3:1). Doubt led to questioning God's Word and then denying it altogether. After doubt and denial came disbelief, which resulted in the disobedience of eating from the Tree of Knowledge of Good and Evil. The disastrous results included disharmony, disease, dismissal from Eden, and ultimately death.

The dire consequences of the Fall can be summed up in one word: *exile*. Exile is about disconnection and distance. There are four aspects to exile that connect to the four aspects of the Fall.

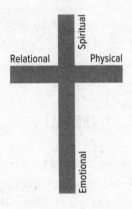

1. Spiritual Exile

   Adam and Eve's disobedience led them to become distant and disconnected from God. Adam and Eve hid in shame and were exiled from the presence of the Lord in Eden. The ultimate consequence of spiritual exile is spiritual death, which means dying while in spiritual exile and being permanently disconnected from God for all eternity.

2. Relational Exile

   Man and woman became disconnected and distant from each other. When questioned by God, the man blamed the woman and even the Lord who gave her to him. The relational disconnection spread to their family and only worsened. Their firstborn son, Cain, murdered his younger brother, Abel, out of jealousy. Humanity has struggled with unhealthy and dysfunctional relationships ever since. Divorce, sibling rivalries, abuse, misogyny, racism, discrimination, and even genocide all have their roots in the relational exile that resulted from the Fall.

3. Emotional and Psychological Exile

After the Fall we became distant from our true selves and God-given identities. Our minds and feelings became fragmented and corrupted, causing emotional and psychological confusion, chaos, and sickness. Our identities were damaged, our destinies blurred and stolen from us.

4. Physical Exile

Adam and Eve were banished from Eden. Humanity became physically distant and disconnected from the creation they were supposed to rule over and steward. Creation was cursed, and the material world began to fluctuate between order and disorder, resulting in natural disasters and physical diseases. The ground was cursed, and humanity needed to work to earn their bread by "the sweat of [their] brow" (Gen. 3:19). Our disobedience affected every aspect of creation and caused misalignment in the material world. The ultimate result of living in physical exile is death. Our physical bodies will die of disease and decay in fulfillment of God's pronouncement (Gen. 3:19).

Finding Hope in Judgment

Exile is a reality, but it's not finality. In God's pronouncement of judgment on the serpent, there is a ray of hope, found in the first direct messianic prophecy in the Scripture:

"I will put animosity
between you [the serpent] and the woman—
between your seed and her seed
He [the Seed of the woman] will crush your head,
and you will crush his heel." (Gen. 3:15)

There is a perpetual cosmic struggle between the serpent and his seed and the woman and her seed. The seed of the serpent (Satan) are those who choose to do his will and harbor hostility toward the woman and her seed, those who follow and worship the One true God and Creator of all (Gen. 3:15). The second half of Genesis 3:15 speaks of a final conflict in which two blows are inflicted. The Seed of the woman deals a death blow by crushing the head of the serpent. The serpent, in turn, deals a fatal blow by striking the Seed's heel. There is, however, a critical difference between these two deaths. The Seed of the woman's death would be temporary, not fatal like the serpent's, and it would lead to the defeat and eternal destruction of Satan and his seed.

Commenting on Genesis 3:15, the rabbis confirm the identity of the Seed of the woman as the Messiah. "But they will be healed in his footsteps (heels) in the days of King Messiah."[5]

MESSIAH, THE SECOND ADAM

The Messiah, the Seed of the woman, would be the second Adam, who would undo the spiritual, relational, emotional, and physical aspects of exile. The New Testament portrays Jesus as this second Adam, the fulfillment of the promised messianic Seed spoken of in Genesis 3:15. Understanding this reveals many mysteries concerning the person and work of the Messiah.

Why the Cross?

The cross is the universal symbol of Christianity. The customary answer given to explain why Jesus had to die on a cross is that crucifixion was a common means of Roman execution. But something as important as the death of God's Son would not be based solely on Rome's proclivity for a brutal means of execution.

When Adam and Eve disobeyed the Lord, sin entered the world. Redemption required a repair (Hebrew, *tikkun*) for their sin. They could not correct what they had done.

Since a tree caused the Fall, the Son of God had to die on a tree as the second Adam to reverse the curse caused by the sin of the first man and woman. Paul wrote that the solution to Adam's sin and the curse is found in Jesus, the Messiah (Rom. 5:12–17). The Lord put Jesus on the tree to restore and make restitution for what had been stolen from the tree in the garden. The first Adam brought death by a tree, but the second Adam brought life by means of His death on one.

The Hebrew word for "the tree" *(HaEitz)* has the numeric value of 165, which is also the numeric value of "curse" (*kelalah*) and "deliver him" (*pedaeihu*). In Greek, 165 is the value of "man" (*andri*) and "image" (*eikoni*). Yeshua died on the tree (165) to free us from the curse (165) that resulted from eating the fruit of the tree (165) so that man (165) could be delivered (165) from the pit and from the image (165) of the beast that would seek to harm the woman's Seed—all who follow the Messiah. The tree is how God sets us free.

Crushing the Curse

Satan tried desperately to undermine the messianic promise of Genesis 3:15. He influenced the soldiers to beat Jesus and place a crown of thorns on His head. He instigated the Jewish leaders to bring charges against Jesus and incited Pilate to execute Him by having His hands and feet nailed to a cross. Satan was confident he could defeat Jesus just as he defeated the first Adam.

Satan did not understand that God is in the business of turning curses into blessings. Satan thought he could humiliate, mock, and destroy the Messiah by means of the cross, but instead he fulfilled God's prophetic plan and provided the means to free humanity from the curse of exile.

Every detail in Jesus' crucifixion connects to undoing the Fall. His hands were pierced because our hands stole from the tree. His feet were pierced to fulfill the promise of Genesis 3:15 that the heel of the messianic Seed would crush the serpent's head. His pierced side made atonement for the sin of Eve, the one taken from man's side, who led Adam into temptation.

Jesus' experience on the cross reverses the four aspects of exile caused by the Fall:

1. Jesus reversed the **spiritual** aspect of exile by allowing Himself to be nailed to a tree, the means of our spiritual exile.
2. Jesus reversed the **relational** aspect of exile by experiencing rejection and betrayal, and even while being mocked on the cross, He chose to extend forgiveness (Luke 23:34).
3. Jesus reversed the **emotional** aspect of exile by allowing Himself to experience the psychological and emotional pain of being mocked by men and feeling abandoned by God (Mark 15:33–34).
4. Jesus reversed the **physical** aspect of exile by physically suffering on the cross. The crown of thorns, the physical sign of the curse of creation, conveyed that the second Adam, the new representative head of creation, was reversing the exile and restoring the blessing.

Jesus, as the promised messianic Seed of the woman, by means of His death and resurrection, not only overcame all four negative aspects of exile that resulted from the Fall but has made healing and transformation possible in each area, allowing us to experience the fullness of the abundant life (John 10:10).

Because of the second Adam, Jesus, we no longer need to live in a state of disconnection with our Creator but can have a deeper spiritual, relational, emotional, and physical connection to God, self, and others that so many of us desire.

The identity of the Seed of the woman, also known as the second Adam, who would come in the distant future to defeat the serpent, vanquish evil, and undo the consequences of the Fall, is not directly revealed in

Genesis. Rather, Genesis 3:15 raises a question that the Five Books of Moses and the rest of Scripture seek to answer. As the chapters ahead reveal, the mysterious and somewhat cryptic promises found in Creation and in Genesis 3:15 come into clearer focus through the progressive revelation of messianic prophecy.

chapter
THREE

THE MESSIAH PROMISED TO THE PATRIARCHS

Abraham, Isaac, and Jacob

Tracing family generations back with a family tree has always been a fun hobby for many people. It's become even more popular in recent years with the ease of DNA testing and the ability to find connections through massive genealogical databases. But there's more to this hobby than gathering data. Reviewing life events helps us better understand ourselves. Looking back offers insights and understanding not found anywhere else.

In the same way, Genesis 12–50 opens up our understanding of the founding generations of Israel. The patriarchs (or fathers) begin with Abraham. The title of patriarch was passed from Abraham to his son Isaac and then to his grandson Jacob. These men became the roots of the ancestral tree of the nation of Israel. "The patriarchs were wealthy nomads, though occasionally they farmed (Gen. 26:12). With the exception of a burial site at Hebron (Gen. 23) and the region of Shechem (Gen. 33:18–34:31; 48:22), they did not 'own' land."[1]

The promised Seed of the woman began to find its fulfillment in Abraham and his offspring. The call and mission of the patriarchs reflect God's original intention for humankind: to experience God's blessing and to be a conduit of blessing to the world. God handpicked Abraham, Isaac, and Jacob to play a foundational role in birthing the line of the chosen Seed who would reverse the curse and bring about the new Eden.

THE CALL OF ABRAM:
THE FIRST SPIRITUAL RADICAL

Then *ADONAI* said to Abram,
"Get going out from your land,
and from your relatives,
and from your father's house,
to the land that I will show you."

—*Genesis 12:1*

The call of Abram (who was later named Abraham) began with a test. The Lord spoke directly to Abram, as He spoke to Adam in the garden. He called Abram to leave three things: (1) his homeland, (2) his relatives, and (3) his father's house. In return, the Lord promised to bless him with (1) descendants, (2) wealth, and (3) a great name.

Abram needed to be tested because God was calling him to become a new Adam who, along with Sarai, a new Eve, would play a critical role in restoring God's plan and blessing for all creation. Abram and Sarai (who was later renamed Sarah) needed to pass the test that Adam and Eve failed. If Abram believed and obeyed, then he would be blessed. But if he doubted and denied God's call, as Adam had, he would be dismissed from the blessing.

In Hebrew, Abram's call began with *Lech lecha*, which means "Go to yourself!" God called and commanded him to embark on physical and spiritual journeys of faith and transformation. Only by leaving would Abram's true identity be revealed. All of us need to *Lech lecha*, "Go!," so we can overcome our past baggage, inherited habits, and spiritual limitations and become all God created us to be.

Abram did not have an illustrious spiritual past. He was from Ur of the Chaldeans, a part of the Babylonian Empire ruled by Nimrod, who, according to tradition, built the Tower of Babel not long after the Flood. Terah, Abram's father, was not just an idol worshiper; he was an idol maker by trade, according to Jewish tradition. Abram, a seeker of truth, had to leave so that he and his family would not have their destiny determined by idolatrous influences.

Abram had to go on an outer journey that accomplished an inner spiritual change. His journey involved testing and struggle that refined his faith and led to receiving and stewarding the promised blessing.

ABRAM THE FIRST MISSIONARY

Abram went by faith, but he did not go alone. Part of God's promise to Abram was that he would become a "great nation"—he would have numerous descendants (Gen. 12:2). The seed of Abram would be both physical and spiritual, which is implied by Genesis 12:5: "Abram took Sarai his wife, and Lot his brother's son, and all their substance that they had gathered, and the souls that they had gotten in Haran; and they went forth to go into the land of Canaan; and into the land of Canaan they came" (KJV). "The souls that they had gotten in Haran" refers to the pagan men and women Abram and his wife brought to faith in the one true God.

Several verbal parallels exist between God's mandate to Abram in Genesis 12:1–5 and the Messiah's mandate to His disciples in the Great Commission. Jesus' words "Go therefore and make disciples [talmidim] of all nations" (Matt. 28:19) are rooted in the divine mission God entrusted to Abram and later to the children of Israel: to be a light to all nations. Too often, believers focus on saving souls without emphasizing making souls—mature followers of Messiah Jesus. We forget that discipleship is the fundamental and long-term aspect of outreach.

THE FAITH OF ABRAM

There were ten generations from Adam to Noah, then ten generations from Noah until Abram.[2] Abram stood out from the ten generations that came before him because of his faith.

Abram is the father of faith. Genesis 15:6 tells us he "believed the LORD, and he credited it to him as righteousness" (NIV). The Hebrew word for "faith" is *emunah*. The root of this word, *aman*, means "firm" or "solid." *Emunah* is a solid and firm belief in God and His Word. More specifically, from a Hebraic perspective, the foundation of *emunah* is both intellectually believing and knowing that God is the sovereign King and Creator of all, who providentially guides and ultimately redeems creation in accordance with His attributes of goodness, kindness, and justice, which are fully actualized through the Messiah. As Hebrews 11:6 states, "Without faith it is impossible to please God, because anyone who comes to him must believe that he exists and that he rewards those who earnestly seek him" (NIV).

Although the Hebraic concept of faith includes a cognitive aspect, *emunah* is much more than an intellectual assent to a set of doctrinal beliefs. *Emunah* is also related to the word *ne'eman*, best translated as "loyalty" or "faithfulness." Thus, *emunah* includes both belief and fidelity, a mindset and an action. True faith results in loyalty to the Lord, faithfulness to His Word, and obedience to His commandments. Habakkuk 2:4 underscores this point: "But the righteous person will live by his faithfulness" (NIV).

Abram's faith was built on several important truths. The first is that God is "the faithful God" (Deut. 7:9). The term for "faithful" (*ne'eman*) in this passage is from the same root as *emunah* as well as the commonly used Hebrew word *amen*. When we respond "Amen!," we are saying that we believe what was spoken will come to pass because the Lord is faithful. We can trust God because "the One who calls" is faithful (1 Thess. 5:24).

Additionally, Abram knew God is good (Ps. 136:1) and loving (1 John 4:8). We can trust the Lord completely because He loves us so much, knows what's best for us, and will always act with our best interest in mind.

Our faith is strengthened to the degree that we understand and take to heart that God is faithful, loving, and good to all His sons and daughters.

THE ABRAHAMIC COVENANT

God entered into a unique covenant with Abram, which set the foundation for all other biblical covenants, including the Davidic Covenant (2 Sam. 7) and the New Covenant (Jer. 31:30–33).

As part of the Abrahamic Covenant, the Lord promised Abram descendants who would inherit and carry forward the blessings divinely promised to Sarai and him. Despite the fact that he and his wife were beyond childbearing years, Abram believed the Lord's promise that Sarai would conceive and bear his son (Gen. 15:4). He believed, by faith, that nothing is impossible with God, and it influenced his actions. Abraham was one hundred and Sarah was ninety years old when Isaac was born.

God made yet another promise to Abram: "I am *ADONAI* who brought you out from Ur of the Chaldeans, in order to give you this land to inherit it" (Gen. 15:7). Abram responded by asking for a sign. How could he believe God's promise that Sarai would miraculously bear a son but then need a sign regarding his inheritance of the Promised Land?

In response, the Lord made a covenant with Abram known as the *Berit Bein Ha-betarim*, which translates as "Covenant Between the Parts." Before this covenant, Abram saw his relationship with God as contractual—if he obeyed the Lord, then he and his family would be blessed, but if he disobeyed, then he and his posterity would lose the blessing. Contracts normally place obligations on all parties who enter into them. Both participants must fulfill prescribed obligations or else there are serious consequences, including the contract's termination.

With this understanding, Abram was concerned that future generations would not remain faithful and thus forfeit the blessing of inheriting the Promised Land. According to the rabbis, Abram was given visions of all the future exiles. This is why he wanted a guarantee from the Lord that his seed would not be permanently exiled from the Promised Land as God exiled Adam and Eve from Eden.

A compassionate and gracious God assuaged Abram's fear in Genesis 15 by helping him understand that their relationship was not contractual but rather based on a special type of covenant, a *brit* in Hebrew. In the ancient Near East, the most common form of covenant was bilateral. When two parties entered into this type of covenant, they would sacrifice animals, cutting them down the middle. Then both parties would walk between the parts, symbolizing that the one who did not keep his end of the covenant agreement would be torn apart. This type of covenant was conditional: all commitments would be voided unless both parties kept the covenantal stipulations.[3]

The "Covenant Between the Parts" that God made with Abram was different: it was unilateral and unconditional. God put Abram into a deep sleep before God *alone* passed through the parts of the covenantal sacrifices (Gen. 15:12–20). The Lord was the guarantor. Even when Abraham's children disobeyed and rebelled, they could temporarily, but not permanently, forfeit the covenantal promises the Lord made to Abram/Abraham.

You can't fully understand God's relationship with believers or salvation history without understanding the concept of covenant. The New Covenant that Messiah Jesus established with us is not transactional but covenantal, which means you don't need to live in fear of messing up and permanently missing out on God's eternal blessing. Like Abram, you enter into the covenant on faith. Paul makes this clear in Galatians 3:18: "For if the inheritance is based on law, it is no longer based on a promise. But God has graciously given it to Abraham by means of a promise."

FROM ABRAM TO ABRAHAM AND SARAI TO SARAH

God promised Abram and Sarai that they would conceive a child, but years passed and they kept waiting. As a sign and affirmation that His promise of a son would be fulfilled, the Lord changed Abram's name to *AbraHam* and Sarai's to *SaraH* (Gen. 17:4–5, 15–16).

There is a one-letter difference between their new names and their former ones—the addition of the letter *hei*, or *h* in English. The letter *hei* connects to Creation. Genesis 2:4 says, "These are the genealogical records of the heavens and the earth when they were created, at the time when *Adonai Elohim* made land and sky." In this verse, the Hebrew verb *bara*, which means "to create out of nothing," has the letter *hei* inserted into it, which is grammatically incorrect. *Hei*, in Jewish thought, is the letter of the divine breath of God, which, along with the Word of God, brought about Creation (Ps. 33:6). So the grammatically incorrect use of this letter in Genesis 2:4 alludes to the divine breath releasing God's creative power. The Lord added this Hebrew letter to Abraham and Sarah's names because it represented His creative power to overcome barrenness in their old age.

The addition of *hei* also gives the phrase "when they were created" the same letters and numeric value as the name Abraham: 248. The Hebrew words for "womb" (Gen. 20:18) and "compassion [or mercy]" (Ps. 103:13) also have the numeric value of 248. The Lord demonstrated His abundant mercy (248) by adding the letter *hei*, miraculously opening Sarah's womb (248) so she could conceive and begin to fulfill the meaning of Abraham's new name: "father of a multitude" (Gen. 17:4).

FROM BARRENNESS TO BIRTH OF THE PROMISED SEED

Sarah's ability to conceive and bear a son was nothing short of miraculous. Not only was she ninety years old, but Sarah "was barren; she did not have a child" (Gen. 11:30). The Talmud states, "The superfluous words: 'She had no child,' indicate that she did not have even a place, i.e., a womb, for a child."[4] The Lord, according to Jewish tradition, performed miracles by creating a womb within Sarah and giving her the ability to produce milk to nurse Isaac.

According to Jewish tradition, the day on which Sarah is said to have conceived is the same day as the Feast of Trumpets,[5] also known as Rosh Hashanah, the Jewish New Year. In traditional Judaism, this is the day God created Adam and Eve. This further underscores Sarah as the new Eve, whom God providentially assisted in bringing forth the promised seed.

The struggle of Sarah's, and later her daughter-in-law Rebekah's, barrenness points to the fact that the promised seed can't be born without the Lord's supernatural intervention. The Lord had a direct involvement in the births of Isaac and Jacob, and His involvement would be much more so for the promised messianic Seed, the One who would be born of a virgin (Isa. 7:14). All of us need divine assistance in birthing God's promises for our lives.

Isaac: The Promised Son

Abraham faithfully named his newborn son Isaac (Gen. 17:19). Isaac (*Yitzhak*) means "one who causes laughter." The Hebrew root of Isaac's name is *tzachak*, which usually refers to an ironic or mocking type of laughter caused by something utterly ridiculous or unthinkable. In part, this refers to Abraham's and Sarah's ages when Isaac was born. It also refers to Sarah's laughter (Gen. 18:12–15). More importantly, Isaac's name communicates a truth that would be key to Israel's future—nothing is impossible or inconceivable. From the outset, the history of the Jewish people and the messianic promise made to them were birthed not from the reasonable, logical, or natural but from the supernatural and outrageous workings of God.

ISAAC AND YESHUA

Isaac was miraculously conceived, and his birth fulfilled the word of the Lord to Abraham. In Jewish tradition, cynics questioned Isaac's paternity. To prove these unbelieving scoffers wrong, the Lord "shaped Isaac's facial features exactly similar to those of Abraham's, so that everyone had to admit that Abraham begat Isaac."[6]

Similarly, Yeshua, as the greater Isaac, also had a supernatural conception that fulfilled prophecy. The Pharisees questioned Jesus' paternity by saying, "Where is your Father?" (John 8:19) and took it a step further when they said, "We were not born as illegitimate children" (John 8:41). The Greek syntax places an emphasis on "we," which implies, "We are not illegitimate, you are." This is said in the context of the Pharisees claiming to be the children of Abraham. Like the scoffers at Isaac's birth, the Pharisees failed to see that the Son bears the image and resemblance of His Father (Col. 1:15; Heb. 1:3).

The Sacrifice of the Only Son

In Genesis 22:2, the Lord told Abraham, "Take your son, your only son whom you love . . . and offer him . . . as a burnt offering [*olah*]." John 3:16 clearly references this verse: "For God so loved the world that He gave His one and only Son, that whoever believes in Him shall not perish but have eternal life."

The numeric value of "as a burnt offering" (*olah*) is 135, the same as *matzah*, the unleavened bread that the Lord commanded the children of Israel to eat at the Passover. This is amazing because Isaac is portrayed as a Passover lamb and as a type of Messiah. Isaac was born on Passover, according to Jewish tradition.

At the Passover Seder,[7] there are three special pieces of *matzah* wrapped together. The upper piece of *matzah* is symbolic of Abraham, the middle of Isaac, and the bottom of Jacob. The middle piece of *matzah* is broken in a special way and becomes known as the *afikomen*—the bread of healing and redemption. The Messiah, like the *matzah* (135), was broken for us and was offered like Isaac in our place (135) so that we might be redeemed and healed.

The Donkey and Divine Mission

Abraham saddling his donkey (Gen. 22:3, 5) is a small but significant detail. The donkey is singled out because it plays an important role in the process of redemption. According to Jewish tradition, Moses rode this same donkey when he went to deliver the children of Israel from Egypt (Ex. 4:20).[8] Abraham and Moses both using the same donkey to fulfill their divine mission prophetically points to the greater work of redemption through the Messiah, who would also ride on a donkey (Zech. 9:9).

The Hebrew word for donkey is *chamor* and derives its name from *chomri*, which means "physical matter." Abraham, Moses, and, ultimately, the Messiah each played a key role in the transformation, elevation, and redemption of the physical world. When Yeshua rode a donkey into Jerusalem on Palm Sunday, He fulfilled prophecy, declaring that He was greater than Abraham (John 8:52–58) and that He was the prophet like Moses (Deut. 18:18) that the people had long been expecting.

The Journey to Mount Moriah

Abraham and Isaac left their homeland to journey to the place of sacrifice—Mount Moriah. This is the same place Solomon began to build the house of the Lord in Jerusalem and the same site where the Lord appeared to David (2 Chron. 3:1). When they had arrived at the location chosen by the Lord, Abraham told his two servants to remain with the donkey while he and Isaac went to "worship." Abraham said they would both return (Gen. 22:5). Commenting on this, Rabbi Shlomo Yitzhaki (Rashi) said, "He [Abraham] prophesied that they would both return."[9]

Yeshua, the only begotten and beloved Son of the Father, also had to leave His home in heaven to go to the place of sacrifice, which was in Jerusalem, on the same mountain range where Abraham offered Isaac. This fulfilled the messianic prophecy that the Messiah would die but come back to life (Gen. 3:15; Hos. 6:2).

The Binding of Isaac and the Passion of the Messiah

The account of the binding of Isaac (Gen. 22) provides many details that parallel the binding and sacrifice of Messiah Jesus. In both accounts the father led his son to be sacrificed. Isaac carried the wood for the burnt offering in the same way Jesus carried his own cross to Golgotha. Even the rabbis alluded to this connection when they wrote that Isaac carried the wood "like one who carries his own cross upon his shoulder."[10] Interestingly the numeric value of "his cross" (134) in Luke 9:23 is the same as "I sacrifice to the LORD" (Ex. 13:15 NIV) and the verb meaning to "pardon [sin]" (Isa. 55:7). This affirms that the Messiah, like Isaac, would carry His own cross and sacrifice Himself to the Lord to forgive our sins.

Isaac asked his father about what they would offer as the sacrifice (Gen. 22:7). He understood that he was going to be slaughtered but continued voluntarily, completely submissive to the will of his father. This foreshadows Jesus, who asked the Father three times to please take the cup from Him but in the end submitted by saying, "Yet not My will, but Yours be done" (Luke 22:42). Jesus, like Isaac, wanted to please His Father and do His will.

Isaac was laid upon the wood as Jesus was laid upon the cross. Both had their hands and feet bound. Jesus was metaphorically bound when the religious leaders "led him away and handed him over to Pilate" (Mark 15:1 NIV); His hands and feet were later bound to the cross.

The Blood of the Lamb

Jesus died and spilled His blood at Passover as the "Lamb of God who takes away the sin of the world" (John 1:29). Not surprisingly, the rabbis associate Isaac with the Passover lamb. Before the exodus from Egypt, the Lord commanded the children of Israel to place the blood of the lamb on their doorposts in order to spare their firstborn sons.

One *Midrash* interprets the lamb's blood on the door as Isaac's: "What did God see [when he passed over the Israelites' houses]? He saw the blood of the binding of Isaac: as it is said, 'God will see for himself the lamb.'"[11]

In that *Midrash*, the blood of the Passover lamb symbolizes the sacrifice of Abraham's only son. "The blood of Isaac serves as an atonement. God remembers Isaac's sacrifice when he sees the lamb's blood, and in the merit of Isaac's willing self-sacrifice, he spares the blood-marked house from wrath."[12]

The offering of Isaac is seen by the rabbis as providing atonement for future generations in the same way the New Testament holds that Yeshua's death brings complete atonement for all generations' transgressions.

The Ram

The Lord tested Abraham and never intended Isaac to be sacrificed. God provided a ram for Abraham to offer "instead of his son" Isaac (Gen. 22:13). According to Jewish tradition, the ram that the Lord provided was no ordinary ram. It had been predestined for this purpose from the sixth day of Creation, having been kept in waiting in the Garden of Eden until that very moment. When Abraham looked up, he saw the ram caught in a thicket of thorns. He took the ram and offered it instead of his son.

God provided Jesus—the One predestined to be slain as the lamb of God from the foundation of the world—to be a substitute for us and atone for our sin. As prophesied, "He was pierced because of our transgressions. . . . The chastisement for our *shalom* was upon Him, and by His stripes we are healed" (Isa. 53:5).

The Resurrection

Isaac is pictured as dying and then resurrected, as Rabbi Yehuda said: "When the blade touched [Isaac's] neck, the soul of Isaac fled and departed . . . [Isaac's] soul returned to his body . . . and Isaac stood upon his feet. And Isaac knew that in this manner the dead in the future will be quickened."[13] The New Testament also makes this connection: "Abraham reasoned that if Isaac died, God was able to bring him back to life again. And in a sense, Abraham did receive his son back from the dead" (Heb. 11:19 NLT).

When does Isaac's resurrection occur? "On the third day" (Gen. 22:4). The third day is the day that God made the trees, the means by which the Fall came. It was on the third day that the Lord revealed Himself on Mount Sinai (Ex. 19:16). The third day is also prophetically seen as a day of redemption, restoration, and resurrection: "After two days He will revive us. On the third day He will raise us up, and we will live in His presence" (Hos. 6:2). This points to Jesus, who performed His first miracle of turning water into wine on the third day, was crucified at the third hour, experienced three hours of darkness on the cross, and rose on the third day in fulfillment of prophecy.

The Son Will Return

Rabbi Hanina ben Dosa explained that the horns of Abraham's ram were made into two shofars.[14] The shorter left horn was blown at Sinai on the third day, when God gave Israel the Torah. Its larger right horn will be sounded to announce the coming of the Messiah: "It will also come about in that day, a great *shofar* will be blown" (Isa. 27:13). This directly connects to the Second Coming of the Messiah. "For the Lord Himself shall come down from heaven with a commanding shout, with the voice of the archangel and with the blast of God's *shofar,* and the dead in Messiah shall rise first" (1 Thess. 4:16). Like Isaac, who figuratively rose from the dead and returned with Abraham, the Messiah, God's only begotten Son, died and rose from the dead, and He will return and cause us to rise from the dead as well.

THE BIRTH OF JACOB: THE DECEIVER

Isaac's life closely paralleled that of his father, Abraham. Isaac and his wife, Rebekah, also struggled with infertility. Like Abraham and Sarah, they dwelled among the Philistines. Isaac bent the truth, as his father did, by telling King Abimelech that Rebekah was his sister and not his wife.

Abraham did not want Isaac to marry a Canaanite woman, a descendant of the cursed line of Ham (Gen. 9:25–27). He was concerned that the immoral practices of the Canaanites might corrupt Isaac and the promised seed forever. So Abraham sent his servant Eliezer to find a bride for Isaac from among his relatives in Aram (Gen. 24:10). The Lord granted success. Bethuel allowed his daughter Rebekah to return to the land of Canaan to marry Isaac. The first time Rebekah laid eyes on Isaac, she literally fell off her camel. It was love at first sight (Gen. 24:64).

Isaac prayed for Rebekah's fertility, and eventually she conceived twins, Esau and Jacob. Although Esau was the older son, Jacob was the one through whom God's covenant with Abraham and Isaac would continue. Jacob, zealous for the blessing from his father, tried to obtain it by worldly and deceptive tactics. Encouraged and assisted by Rebekah, Jacob dressed up like his brother, Esau, and tricked Isaac into giving him the promised family blessing. Upon hearing that Esau was plotting to murder Jacob for stealing his rightful blessing, Rebekah convinced Isaac to send Jacob to Haran, both to protect his life and to find him a wife.

JACOB'S TRANSFORMATION

Then Jacob left Beer-sheba and went toward Haran.

—*Genesis 28:10*

The name *Beer Sheva* ("Beer-sheba," Gen. 28:10) means "Well of the Seven." In Hebrew, the number seven represents process, progress, completion, and time (such as the seven days of the week). The name "Haran" means "anger" and symbolizes the barriers that prevent us from reaching higher levels of spiritual growth and transformation. Jacob's journey from *Beer Sheva* to Haran points to the process for Jacob to progress to a new spiritual level.

Jacob's name means "supplanter" or "heel." In English, a heel is a person who steps on others to get ahead. This was Jacob at first; he was willing to use any means necessary to obtain the coveted blessing. But through the spiritual journey of transformation, he went from being a heel to being called Israel—"Prince of God." He became one who wrestled with God and was victorious (Gen. 32:29). Jacob needed to go through the process to gain the promise.

Jacob's Dream

He happened upon a certain place and spent the night there, for the sun had set. So he took one of the stones from the place and put it by his head and lay down in that place. He dreamed: All of a sudden, there was a stairway ["ladder" in Hebrew] set up on the earth and its top reaching to the heavens—and behold, angels of God going up and down on it! Surprisingly, *Adonai* was standing on top of it. (Gen. 28:11–13)

On his way to Haran, Jacob had a life-changing encounter. He dreamed of "a ladder standing earthward and its top reached the heaven."[15] The ladder originated in heaven and was sent to earth by the Lord Himself. The ladder is a vehicle of revelation, the means by which heaven and earth communicate. The Hebrew word for "ladder" is *sulam*, which has the same numeric value as "Sinai" and "voice" (130). God's voice (130) was heard at Sinai (130). Through the Torah given at Sinai (130), God's voice (130) can still be heard. The Torah—representative of God's Word, like Jacob's ladder (130)—is God's primary means of speaking to us.

Jesus said to His disciple Nathaniel, "Amen, amen I tell you, you will see heaven opened and the angels of God going up and coming down on the Son of Man!" (John 1:51). The ladder (130) Jacob saw is a symbol of the Messiah. In and through Him, the fullest revelation of God is made manifest to the world. The Voice (130) that spoke at Sinai (130) now speaks through the Messiah. "In these last days He has spoken to us through a Son" (Heb. 1:2).

As God, Jesus has origins in heaven but descended to earth by means of the incarnation. When Adam and Eve sinned, they broke the connection between heaven and earth. This connection would be restored through Jesus, the ladder. Believing in Him, listening to His voice, and walking with Him will lead you to new spiritual heights. Jesus has the power to turn you from a Jacob, or even an Esau, into an Israel—a prince/princess of God.

The Miracle of the Stone

Before Jacob went to sleep and dreamed of the ladder, he put a stone by his head (Gen. 28:11). When he awoke from his divine encounter, "Jacob got up and took **the stone [singular]**, which he had placed by his head, and set it up as a memorial stone and poured oil on top of it" (Gen. 28:18). According to one Jewish tradition, a miracle occurred, and three rocks became one stone. The three stones becoming one prophetically communicated to Jacob that the Lord would unite His name, His plan, and His promises with Jacob as He had done with Isaac and Abraham. Even though Jacob had used deceptive means to obtain God's blessing, the Lord assured him, by this miracle, that He would use Jacob to help advance the promised Seed and divine plan.

The three rocks in the Jewish tradition are an allusion to the essential triune nature of God. The word for "stone" in Hebrew (*evan*) has three letters, *aleph*, *bet*, and *nun*, and can be seen as an acronym for the Godhead: The *aleph*, which has a numerical value of 1, represents the *Abba/Av* (Father). The *bet* is symbolic of the Son; it is the first letter of the word *ben* and has a numerical value of 2. The *nun* has a numerical value of 50, which is associated with the Holy Spirit (*Ruach HaKodesh*) because the Holy Spirit was given at Pentecost, the fiftieth day. Fifty in Jewish thought is associated with freedom ("Where the Spirit of the Lord is, there is freedom," 2 Cor. 3:17 NIV). *Evan* can also be read as a contraction of the words *Av* (Father) and *Ben* (Son). This points to the fact that the Father is **seen** and made **manifest** through the Son. It also alludes to the oneness that exists between the two, as Jesus declared, "I and the Father are one" (John 10:30).

Wrestling for the Blessing

After Jacob spent twenty years serving his uncle Laban, the father of Rachel and Leah, the Lord told him to return to the land of his father (Gen. 31:3). Jacob obeyed the voice of God and headed home, despite being fearful of Esau's reaction.

The evening before seeing his brother, Esau, for the first time in two decades, Jacob had another spiritual encounter. A divine being appeared and wrestled all night with him. Jacob had previously wrestled with his father (Gen. 27:14–27), with his brother (Gen. 25:21–26; 27:30–41), and with his father-in-law (Gen. 29–31), but the only One he really needed to wrestle with to receive the blessing was the Lord (Gen. 32:25–31). This process of wrestling with God transformed him, causing the Lord to change his name in Genesis 32:29 from Jacob (which means "heel") to Israel, which means "the one who struggles with God and overcomes."

Jacob had to be broken before he could be blessed. The dislocation of his hip symbolized that he was broken but not fragmented. Brokenness is a prerequisite for becoming a person God can extraordinarily use. We should never trust a leader who does not walk with a limp.

The Sun Rose on Him

Jacob's all-night encounter with "the man" led to blessing as dawn approached. At the close of this incident, the text provides a seemingly superfluous detail: "The sun rose on him [Jacob]" (Gen. 32:31 NKJV).

This divine encounter left Jacob seriously wounded and in need of healing. Therefore, according to Jewish tradition, the Lord miraculously caused the sun to rise prematurely upon Jacob so that he might be healed in preparation for his confrontation with Esau.

How could an early sunrise bring about a special healing for Jacob? According to Jewish sages, this was no ordinary light that rose for Jacob; it was the *Ohr Haganuz*, the primordial divine light of Creation that originally lit the world. Adam and Eve basked in this supernatural light for three days until God hid it because of humanity's sinfulness.

In the phrase "sun rose on him" (Gen. 32:31 NKJV), the numeric value of "on him" is 36 (*lamed* = 30 and *vav* = 6), which is the exact number of daylight hours that Adam and Eve experienced the special light of Creation, according to Jewish tradition. In addition, the concept of light appears exactly thirty-six times in the Torah. Therefore, the numeric value of "on him" refers to the divine light the Lord used to bring healing to Jacob.

Jewish tradition also connects this special light with the Messiah: "The Jewish people are yearning for the light of the Messiah, as it is written, 'And God saw the light that it is good.' This teaches us that God foresaw Messiah and his activities even before the Creation of the world."[16]

It is even taught that the name of the Messiah is connected to the continued existence of the sun and to light itself, as Midrash Rabba stated:

What is the name of the Messiah? In the house of R. Yannai they said "*YINNON* is his name, for it is written May his name **be continued** [yinnon] as long as the sun (Ps. 72:17)." R. Biva said "*NEHIRA* ['Light'] is his name, for it is written, And the **light** [nehira] dwelleth with Him (Dan. 2:22), and it is spelled *nehira*."[17]

The New Testament writers stand in agreement with these texts and elaborate even further. For example, John wrote, "In Him was life, and the life was the light of men. And the light shines in the darkness, and the darkness did not comprehend it. . . . That was the true Light which gives light to every man coming into the world" (John 1:4–5, 9 NKJV). The apostle also wrote, "Then Jesus spoke to them again, saying, 'I am the light of the world. He who follows Me shall not walk in darkness, but have the light of life'" (John 8:12 NKJV).

John also wrote in Revelation 21:23 of the divine light: "The city was full of light, not the light of the sun, nor the moon, nor of candles, nor any artificial illumination; the Lord God was its light."[18]

The Messiah is both the source of this special light and the One who will bring it forth again in the messianic age, so that all might bask in the Lord's divine light and find healing and blessing as Jacob did. Yeshua told His followers, "You are the light of the world" (Matt. 5:14). You are called, like Yeshua, to be the light and help bring healing to this hurting world.

THE BLESSING REAFFIRMED

The faithful Lord watched over Jacob and brought him safely home. God appeared to Jacob once again at Bethel, the place where the ladder from heaven descended, and renewed the promise He had originally made with Abraham and Isaac. The words of this blessing connect directly to God's original promises to Adam and Eve. By telling Jacob to "be fruitful and multiply" (Gen. 35:11), the Lord was underscoring the fact that He was still in the process of bringing forth His original blessing for creation through the seed of Jacob. Jacob's twelve sons, whose descendants became the twelve tribes of Israel, tangibly demonstrated the Lord's faithfulness to this promise. God also promised that kings would come forth from Jacob's seed (Gen. 35:11). From Jacob and one of his twelve sons came the royal Seed, King Messiah, who was promised in Genesis 3:15.

The promise of the land, originally made to Abraham, then to Isaac, was reaffirmed with Jacob. The geographical boundaries of the land originally promised to Abraham "from the river of Egypt to the great river, the Euphrates River" (Gen. 15:18) appear to match the geographical borders of the Garden of Eden.[19] The prophet Isaiah confirmed this:

> For *Adonai* will comfort Zion.
> He will comfort all her waste places.
> He will make her wilderness like Eden,
> her desert like the garden of *Adonai*. (Isa. 51:3)

The three blessings that God gave to the patriarchs—(1) numerous descendants, (2) royalty who would culminate in the coming of King Messiah, and (3) the Promised Land, which was originally Eden—bring together the primary themes of Genesis, which will lead to the restoration of God's original blessing and plan for all creation.

chapter
FOUR

THE MESSIAH, SON OF JOSEPH AND JUDAH

Siblings! Who needs them? We can't live with them, and sometimes we can't live without them. I have two boys, and sometimes there's rivalry and a rumpus of emotions. Other times they band together and actually love and support each other. Joseph and Judah were part of a big family. There was rivalry and reconciliation and, in between, a story not only about two brothers but one that points to Messiah.

Joseph and Judah, two sons of Jacob, also provide two of the clearest prophetic portraits that point in great detail to the person and work of the Messiah. In Jewish thought, the stories of Joseph and Judah lead to the belief that there are two Messiahs: Messiah, Son of Joseph and Messiah, Son of David (the descendant, or "seed," of Judah). Their lives reveal two different yet critical aspects in the redemption process. Let's explore the lives of Joseph and Judah to discover some of the many mysteries of the Messiah.

THE SON OF JOSEPH

Joseph's life paints a powerful picture that foreshadows the Messiah's rejection and suffering. In Jewish tradition, the suffering Messiah is referred to as

Messiah, Son of Joseph (*Mashiach Ben Yosef*) or Ephraim, the son of Joseph who received the blessing of the firstborn. An examination of Joseph's life reveals that what happened to the first Joseph also happened to the second Joseph—Jesus.

Joseph, the Beloved and Favored Son

The story of Joseph begins with these words: "These are the genealogies of Jacob. When Joseph was 17 years old . . . he was shepherding" (Gen. 37:2). Commenting on this verse, Rabbi Sforno wrote, "The events which occurred to him . . . foreshadow our history during the second temple and our subsequent exile—the redemption at the end of time."[1] This underscores the idea that the events of Joseph's life point to future redemption through the Messiah.

There are several parallels between the lives of Joseph and Jesus. Joseph was the most loved and favored son of his father, Jacob. Similarly, Jesus is referred to by God the Father as "My beloved Son, in whom I am well pleased" (Matt. 3:17 NKJV). Joseph served his father as a shepherd, and Messiah Jesus is called the "Good Shepherd" (John 10:11). They both spent time in Egypt and were raised in Israel.

Joseph and Yeshua were both prophets who understood their callings to save Israel and the nations. Joseph's prophetic dreams that he shared with his brothers, as well as the dreams of Pharaoh that he interpreted, point to his role as the prophet and savior of Israel and Egypt. Yeshua, like Joseph, knew from a young age that He was called to be about His heavenly Father's business (Luke 2:49). Joseph was clothed by his father with a beautiful tunic as a sign of his father's favor and love (Gen. 37:3). Some early rabbinic commentators believe that Joseph's tunic was a sign of his elevated status and the leadership role he played as the son who was chosen to serve his father.[2] Yeshua was clothed with the Spirit and power by the Father as a sign of His elevated status and call to serve as the Messiah (Matt. 3:16; Luke 4:1). Despite all the signs that the Lord had anointed and appointed Jesus to be the promised Redeemer, "Even His brothers did not believe in Him" (John 7:5 NKJV). Similarly, Joseph's brothers had no faith in Joseph's dreams (Gen. 37:11).

Hatred of Joseph and Jesus

Joseph's brothers could not stand that their father loved their younger brother more than he loved them. Their disdain for Joseph grew deeper after Joseph shared his two dreams with them. They were unwilling to accept that Jacob and the Lord had chosen Joseph as the generational leader of the family. The senseless hatred they felt toward their brother was the sort of hatred exhibited toward Jesus by the religious leaders of His day (John 15:25).

This same senseless hatred led to the destruction of the second temple according to the rabbis.[3] The root cause of the second temple's destruction was the rejection of Yeshua and His message. He provided the antidote that would have cured the hatred that led to the destruction of God's house and the subsequent two-thousand-year exile from the Promised Land. The only way to overcome gratuitous hatred is with unconditional love, which is what Yeshua preached and lived. The leaders were unwilling to listen to His message. As a result, He said, "Look, your house is left to you desolate!" (Matt. 23:38). This was fulfilled in AD 70 when the Romans destroyed Jerusalem.

A Jewish teaching says that in AD 70, after the Romans broke down the walls of Jerusalem and were approaching the temple, the priest who was in charge, who held the keys of David, knew what was going to happen. These keys had the ability to open the gates of Jerusalem that David and Solomon built and that their descendants were responsible for. The priest threw the keys into the air, and a hand came down from heaven, captured the keys, and brought them to heaven—where they are to this day.

Concerning the keys of David, Isaiah wrote, "I will place on his shoulder the key of the house of David; he shall open, and no one shall shut; he shall shut, and no one shall open" (Isa. 22:22 NRSV). The only other place we read about the keys of David is in Revelation 3:7: "To the angel of the church in Philadelphia write: These are the words of him who is holy and true, who holds the key of David. What he opens no one can shut, and what he shuts no one can open" (NIV). The name *Philadelphia* means "city of brotherly love." Brotherly love is the key that opens the door that no man can shut.

When we have love for one another, doors begin to open on many levels. If you do not possess the keys of love, you do not possess the keys of David. Joseph and Jesus expressed this kind of love for people in the face of senseless hatred. As followers of the Messiah, we need to express this same sort of radical love to a world that increasingly hates us as people hated Joseph and Jesus.

Rejection of Joseph and Jesus

Joseph's brothers "plotted together against him in order to kill him" due to their jealousy and hatred (Gen. 37:18). Reuben, in an effort to prevent the death of his younger brother Joseph, suggested that they throw Joseph into a pit. Before casting him into the empty pit, they stripped Joseph of the special tunic his father had given him. Judah then suggested that they sell Joseph for twenty pieces of silver to some Ishmaelite slave traders. The brothers agreed and sold Joseph into slavery.

The life of Jesus had a similar pattern. The religious leaders—His Jewish brothers—"plotted to kill Him" (John 11:53). Yeshua was sold for silver by Judas, just as Joseph was sold by Judah. (This detail is often missed because, like many Jewish names in the New Testament, *Judah* was changed to *Judas* in the translation from the Hebrew into Greek and later English.)

Jesus, like Joseph, was stripped of his tunic (*ketonet passim*). According to the rabbis, "The tunic is called *passim* because [the ten brothers] cast lots over it . . . and the lot fell to Judah."[4] In the same way, the Romans stripped Jesus of His clothing (Matt. 27:28), cast lots for the garments, and divided His clothing among themselves (Matt. 27:35). This was to fulfill the messianic prophecy found in Psalm 22:18 (NIV).

There's more as we look at the numbers. The adjective describing Joseph's tunic is *passim* and can be interpreted as the garment's material or "fine wool." Its numeric value is 190, which is the same as the word for "end," *kets* ("the end of time"). Some rabbis believe this shared numeric value hints at Joseph having key aspects of the Messiah and that the end times were revealed to him by his father, Jacob, who had learned from Isaac, who was taught by Abraham. As it is written, "Abraham rejoiced to see My day; he saw it and was thrilled" (John 8:56).

The Hebrew word for "summer," *kayeets*, is related to the Hebrew word for "end," *kets*, for summer is the end of the agricultural season. This connection is seen in Mark 13:28: "Now learn the parable from the fig tree. When its branch becomes tender and puts forth leaves, you know that summer is near." Jesus used "summer" as an allusion to the end, which makes perfect sense in Hebrew.

The words "Canaan" and "curse" also equal 190. The rejection of Joseph points to the Messiah, who allowed His life to be ended to put an end to the curse (190) of sin, death, and exile so we can inherit the land of Canaan (190), the new Promised Land at the end of time when the Messiah returns.

Yeshua was placed in an empty tomb (John 19:41–42). Joseph's pit was empty and waterless (Gen. 37:24). There is a messianic allusion to this in Zechariah 9:11: "As for you also, by the blood of your covenant, I will release your prisoners from the waterless Pit." The grave is like a dungeon from which there is no escape, but the Messiah broke free, like Joseph, to save you and me.

The numeric value of the Hebrew word for "pit" (*haborah*) is 212, which is the same value as "in the valley" (*b'emek*). It is also the same as "the light" (*haohr*) in Genesis 1:4 and "brightness" (*zohar*) in Ezekiel 8:2. In your own life, your **valley** (212), **pit** (212), and prisons are not meant to be your death but the means of your promotion that cause **the light** (212) of God's presence to shine through you. This light reveals your hidden brightness as you "**wait**[5] [212] for His Son from heaven, whom He raised from the dead—*Yeshua*, the One delivering us from the coming wrath" (1 Thess. 1:10).

THE GOAT'S BLOOD

To cover their crime and deceive their father, Joseph's brothers killed a goat and dipped Joseph's tunic into it. Why a goat? The book of Jubilees and the later rabbis (such as Maimonides) connect the goat used by Joseph's brothers with the scapegoat used on Yom Kippur (Day of Atonement) to atone for the sins of God's people:

For this reason it is ordained for the children of Israel that they should afflict themselves on the tenth of the seventh month—on the day that the news which made him weep for Joseph came to Jacob his father—that they should make atonement for themselves thereon with a young goat on the tenth of the seventh month, once a year, for their sins; for they had grieved the affection of their father regarding Joseph his son.[6]

There are some amazing connections between the goat in Joseph's story and the scapegoat used on the Day of Atonement (Lev. 16). Both goats were killed in the desert and lots were cast. The same Hebrew word for "tunic" used in the Joseph account was also used to refer to the garment worn by the high priest. The high priest stripped off his tunic before immersing in water. With Joseph and on the Day of Atonement, the offense is placed on the goat. Both end in repentance and forgiveness.

More importantly, this detail of the goat/scapegoat connects to one of the primary roles of the Messiah, Son of Joseph: to suffer and die to make atonement for sin.

Of the various Day of Atonement sacrifices, the most central was that of the two he-goats. They were to be equal in height, weight, and cost. Next, lots were cast to determine which he-goat would be sacrificed as a sin offering upon the altar to the Lord and which would be designated as the scapegoat "for Azazel."[7]

The high priest then fastened a scarlet woolen thread to the head of the goat "for Azazel"; a second scarlet cord was tied to the entrance of the doors to the most holy section of the temple. Next, the high priest laid his hands upon the scapegoat again, reciting a confession of sin and prayer for forgiveness. After all those present responded to this prayer, an individual was chosen, preferably a priest, to take the goat to the precipice in the wilderness, where the scapegoat would be thrown over a steep and jagged cliff, so that its body would be completely torn apart before it reached the bottom.

The he-goat singled out for the Lord was a sin offering to make atonement for the national transgressions of Israel (Lev. 16:8–9). According to *halakhah*, Jewish law, the scapegoat brought atonement for all of Israel's sins, both large and small, except for the contamination of the sanctuary and the holy place, which were atoned for by the other he-goat.[8]

The teachings of Rabbi Alshich argue that the scapegoat did not completely wipe out Israel's sin but only prevented the negative consequences of sin from being manifested against the people. What is true of the scapegoat is true of all the sacrifices offered on the Day of Atonement: they only provided a covering for Israel's sins but did not remove them altogether.[9]

Ultimately Israel's Messiah would be the One to remove the nation's sin once and for all. The *Brit Chadashah*, New Testament, makes it clear that the scapegoat offering, as well as all the other sacrifices, foreshadowed the better sacrifice provided by Messiah Yeshua. Like the scapegoat, Messiah Yeshua has borne all our sin (Isa. 53:6, 11). He not only acts as our sin bearer but also completely removes our sins and purifies us from them.

An ancient Jewish practice ascribed by the rabbis in the Talmud tells us the red cords that were tied to the horns of the scapegoat and placed at the entrance of the Holy Place supernaturally turned from red to white to symbolize that God had washed Israel's crimson sins white as snow (Isa. 1:18). When this occurred, it publicly bore testimony that Israel had been forgiven. Like the high priest on Yom Kippur, Yeshua has the power to turn the crimson cords of our sin from red to white—not just on Yom Kippur but whenever we turn to Him and call upon His name for forgiveness.

According to the Talmud, forty years before the destruction of the temple, the scarlet cord stopped turning from red to white, proof that the Yom Kippur sacrifices were no longer efficacious.[10] The temple was destroyed in AD 70, which means that the cord stopped turning around AD 30, the time when the Messiah began His spiritual mission to bring redemption.

Yeshua's sacrifice as the Messiah, Son of Joseph is much greater than the he-goats offered by the high priest on Yom Kippur, for He removes our sin, brings forgiveness, and purifies us for all time through His one-time self-sacrifice.

There are many other parallels between Joseph and Jesus:

- Both were raised from the pit.
- Both overcame temptation and testing.
- Both were falsely accused and imprisoned.
- Both were elevated to positions of rulership at age thirty.
- Both had people come to them for food.
- Both would have their brothers bow down to them.
- Both were rejected by their family.
- All Israel and the nations were ultimately saved by them.

There are a couple of other parallels between Joseph and Jesus that are worth mentioning. First, Pharaoh and the Egyptians recognized that God was with Joseph and received Joseph before his Hebrew family received him. This pattern happened with Yeshua as well. Although the apostles and first followers of Yeshua were nearly all Jewish, the Gentiles—the nations of the world—were the ones who first received Yeshua on a large scale. Today there are over one billion Gentiles who claim Christianity as their religion, but there are only about two hundred thousand messianic Jews.

Second, Joseph's brothers did not recognize him at first when they traveled to Egypt. Joseph is a picture of Messiah, Son of Joseph—the hidden Messiah—the One who would be rejected by His brothers and hidden from them (Isa. 53:3–5). Joseph, like the Messiah, intentionally hid his identity from his brothers: "He made himself unrecognizable to them" (Gen. 42:7).

Another reason Joseph's brothers did not recognize him was because Joseph walked, talked, and looked like an Egyptian. He was a Hebrew concealed among the Gentiles. The same is true of Jesus. At His First Coming, He was literally the son of Joseph, fulfilling His role as Messiah, Son of Joseph, the hidden Messiah.

Joseph's brothers also didn't recognize Joseph because they thought he was dead. Their rejection of Joseph represents the Jewish political and spiritual leaders who have rejected Yeshua throughout the centuries. Joseph and his brothers were the founders of the twelve tribes of Israel. Only a remnant of Jews became followers of Messiah Yeshua, but they were the ones who originally brought the Gospel to the nations.

The large number of Gentiles who embraced the promised Jewish Messiah believed the Gospel, which is Jewish to the core. Jesus said to the Samaritan woman, "Salvation is from the Jews" (John 4:22). These Gentiles embraced the Old and New Testaments, which were written almost exclusively by Jews. However, the Gentiles quickly forgot and rejected the Jewish roots of their faith. As a result, Jesus was concealed among the Gentile nations as Joseph was concealed among the Egyptians. The Jewish Yeshua has become the Gentile Jesus.

Joseph's brothers did not recognize him until he took off his Egyptian garments and spoke to them in Hebrew: "I am Joseph!" (Gen. 45:3). If Yeshua's Jewish brothers are going to recognize Him today, Yeshua needs to dress in Jewish garments and be put back into His Jewish context. This context is key to preparing the way for the Messiah's return.

Joseph's name, in Hebrew, totals 156, which is the same as the phrase "Who is this coming from Edom?" (Isa. 63:1). According to Isaiah, the Messiah must come out of Edom. In Jewish thought, Edom is equated with Rome and Christianity. Yeshua has been in the church in disguise, but in the end of days, Messiah will open the eyes of the Jewish people and reveal Himself as Joseph did with his brothers. I believe that this time has come. God is starting to move in amazing ways among the Jewish people, preparing the way for the Lord's return.

The fact that you are reading this book is just one sign of the times. The eyes of the church must be opened to the Jewishness of Jesus, His Hebrew identity must be restored, and the church must embrace the Jewish followers of Yeshua—messianic Jews—as Pharaoh embraced Joseph. This must happen in preparation for the great move of the Lord in the last days. By embracing the message of this book, you, like John the Baptist, are preparing "the way for the Lord" (Matt. 3:3 NIV).

AN IMPORTANT DETOUR: JUDAH AND THE MESSIAH

Joseph is the focus of the Genesis narrative, from the mention of his birth to the closing chapter. Why, then, after recounting how Joseph's brothers sold him into slavery, does the narrative turn its attention from the fate of Joseph to highlight a seemingly seedy and strange event in the life of Joseph's brother Judah? In Genesis 38, Judah left his brothers, married a Canaanite woman, and had three sons. His firstborn son, Er, also married a Canaanite woman by the name of Tamar. Judah's son was evil, so the Lord took his life prematurely. Then Judah's second son, Onan, married Tamar in a levirate marriage.[11] Onan acted wickedly by intentionally not impregnating her. Due to this evil, the Lord also took Onan's life.

Judah sent Tamar back to her father's house and told her to wait till his youngest, Shelah, was old enough to give her a child. But when Shelah came of age, Judah refused to send him, fearing that he might die as well. Tamar, after hearing about the death of Judah's wife, and knowing that Judah was not going to fulfill his obligation to raise up seed in the name of his deceased son, dressed like a prostitute and tricked Judah into having sexual relations with her.

Upon hearing that Tamar was pregnant a few months later, Judah demanded she be put to death for her harlotry. Tamar responded by sending her father-in-law his own signet, its cord, and the staff Judah had given her in pledge for her services. Upon seeing them, Judah exclaimed, "She [Tamar] is more righteous than I, since I didn't give her to my son Shelah" (Gen. 38:26).

Rabbi Shmuel explained the great importance and purpose of this account:

The tribes [i.e., the brothers] were preoccupied with the selling of Joseph; and Joseph was preoccupied with his sackcloth and fasting; Reuben was preoccupied with his sackcloth and fasting; Jacob his sackcloth and fasting; and Judah was preoccupied with selecting a wife; and at that very time the Holy One, blessed is He, was busy creating the light of the Messiah.[12]

While it might have seemed that Israel's future was in jeopardy, the Lord was providently orchestrating all the events so that the line of the Messiah would be birthed. "The light of the Messiah" mentioned above refers to Perez (*Peretz* in Hebrew), the offspring of Judah and Tamar from whom the root of David, and ultimately the Messiah, would come (Gen. 38:29).

Peretz means "to break forth" or "breakthrough" and alludes to the Messiah. One of the names of the Messiah, according to Micah 2:13, is *Poretz*, which comes from *Peretz*:

> "One breaking through [*Poretz*, "the Messiah"] will go up
>   before them.
> They will break through,
> pass through the gate and go out by it.
> Their King will pass through before them
>   —*Adonai* at their head!"

This seemingly incongruous passage is significant as the author of Genesis was helping us keep our eyes on Judah. Even though Joseph was the one God used to save the family, the future of Israel resided with Judah. The promised Seed would come from the tribe of Judah through the *Peretz*, as seen in the book of Ruth and Jesus' genealogy. *Peretz* is one of the key links in the lineage of the Messiah, Son of David.

THE MESSIANIC CONTEXT

On his deathbed, Jacob gathered all his sons to bless them and to reveal to them what would befall "in the last days" (Gen. 49:1). The phrase "in the last days" (*beacharit hayyamim*) always refers to the time of the coming of the Messiah and has the numeric value of 726.

Incredibly, the number 726 connects to several key messianic prophecies in Isaiah, including "a child is born, a son will be given to us" (Isa. 9:5), "One from whom people hide their faces" (Isa. 53:3), and "like a lamb led to the slaughter, like a sheep before his shearers is silent, so He did not open His mouth" (Isa. 53:7). The numeric value of "the Messiah" in Hebrew is 363. When multiplied by two it equals 726, which hints that Genesis 49 will reveal truths about both Messiah, Son of Joseph, and Messiah, Son of David.

The Greek phrase for "that Messiah" (*O Messia*, John 4:25) and the Hebrew for "Yeshua's name" (*shem Yeshua*) also total 726. I believe the secret that Jacob wanted to reveal is "Yeshua's name" (726), who will come at the beginning of the end to die in fulfillment of Isaiah 53 as Messiah, Son of Joseph (the suffering servant) and at the actual end as the Messiah, Son of David (the conquering King).

There are not two Messiahs, as many traditional Jews believe, but two comings. The first time He came as Messiah, Son of Joseph, the suffering servant and the Lamb of God. He will return a second time as the Son of David, the warrior Messiah and conquering King who, like his ancestor David, will usher in a time of *shalom* (peace[13]) and blessing as the Lion of Judah. Jacob's blessing in Genesis 49:8–12 reveals secrets about both the First and Second Comings of the Messiah.

Genesis 49:8–12 is one of the Bible's most significant messianic prophecies. These verses contain the Shiloh prophecy, which provides insight into the lineage of the promised messianic Seed, some of the key signs that will accompany the Lord's anointed, and the time frame for the coming of the Messiah.

THE SHILOH PROPHECY: THE FIRST COMING

After Jacob assembled his sons, he began to prophesy over each of them. When it came time to bless his son Judah, Jacob gave a seminal prophecy about the Messiah:

> The scepter will not pass from Judah,
>   nor the ruler's staff from between his feet,

until he to whom it belongs will come.
To him will be the obedience of the peoples. (Gen. 49:10)

This unusual prophecy has several key words that need to be defined to understand it accurately. The first term, *shevet*, is usually translated as "scepter." In Hebrew, it means "tribe" and is best translated as "tribal rod." Each of the leaders of the twelve tribes had a tribal rod that represented tribal identity and leadership. This prophecy tells us something important about the identity of the promised Seed of the woman who will defeat the serpent (Gen. 3:15). He will be a King from the tribe of Judah.

The second key word is *me-cho-kek*, usually translated as "the ruler's staff" but best interpreted as "the judge's staff" or "lawgiver's staff." When a king sat on his throne, he was exercising both political power and judicial authority. It was common practice for a king to rest his judge's staff on his knee. Today this would be analogous to the judge's gavel.

The third key term is *Shiloh*, as in "until Shiloh comes" (Gen. 49:10 NKJV). All the Jewish commentators and rabbis understand this as a reference to the Messiah. For example:

> The transmission of dominion shall not cease from the house of Judah, nor the scribe from his children's children, forever, **until Messiah comes.**[14]

> Kings shall not cease from the house of Judah . . . **until the time of the coming of the King Messiah** . . . to whom all the dominions of the earth shall become subservient.[15]

The Hebrew phrase "until Shiloh comes" (*yavo shiloh*) has the numeric value of 358. The value of "Messiah" (*Mashiach*) and "serpent" (*nachash*) also total 358. Messiah (358), the Seed of the woman, will defeat the serpent (358) once and for all by "His sacrifice" (*korbono*), which equals 358. Jesus said, "Just as Moses lifted up the serpent in the desert, so the Son of Man must be lifted up, so that whoever believes in Him may have eternal life"

(John 3:14–15). The Messiah, at His First Coming, defeated the serpent spiritually. But when He returns, He will completely crush his head and all will know **the Lord reigns, the Lord has reigned, and the Lord will reign** (which is 358 in Hebrew).

"Shiloh" clearly refers to the Messiah but can also be interpreted as "the one to whom it belongs," as in the power and authority of kingship given to the Messiah. Let me paraphrase Genesis 49:10 to provide a clearer understanding: **Tribal identity and judicial authority will not cease from Judah until the Messiah, the one to whom these legitimately belong, comes. And people from every nation will acknowledge and obey Him as King.**[16]

One of the amazing mysteries revealed by interpreting Genesis 49:10 in this manner is that it provides the time frame for the First Coming of the Messiah. This verse prophetically discloses that judicial authority and tribal identity will not be lost from Judah until the Messiah arrives.

"Judicial authority" is the right to administer and enforce Torah law upon the Jews living in Judea, including the right to adjudicate capital cases and apply capital punishment. According to Josephus, judicial authority was lost around AD 6–7, when Archelaus, the son and heir of King Herod, was dethroned and replaced by a Roman procurator named Coponius. From this point on, the legal power of the Sanhedrin was greatly restricted.

The rabbis in the Talmud also mentioned the loss of judicial authority:

> Forty years before the Temple was destroyed, the Sanhedrin was exiled from the Chamber of Hewn Stones and sat in the stores on the Temple Mount. With regard to the last statement, the Gemara asks: What are the halakhic ramifications of this statement? . . . That they no longer judged capital cases. The authority to impose the death penalty was stripped from the Sanhedrin, and therefore they willingly left the Chamber of Hewn Stone.[17]

The temple was destroyed in AD 70. This puts the time mentioned here around AD 30. It appears that judicial authority was lost sometime between 6 BC and AD 30.

Julius Magath, in his book *Jesus Before the Sanhedrim*, recorded a statement by Rabbi Rachmon:

> When the members of the Sanhedrin found themselves deprived of their right over life and death, a general consternation took possession of them: they covered their heads with ashes, and their bodies with sackcloth, exclaiming: **"Woe unto us for the scepter has departed from Judah and the Messiah has not come."**[18]

Based upon a rabbinic understanding, the Messiah had to come between AD 30—which is forty years before the destruction of the temple, the exact time Jesus' ministry began—and AD 70, which is when the official genealogical records were destroyed and the Jewish people were exiled.

THE SHILOH PROPHECY: THE SECOND COMING

> To him will be the obedience of the peoples.
> Binding his foal to the vine,
>> his donkey's colt to the choice vine,
>> he washes his garments in wine,
>> and in the blood of grapes his robe.
> His eyes are darker than wine,
>> and teeth that are whiter than milk.
>
> —*Genesis 49:10–12*

Another way to interpret *Shiloh* is based on the Hebrew phrase "a gift unto him" (*shai lo*). As it is written, "Let all around Him bring tribute [*shai*] to the One who is to be feared" (Ps. 76:12). This interpretation suggests the gifts that kings and world leaders would offer as tribute to King Messiah.

> Nations will come to your light,
> kings to the brilliance of your rising.

The wealth of nations will come to you.

They will bring **gold and frankincense**,

and proclaim the praises of *Adonai*. (Isa. 60:3, 5, 6)

"Let all kings bow down before him, / and all nations serve him" (Ps. 72:11).

These prophecies were partially fulfilled when Jesus was born and the wise men, kings from the East in Christian tradition, came to visit Him. They "fell down and worshiped Him" and "presented to Him gifts of **gold, frankincense**, and myrrh" in recognition that Jesus was the messianic King of Israel (Matt. 2:11). The Messiah, Son of David will be much greater than King David, His ancestor, for He will not just rule over Israel, but all the nations of the world will acknowledge His kingship and will serve and honor Him with their wealth.

Several of the prophets built on the imagery of Genesis 49 when they described the idyllic state of the messianic age. "'In that day,' declares *Adonai-Tzva'ot*, 'every man will invite his neighbor to sit under the vine and under the fig tree'" (Zech. 3:10; see also Mic. 4:4). Jesus, at His First Coming, provided a sneak preview of this when He performed His first miracle at the wedding in Cana.

Knowing the wine had run out, Mary asked Jesus to help. He had the servers fill six stone pots to the brim with water. Then He miraculously turned it to wine (John 2:1–11). The abundance of wine that accompanied this miracle points to Jesus as the messianic King who came to bring abundant life and blessing, in partial fulfillment of Genesis 49 and the many other prophecies that associate wine with the coming Kingdom. Amos 9:13 says, "Behold, days are soon coming . . . when . . . the mountains will drip sweet wine and all the hills will melt over." When Yeshua turned the water into wine, He was proclaiming, "I am the Messiah you have been awaiting."

Living Out of the Overflow

Jesus said, "I have come that they might have life, and have it abundantly!" (John 10:10). With His death and resurrection, the Kingdom of

God became a reality. We can already begin to experience, in part, the abundance of the Kingdom today. We are meant not to merely survive but to thrive—to live in the overflow, not in the shortage or out of the lack.

After Jesus turned the water into wine, the stone pots overflowed, and there was enough wine for the future. When God multiplied the loaves and the fishes (Mark 6:30–44), there was some left over. There's always more than enough with God.

No matter how difficult the situation, we have to understand that God is generous, He is good, and He desires to bless us and provide for our needs. He wants us to have prosperity of our souls—spiritually, emotionally, and relationally.

JOSEPH AND JUDAH: THERE'S MORE

God created the world in six days and rested on the seventh. In Jewish thought, the six days of Creation indicate that the world can exist for a maximum of six thousand years before the Messiah has to come and reign for one thousand years. As the Midrash Pirkei De Rabbi Eliezer stated, in the Hebrew reckoning of time, "Six eons for going in and coming out, for war and peace. The seventh eon is entirely Shabbat and rest for life everlasting."[19] There is a universally acknowledged belief in Judaism that the Messiah must come by the seventh millennium. The Messiah can come earlier, but not later. Currently on the Hebrew calendar we are in the decade of 5780.

Each day of Creation prophetically points to one millennium, which is based on Psalm 90:4: "For a thousand years in Your sight are like a day." The six days of working and the seventh day of resting, like the sabbatical year, become a prophetic picture of the messianic Kingdom. The messianic Kingdom is known as the time that is "all Shabbat,"[20] for the world will enter into a time of *shalom* and rest under the Messiah's reign. This is alluded to by the Hebrew word *sheishet* ("six"), which has the numeric value of 1,000. The Messiah must come and establish the millennial Kingdom by the end of the sixth millennium, and we're in that now.

As previously mentioned, there are two aspects of the Messiah: Messiah, Son of Joseph and Messiah, Son of David. Messiah, Son of Joseph will be rejected and suffer to atone for the sins of Israel, like Joseph in the book of Genesis. The Messiah fulfilled this role at His First Coming when He prophetically fulfilled the spring holidays of Passover, Firstfruits, and Pentecost. The Messiah, at the Second Coming, will return and fulfill the role of Messiah, Son of David. As the descendant of King David, Messiah Yeshua will defeat God's enemies and establish the messianic Kingdom for one thousand years from Jerusalem. On that day the Messiah will also fulfill the fall holidays of the Feast of Trumpets, Day of Atonement, and Feast of Tabernacles.

In Hebrew, "Messiah, Son of Joseph" has a numeric value of 566 and "Messiah, Son of David" totals 434. When you add these two aspects of the Messiah together, you get 1,000. When Yeshua—the "Holy One" (1,000)—finally fulfills both messianic roles, as the sacrificial Lamb of God and as the Lion of Judah, the lion will lie down with the lamb, and the Lord will establish the millennial Kingdom of God. May it come speedily and soon.

chapter
FIVE

THE MESSIAH REVEALED IN MOSES

His Good Birth

Moses, the greatest prophet of the Hebrew Bible and central figure in Judaism, was used by God not only to free Israel from slavery to the greatest superpower of its day but also to give the Ten Commandments and the Torah to the Hebrew people. No leader or prophet is as loved and revered by the Jewish people as Moses. Let's explore Moses' life and his uniqueness as a leader and prophet to understand how he points to Messiah Jesus and what practical transformative lessons this holds for us.

What did Moses do for his people, and how does he connect to the Messiah? Before we look into those questions, we need to understand the times that foreshadowed Moses' birth, his upbringing in Pharaoh's palace, and the leader he became.

THE ISRAELITES IN EGYPT

Initially seventy Jewish people settled in Egypt (Gen. 46:27). As we expound later in chapter 10, Egypt was like a womb for the children of Israel. The womb is a tight and confining space, but it provides the perfect environment for babies to grow and develop.

Due to God's blessing, Egypt became a fertile womb for the Jewish people: "The Israelites were exceedingly fruitful; they multiplied greatly, increased in numbers and became so numerous that the land was filled with them" (Ex. 1:7 NIV). The language used to describe Israel's growth in Egypt is the same as the Creation account, where the Lord told Adam and Eve to "be fruitful and multiply, fill the land" (Gen. 1:28). God's original blessing to mankind, which the Lord swore to restore through Abraham by promising that his seed would be as numerous as the stars of the sky (Gen. 15:5), began to come to fruition in Egypt.

The growth of Israel also caused its people to experience the negative side of Egypt, which led to their physical confinement as slaves. Many years after Joseph's death, Pharaoh enslaved the children of Israel out of fear. He said, "We must deal shrewdly with them, or else they will grow even more numerous, so that if war breaks out, they may join our enemies, fight against us, and then escape from the land" (Ex. 1:10). With Pharaoh's decree, Egypt became a place of restriction for the Israelites in the most negative way possible, as the Scripture states: "They put slave masters over them to oppress them with forced labor . . . and worked them ruthlessly. They made their lives bitter with harsh labor. . . . the Egyptians worked them ruthlessly" (Ex. 1:11, 13–14 NIV).

Pharaoh thought that the backbreaking labor would cause a decrease in the explosive growth of the Israelites, but by God's grace, "the more they were oppressed, the more they multiplied and spread" (Ex. 1:12 NIV).

In the midst of all this hardship, we find a spiritual principle that is a source of encouragement in tough times: **God can use persecution to cause you to prosper**. This paradox of persecution and the resulting blessing demonstrates the power, goodness, and kindness of God. The more physically weak the people became, the more God's blessing was released.

The apostle Paul, a true Hebrew, experienced that same truth. He wrote in 2 Timothy 3:11, "Persecutions and sufferings . . . happened to me in Antioch, Iconium, and Lystra. What persecutions I endured! And the Lord rescued me from them all!" What was true for Israel in Egypt can be true for all faithful followers of the Messiah. Dr. J. Paul Nyquist gave this perspective on persecution: "Persecution means we're blessed, not cursed. Persecution brings blessing because it allows us to know Christ more."[1]

Things went from bad to worse for the Israelites. In response to his ineffective population-control plan, Pharaoh decreed that every Hebrew son born was to be thrown into the Nile River (Ex. 1:22). What motivated this diabolical decision? According to Jewish tradition, the astrologers of Egypt saw in a vision that the savior of Israel would soon be born and that his downfall would come by means of water. They thought their vision indicated that Moses would be killed in the water. When Moses' mom, Jochebed, cast baby Moses into the water, although he was protected in an ark, the astrologers said they no longer saw in the stars the sign they had seen as the downfall of the leader of the Hebrews by water; therefore, they canceled their decree. But they did not know that their vision foretold that Moses would be stricken because of the waters of Meribah (Num. 20:2–13).[2]

The divine irony is amazing. What was meant to bring about the demise of Israel's redeemer led to his deliverance. What's even more ironic is that it was Pharaoh's own daughter who rescued Moses and raised him as a prince of Egypt. Nothing can hinder God's plan. He works all things according to His will. **What others use to try to harm you, God can use to help you.**

Amazingly Pharaoh's decree to kill the Hebrew baby boys foreshadows and prophetically connects to the birth of Jesus. After the birth of Jesus, astrologers known as magi came to Herod and asked, "Where is the One who has been born King of the Jews? For we saw His star in the east and have come to worship Him" (Matt. 2:2). Herod, who was greatly disturbed, inquired of the Jewish religious leaders and was told that the Messiah would be born in Bethlehem, as the prophet Micah wrote:

> "But you, Bethlehem, in land of Judah,
>   are by no means least among the rulers of Judah;
> for out of you will come a ruler
>   who will shepherd My people Israel."
>   (Matt. 2:6 NIV; see Mic. 5:1–3)

As a result, Herod made a decree that all boys age two and under should be put to death (Matt. 2:16).

The parallels between Pharaoh's and Herod's actions are unmistakable. Both learned from astrologers about Israel's Savior. Both leaders decreed the murder of Jewish boys, which was satanically motivated to kill the promised Seed of the woman (Gen. 3:15) to prevent God's plan of redemption from being fulfilled. In these two acts we get a glimpse of how the seed of the serpent continually tried to attack and bruise the Seed of Eve but to no avail.

MOSES' BIRTH AND DIVINE LIGHT

Supernatural events accompanied the births of Moses and the Messiah. Their birth accounts parallel each other in important ways, providing proof that Jesus is the prophet like Moses (Acts 3:22).

According to Jewish tradition, when Moses was born, the whole house in its entirety was filled with light.[3] This was the divine light, the same light that shone on the first day of Creation. The light that radiated from Moses was a sign to his family, and, ultimately, to the children of Israel, that the night of exile was coming to an end. The darkness was going to give way to the light of salvation. Scripture states, "The LORD is my light and my salvation" (Ps. 27:1 NIV) and "Weeping may stay for the night, but rejoicing comes in the morning" (Ps. 30:5 NIV). The divine light that illuminated the house was a sign that Moses was the redeemer of Israel who would bring the light of redemption.

Where do rabbis derive this interpretation? At Moses' birth, his mom "saw that he was good, and she hid him for three months" (Ex. 2:2 literal translation). The first time the term "good" (Hebrew, *tov*) is used in the Bible is in reference to the light of the first day of Creation. This was no ordinary light. It was the divine light of the Lord, for the sun and other luminaries were not created till the fourth day. The first thing God "saw" and called "good" in the beginning was the divine light in Genesis (Gen. 1:4). This connects to Moses, for in the same way his mother "saw" him, and he is called "good" at the beginning of Exodus.

Jewish tradition says that God hid the divine supernatural light because He saw that people would misuse it due to the Fall. One place that the Lord hid the light was in the Torah. The Torah, the foundation of the Word of God, was the repository for the divine light that brings life and blessing, as the Scriptures teach: "Your word is a lamp to my feet and a light to my path" (Ps. 119:105). Through the study of the Word, the light of the Lord is released into our lives and provides abundance and blessing.

The Torah, also known as the Five Books of Moses, was given through Moses. He emanated the divine light of the Torah at his birth, for he was the one who was destined to bring the light of the Torah into the world. That light became hidden when Moses was placed in the basket that would be put into the Nile River. This light was once again made manifest when Moses descended from Mount Sinai with the Ten Commandments:

Now it happened, when Moses came down from Mount Sinai with the two tablets of the Testimony in his hand when he came down from the mountain, that Moses did not know that the skin of his face was radiant, because God had spoken with him. When Aaron and all *Bnei-Yisrael* saw Moses, the skin of his face shone in rays, so they were afraid to come near him.

When Moses was done speaking with them, he put a veil over his face. But when Moses went before *ADONAI*, so that He could speak with him, he took the veil off until he came out. When he came out and spoke to *Bnei-Yisrael* what he was commanded, *Bnei-Yisrael* saw the face of Moses and that the skin of his face glistened. So Moses put the veil back over his face until he went in to speak with Him. (Ex. 34:29–30, 33–35)

Light shone forth from Moses at his birth as a sign that through him the light of salvation and redemption would spring forth.

The birth of Moses was a sneak preview of the birth of the Messiah, who was to be greater than Moses (Heb. 3:3). Therefore, it is significant that the birth of the Messiah is associated with the divine light of the Lord's glory. At the birth of Jesus, an angel of the Lord appeared to shepherds in the field, "and the glory of *Adonai* shone all around them" (Luke 2:9). The angel proclaimed, "Good News. . . . A Savior is born to you today in the city of David, who is Messiah the Lord. . . . And suddenly a multitude of heavenly armies appeared with the angel, praising God and saying, 'Glory to God in the highest,' and on earth *shalom* to men of good will'" (vv. 10–11, 13–14).

Approximately thirty-one days after Jesus' birth, His parents took Him up to Jerusalem for His *pidyon haben*, the redemption of the firstborn son ceremony. Simeon the priest was the one who performed this ceremony to fulfill the requirement of the Torah. Upon receiving the baby Yeshua in his arms, Simeon, who was in the Spirit, prophetically declared:

> "Now may You let Your servant go in peace, O Sovereign
>   Master,
> according to Your word.
> For my eyes have seen Your salvation,
>   which You have prepared
>   in the presence of all peoples:
> 'A light for revelation to the nations'
> and the glory of Your people Israel." (Luke 2:29–32)

According to Jewish tradition, the same light that accompanied the birth of Moses was made manifest and recognized by both the shepherds and Simeon the priest. Through the Messiah, the One who was greater than Moses (Heb. 3:3), the fullness of the light of redemption and the Word was revealed. At His advent, as at Moses' birth, the light of salvation and revelation was being revealed as a sign that the dark night of exile was coming to an end. As the prophet said, "The people walking in darkness" were beginning to see "a great light" (Isa. 9:2 NIV).

The divine light that appeared at Moses' birth is associated with the "good" light that shone in the heavens at Creation and was revealed once again in the heavens at the birth of the Messiah. The magi, wise men from the East, saw a brilliantly shining star in the heavens and followed it to Jerusalem. After taking leave of King Herod, they departed and "the star they had seen in the east went on before them, until it came to rest over the place where the Child was" (Matt. 2:9).

NO ORDINARY STAR

Messianic teacher and scholar Arnold Fruchtenbaum gave five reasons that it was not a literal star that the wise men saw:

1. It is called the Messiah's star.
2. It appeared and disappeared on at least two or more occasions.
3. It moved from east to west.
4. It moved from north to south.
5. It literally came down and hovered over one particular house in the town of Bethlehem.[4]

The Hebrew word for "star" is *cocav*, which can mean "radiance" or "glory." The wise men found Him not by a star but through the *Shechinah* Glory, which is God's manifest presence. This connects the light of Creation, which is called "good" (Gen. 1:4), with the same light that appeared at the birth of Moses, whose mother saw he was "good" (Ex. 2:2), and with the light that appeared in the heavens, both to the shepherds and the wise men, as a sign of the good news that a greater Savior than Moses had been born.

But what does this mean practically for us? This light was and is the light of hope. The light of redemption that was revealed through Moses' birth took years to manifest in Israel's redemption. In Yeshua, we get a glimpse of this light and begin to experience salvation, but this will not fully materialize until His return. This is known as the blessed hope. The Old and New Testaments testify to it. Don't lose heart.

The birth of Jesus is the birth of hope. Pharaoh tried to extinguish the light of hope, the light of Israel's salvation and freedom, but he could not.

The Roman rulers and the religious leaders tried to extinguish this light that shone through Yeshua, and they failed as well. They are all in the grave, but the light of Jesus still burns bright centuries later. Don't let anyone steal your hope. Hope declares that things will be different. The ultimate source of hope is found in Yeshua, as Paul wrote:

> Now we do not want you to be uninformed, brothers and sisters, about those who are asleep, so that you may not grieve like the rest who have no hope. For if we believe that *Yeshua* died and rose again, so with Him God will also bring those who have fallen asleep in *Yeshua*. For this we tell you, by the word of the Lord, that we who are alive and remain until the coming of the Lord shall in no way precede those who are asleep. For the Lord Himself shall come down from heaven with a commanding shout, with the voice of the archangel and with the blast of God's *shofar*, and the dead in Messiah shall rise first. Then we who are alive, who are left behind, will be caught up together with them in the clouds, to meet the Lord in the air—and so we shall always be with the Lord. Therefore encourage one another with these words. (1 Thess. 4:13–18)

> Behold, I tell you a mystery:
>> We shall not all sleep,
>> but we shall all be changed—
>> in a moment, in the twinkling of an eye,
>> at the last *shofar*.
>> For the *shofar* will sound,
>> and the dead will be raised incorruptible,
>> and we will be changed. (1 Cor. 15:51–52)

The Lord will return, hope will be fulfilled, and your future will truly be so much better than your past. And what do we need to do? In John 11:40, Yeshua said to Martha, who was grieving the death of her brother, Lazarus: "Didn't I tell you that **if you believed**, you would see the glory of

God?" Martha was stuck. She didn't believe as strongly as she needed. But Yeshua made it clear to her, and to us, that we can find hope when we come to Yeshua as little children and believe. We will see His glory, and we can put our past behind us if we only believe.

chapter
SIX

THE MESSIAH, GREATER THAN MOSES
His Divine Calling

I f you've ever seen anything on fire, especially a hay meadow or a tree, you know how fast it burns up. It's pretty much *whoosh*, and it's gone. That's not what Moses experienced. He was tending his father-in-law's flock of sheep one day when he came upon a bush that was burning. The strange thing was that it was on fire, but it wasn't being consumed. As he stepped over to investigate, he heard a voice coming out of the fire, calling his name, "Moses! Moses!" We can only imagine the shock he had to have felt.

What was happening? God was speaking to Moses from a burning bush and calling him to redeem the children of Israel (Ex. 3:1–2). Of all the ways the Lord could have spoken to Moses, why did He choose to do so in this way? At first glance it seems a bit strange. The Lord was about to display His power and might through miraculous signs and wonders in a way the world had never seen, yet it all began with God speaking from a lowly bush in the desert.

This was no ordinary bush; it was a thornbush (Hebrew, *hasineh*). This small detail communicates a deep and beautiful message. Beginning in Genesis 3, thorns are associated with hardship, suffering, and exile. Thus, it is no surprise that God commissioned Moses to redeem Israel out of the Egyptian exile from a thornbush. Commenting on this point, the *Midrash* says:

> Why did He appear in the midst of a bush of thorns rather than in a large tree or a column of smoke? The Holy One, blessed be He, said: I have stated in the Torah: I will be with him [Israel] in trouble (Ps. 91:15); inasmuch as they were enslaved, I appeared in a bush of thorns, which is a place of trouble. Therefore, out of the midst of a bush which is full of thorns, I appeared unto him.[1]

By appearing to Moses in a thornbush, God was telling Israel that He had heard their cries and identified with their suffering. When Moses shared this reality with his enslaved sisters and brothers, they were overwhelmed:

> Aaron told them everything the LORD had said to Moses. He also performed the signs before the people, and they believed. And when they heard that the LORD was concerned about them and had seen their misery, they bowed down and worshiped. (Ex. 4:30–31 NIV)

The Lord is attuned to the pain of His children and, like any loving parent, wants to alleviate it. His loving care for us should give us pause and cause us to praise our heavenly Father. The fact that the Creator of the universe sees our pain and cares deeply for us is truly amazing and should be a source of comfort for us in difficult times.

Thorns are connected not only to redemption from Egypt but also to the even greater exodus that comes through the prophet greater than Moses (Deut. 18:18), the Messiah. This connection is one of the reasons Jesus had a crown of thorns placed upon His head right before He died as the Passover Lamb (Matt. 27:29).

In the person of Yeshua, the Lord not only appeared in a thornbush but also wore a crown of thorns to demonstrate how much He was willing to identify with us and feel human pain so He could set us free from the slavery to sin and from death. The crown of thorns on Yeshua's head, and the cross in general, declare loudly that the Lord loves and cares for you and was willing to feel your pain.

Moses had this encounter with the Lord in the thornbush while he was alone, going about his ordinary routine of shepherding his father-in-law's flock in the desert. God prepares us through the seemingly mundane. All of life is preparing you for who you are called to be and what you are called to do. When God calls you to step into your destiny, it often happens unexpectedly. There are many biblical examples of this, such as King David being called suddenly, like Moses, while he was shepherding. Yeshua calls people to leave everything and follow Him. His disciples did follow, but many didn't (Luke 9:56–62).

Often it's not convenient when God calls us. Sometimes it seems like forever—even Jesus, the Son of God, had to wait thirty years before starting His earthly ministry. But when it happens, it can happen in a moment, as it did for Moses and David. When we are called, we must be willing to drop everything, just as some of the disciples dropped their nets, and go where the Lord calls us.

What has the Lord called you to drop? When the Lord calls, will you follow? God is looking for modern-day Moseses. God's appearing to Moses in the midst of a burning thornbush was an eternal promise that the Lord would forever be with His people in their pain and suffering until the curse is reversed and exile has ended. Yeshua embodied this truth more than anyone, and we are called to follow His example. The world needs people who will hear the Lord's call and bring His message of salvation and healing to a hurting and dying world.

TAKE OFF YOUR SANDALS

When *ADONAI* saw that he turned to look, He called to him out of the midst of the bush and said, "Moses, Moses!"

So he answered, "*Hineni*" [Here I am].

> Then He said, "Come no closer. Take your sandals off your feet, for the place where
> you are standing is holy ground."
>
> —*Exodus 3:4–5*

The Lord told Moses not to come any closer until he removed his sandals because Moses was standing on "holy ground" (Ex. 3:5). What made it holy was the presence of the Lord, the Holy One of Israel. The ground was also holy because the place where God appeared to Moses and spoke with him from the burning bush was the same place that the Lord would speak to all Israel from a blazing fire on the mountain.

Removing Spiritual Barriers

The purpose of shoes is to create a barrier that protects your feet from experiencing pain or discomfort. Shoes, therefore, represent a barrier and symbolize disconnection. God told Moses to take off his shoes because He wanted Moses to be completely connected to Him on a spiritual level. He wanted Moses to fully experience His holy presence.

Removing the Locks That Limit You

The Hebrew word for "sandals" in Exodus 3:5 is *na-a-laim*. This word comes from the same root as "lock"—*na'al*. Like Moses, we must remove those things that keep us locked up and confined. Moses was locking himself out of his calling and destiny by focusing on all his shortcomings—the things he felt made him an unworthy candidate to become the redeemer of Israel.

Moses struggled with inner barriers and had physical limitations, such as his speech impediment, that made him feel unqualified and insufficient. These types of barriers tend to separate us from God, our true selves, and others. The removing of the shoes is symbolic of the removal of physical, emotional, and spiritual limitations that keep us from the deeper connection and calling on our lives. When we live from the place of connection, we begin to experience God differently.

Removing Disconnection and Desensitization

Moses' removal of his shoes also symbolized removing the barriers that keep us from connecting to God and others. Taking off one's shoes is symbolic of connecting with people on a deeper level.

The foot is one of the most sensitive parts of the body. Each foot has more than seven thousand nerve endings that connect to every organ and system in your body, according to reflexology. Shoes create a barrier that protects our feet from feeling pain. Shoes limit sensitivity and thus are symbolic of spiritual disconnection and desensitization to the feelings and pain of others. This relates back to why God appeared to Moses in the midst of a burning thornbush, which was to communicate that He feels the pain of His people. In the same way, God wants Moses, and all of us, to feel and identify with the pain of His people.

The priests of Israel wore no shoes or sandals anywhere in the temple. There could be nothing that prevented contact between the foot of the priest and the temple floor. Any barriers rendered the services the priest performed invalid.[2] The priests' lack of shoes demonstrated their connection to the people, whose burdens and pains they were to help bear before the Lord. In addition, the entire temple complex was seen as holy ground. The priests could not allow anything to create a barrier between them and the Lord's holy ground.

These reasons for Moses' removal of his sandals underscore Jesus' motives for washing His disciples' feet at the Last Supper, which was a Passover Seder. They give meaning to why He walked barefoot to the cross and had His bare feet pierced. He was identifying with our pain. His life and death were about removing barriers, restoring connection, and deepening our sensitivity to the hurts of others so that they might find healing and wholeness. We are called to follow His example by being willing to take off our shoes and be sent by God, like Moses and the disciples, to proclaim the good news of salvation and transformation. As the Scripture says, "How beautiful on the mountains are the feet of him who brings good news" (Isa. 52:7).

Through Jesus, you can overcome your limitations. You can break through barriers. The Lord wants you to have a deeper level of connection and sensitivity to things of the Spirit. Ask Him to help you take off your shoes so you can unlock the fullness of His blessing for your life.

USE WHAT'S IN YOUR HAND

In response to the Lord's command to deliver the children of Israel from Egypt, Moses said to God, "But look, they will not believe me or listen to my voice. They will say, '*ADONAI* has not appeared to you'" (Ex. 4:1). Moses did not think the Israelites would believe that the Lord had sent him to free them, given his past experiences with them and his personal limitations. But the Lord was not going to take no for an answer.

He responded to Moses, "What is that in your hand?" (Ex. 4:2). The Lord then proceeded to give Moses three signs that would prove he was being sent from God.

The First Sign: Moses' Staff Turned to a Serpent

The first sign involved his staff.

> Then He said, "Cast it on the ground." When he cast it to the ground, it became a serpent, so Moses fled from before it. Then *ADONAI* said to Moses, "Stretch out your hand, and take it by the tail." So he put out his hand, laid hold of it, and it became a staff in his hand.
>
> "This is so that they may believe *ADONAI*, the God of their fathers—the God of Abraham, Isaac and Jacob—has appeared to you." (Ex. 4:3–5)

How was this sign meant to produce faith? The serpent, in the form of a cobra, represented *Wadjet*, one of the most ancient deities worshiped in Egypt. Her symbol, in the form of a reared snake known as a *Uraeus*, was found on the royal crown of Pharaoh for three reasons. First, it symbolized that the pharaoh was divinely appointed by the gods and invested with royal power and absolute authority to rule over Egypt. Second, it was meant to divinely guard the pharaoh from all harm as an embodiment of the cobra goddess; she was literally protecting him. Last, the pharaoh, who was seen as semidivine, was responsible for maintaining order in Egypt.

Moses, as a former prince of Egypt, would have been very familiar with this serpent on the gold crown of Pharaoh and what it represented. God wanted Moses and all Israel to know that God, not Pharaoh, was the one with true power and authority, that the gods of Egypt were powerless to protect before the Lord, and that the Lord God of Israel was sovereignly in control of all Creation, including Egypt.

When Moses first saw the snake, he ran in fear. But God told Moses to grab the serpent by the tail. This is interesting because the tail is the worst place to grab a cobra—it's absolute suicide. The snake represents Moses' fear of Pharaoh, who at one time sought to take his life, and his personal doubts about the Lord using him.

By telling Moses to stretch out his hand and take the serpent by the tail, the Lord was telling Moses to face his greatest fears by grabbing hold of them. Likewise, we must not flee from our fears but face them. Too often we succumb to our doubts and fears, but the thing you fear might be the very thing the Lord wants to use in your life.

Everything in this biblical scene, even Moses' staff, points to the Messiah. This first sign is no exception. The Hebrew word translated "serpent" in this passage, *nachash*, is the same word used for the serpent in the garden. In Hebrew, *nachash* has the same numeric value of "Messiah" (*Mashiach*)—358. Part of the miracle is that a dead, inanimate staff comes to life and will also be used to swallow the living serpents of the Egyptian magicians. The Messiah (358), who symbolizes life, will swallow up death, represented by the Egyptian serpent (358). Then, as Scripture states, "He will swallow up death forever" (Isa. 25:8). Or, as Paul said, "Death is swallowed up (utterly vanquished forever) in and unto victory" (1 Cor. 15:54 AMPC).

There is also a connection between the thorns and the staff in the Gospels. According to Matthew's Gospel, the Roman soldiers mocked Jesus by placing a braided crown of thorns on His head and by putting "a staff in His right hand" (Matt. 27:29). This connects to Moses, who was called from the thornbush to redeem Israel and who was given a staff in his hand to perform signs before Israel and the Egyptians, demonstrating that he was the promised redeemer.

The Second Sign: Moses' Hand Turned Leprous

The Lord gave Moses a second sign:

> ADONAI also said to him, "Now put your hand within your cloak." So he put his hand inside, and when he took it out, his hand had *tza-ra'at*—white as snow. Then He said, "Put your hand back into your cloak." So he put his hand back in, and when he took it out it was restored again as the rest of his skin. (Ex. 4:6–7)

There is a dual purpose to this sign. "Leprosy" in Hebrew is *tza'raat*, and in the Torah it occurs primarily as a result of evil speech in the form of gossip (*lashon harah*) and pride (*ga'avah*). The letters of the word "pharaoh" in Hebrew can be read *peh rah*, which means "evil speech." This alludes to Pharaoh's use of evil speech in the form of lies, slander, witchcraft, and wicked anti-Semitic decrees to enslave and harm Israel physically and spiritually. This sign clearly demonstrates that the Lord would judge the pharaohs of Egypt who, in their pride and arrogance, thought they were semi-gods who could oppress and abuse the children of Israel.

Just as the sign of leprosy showed how the pharaohs forgot the ways they were blessed through Joseph, the Israelites, and their God, it was also a reminder to the Jewish people of God's blessings to them. This sign connects the promise of redemption back to the patriarchs. Shortly after God called Abraham, he and his wife, Sarah, went to Egypt due to a famine. Pharaoh, struck by Sarah's beauty, lusted after her and wanted her as one of his wives. The Lord responded by afflicting Pharaoh with a plague (Gen. 12:17). According to Jewish tradition, it was leprosy.[3]

Moses' leprous hand was a sign that what the Lord did for Abraham He would do again for Israel. This pharaoh, like his predecessor, would also be plagued if he didn't release the Israelites from Egypt as in the days of Abraham. The sign of leprosy would also have been a reminder that the Lord's promise in Genesis 15 was about to be fulfilled:

> Then He said to Abram, "Know for certain that your seed will be strangers in a land that is not theirs, and they will be enslaved and oppressed 400 years. But I am going to judge the nation that they will serve. Afterward they will go out with many possessions." (vv. 13–14)

The time of Israel's redemption had come. God had not forgotten His covenant with Abraham and would curse those who cursed Israel. Pharaoh, powerless, would send them away—as an earlier pharaoh had done with Abraham and Sarah—with great wealth.

Moses' leprous hand also points to the Messiah. Several rabbinic texts describe the Messiah as a *metzora*: a leper who suffers on behalf of the Jewish people: "What is his [the Messiah's] name? . . . [His name is *metzora*—the white one] the leper . . . as it is stated, 'Indeed our illnesses he did bear and our pains he endured; yet we did esteem him injured, stricken by God, and afflicted' (Isaiah 53:4)."[4] The Messiah was to be the leper of Israel. (Isa. 53)

The Third Sign: Water Turned to Blood

The Lord gave Moses a third sign, in case the children of Israel didn't believe the first two:

> Then He said, "If they do not believe you, or listen to the voice of the first sign, they will believe the message of the latter sign. But if they do not believe even these two signs nor listen to your voice, you are to take the water of the river and pour it on the dry land. The water which you take out of the river will become blood on the ground." (Ex. 4:8–9)

Moses was to take water from the Nile, and when he poured it on dry ground it would turn to blood. This sign would have instilled hope and touched the hearts of the people. The water turning to blood was a sign that God remembered the Hebrew babies that had been thrown into the Nile.

Justice was about to be served. The sign of water into blood is also the first plague that God brought upon Egypt, which also points to the Messiah.

MOSES' CALLING AND HIS CHARACTER

Why did Moses resist the call of God? Strangely, it had to do with his character. Moses' humility endeared him to God and made him a great man and leader. This one trait also explains why Moses resisted the Lord's call to become Israel's redeemer, even though it was a tremendous honor.

Moses embodied the trait of humility more than any other prophet or leader in the Hebrew Bible. God Himself testified to Moses' humility and named it as the primary reason He spoke to and through Moses unlike any other prophet:

> Now the man Moses was very humble, more so than anyone on the face of the earth.

> "Hear now My words!" He said. "When there is a prophet of ADONAI, I reveal Myself in a vision, I speak to him in a dream. Not so with My servant Moses. In all My house, he is faithful. I speak with him face to face, plainly and not in riddles. He even looks at the form of ADONAI! Why then were you not afraid to speak against My servant Moses?" (Num. 12:3, 6–8)

The Lord said this in response to Miriam and Aaron, Moses' own family, who complained, "Has ADONAI spoken only through Moses? Hasn't He also spoken through us?" (Num. 12:2). Moses' humility marked him for the Lord and is one of the reasons the Lord called him as Israel's redeemer. Calling and character are always connected.

But what is humility? The book of Leviticus provides some insight into this question and shows the depth of Moses' humility. Leviticus is the name of the third book of the Bible in English. In the Hebrew Bible, the book of

Leviticus is called *Vayyiqra*, which is also the book's opening word, which means "and [God] called [Moses]." In the Torah, the last letter of this word is written with a small *aleph*. Tradition tells us that Moses did not want to begin the third book of the Torah with the word *vayyiqra* because he felt it afforded him too much honor and distinction. He was reluctant to have it recorded for all time that God directly called him alone to be the first person to enter the newly completed tabernacle, which contained the glory of God. As a testimony to Moses' humility, God allowed him to write the letter *aleph* in a smaller case.

The letter *aleph* is the first letter of the Hebrew alphabet and is therefore the "lead" or "chief" letter. Although Moses was one of Israel's greatest leaders and regularly spoke with God face-to-face, he never thought of himself as greater than any of the other children of Israel, despite numerous suggestions to the contrary. His request to reduce the *aleph* demonstrates to us that Moses made himself small in the sight of both God and Israel.

A couple of years ago I had a dream that illustrates the spiritual significance of the small *aleph* (א) in the opening word of Leviticus. In the dream I was standing on the red carpet at a Hollywood premiere. There were many paparazzi and several large spotlights lighting up the evening sky. Suddenly all of these intensely bright spotlights were pointed at me, and I became completely blinded by them. I cried out and asked that they be pointed away from me. Then I heard a heavenly voice say, "If you ever try and take the light of My glory and place it upon yourself, you will become blinded. But if you remain small in your own sight, you will always remain significant in Mine."

All of us should follow Moses' example and strive to be humble, for humility is necessary for godliness and is a prerequisite for Spirit-empowered leadership. Jesus demonstrated an even greater humility than Moses.

Yeshua, speaking to the mother of John and James, said, "The Son of Man did not come to be served, but to serve, and to give His life as a ransom for many" (Matt. 20:28). Yeshua showed us later, at the cross, how far a humble man will go to serve God and people. Paul later wrote that Yeshua would empty Himself for us. Humble people give of themselves.

In Matthew 23, Jesus told a group of Pharisees and scribes, "But the greatest among you shall be your servant. Whoever exalts himself shall be humbled, and whoever humbles himself shall be exalted" (vv. 11–12). He was telling them that God will honor humility. He was teaching from His own gift of humility. Jesus' sacrificial humility was one of the proofs that He was the prophet like Moses (Deut. 18:18) that Israel had been eagerly awaiting.

What does it mean to have humility like that of Jesus and Moses? Specifically, it means

1. not thinking too highly of yourself (Rom. 12:3),
2. not thinking you are especially deserving of praise and honor,
3. esteeming others as greater than yourself (Phil. 2:3),
4. bearing insults (2 Cor. 12:10),
5. not desiring positions of authority and fleeing honor, and
6. showing honor to all people (Rom. 12:10).

Moses and Messiah Jesus embodied the essence of humility in thought, word, and deed. They constantly put others' needs and honor before their own.

This is the meaning of the small *aleph*—greatness comes through smallness. Even more than Moses, Jesus embodied this kind of humility. As Messiah Yeshua taught, "Whoever then shall humble himself like this child, this one is the greatest in the kingdom of heaven" (Matt. 18:4). This type of person will be used to transform lives and unlock our potential to live and lead like both Moses and Messiah Jesus.

Humility is about smallness. It's about occupying the right amount of space—not too much, which is pride, nor too little, which is false humility. Moses' understanding of this truth made him one of the greatest spiritual leaders in the Bible. All of us should strive to be humble—small in relationship to God, others, and ourselves. Humility is the foundation of spiritual service and key to the Lord speaking to and working through you in powerful ways. Humility is one of the defining marks of a true disciple of Jesus and comes with the promise of great blessing, according to the Sermon on the Mount: "Blessed are the humble, for they will inherit the earth" (Matt. 5:5 csb).

FAITHFUL SERVANT

One of the loftiest praises that the Lord gave Moses was to call him an *eved HaShem*: a "servant of the LORD." This title is one of the highest honors God could bestow on an individual. It might not seem fashionable today, but biblically speaking, being a servant is the essence of spiritual leadership.

Moses was the servant par excellence. A servant is one who puts the needs of others ahead of his own. The rabbis refer to Moses as a *noseh be' ol*—one who bears the yoke of others. What made Moses special as a leader was that he was a compassionate servant-leader who always sought to lighten the load of those around him. He risked his position in the palace and even his own life to help a fellow Hebrew who was being beaten by an Egyptian taskmaster (Ex. 2:11–12). After leading the children of Israel out of Egypt, Moses would spend all day—morning to evening—instructing the people who came to inquire of God (Ex. 18:13–15). Moses was selfless and sacrificial in his service to the Lord and to the people. He was faithful to the end: "And Moses the servant of the LORD died there in Moab, as the LORD had said. He buried him" (Deut. 34:5–6 NIV).

Two other leaders in the Hebrew Bible earned this title of "servant of the LORD." Joshua, Moses' protégé and disciple, who led Israel in their conquest of the Holy Land, is called this upon his death (Judg. 2:8 NIV). Israel's legendary and beloved king also received this lofty title in Psalm 18, which opens with these words: "A psalm of David the servant of *ADONAI*" (v. 1). Few others embodied the essence of being a servant like Moses and these men.

But Moses was not just called "servant of the LORD." God publicly called him a faithful servant:

"In all My house, he is faithful. I speak with him face to face, plainly and not in riddles. He even looks at the form of *ADONAI*! Why then were you not afraid to speak against My servant Moses?" (Num. 12:7–8)

Moses embodied the essence of a faithful and humble servant like none other except one. That one is Jesus. The writer of Hebrews makes this connection between Moses and Jesus:

> Therefore, holy brothers and sisters, partners in a heavenly calling, take notice of *Yeshua*—the Emissary and *Kohen Gadol* [High Priest] we affirm. He was faithful to the One who appointed Him in His house—as was Moses also. For He has been considered worthy of more glory than Moses, even as the builder of the house has more honor than the house. For every house is built by someone, but the builder of all things is God. Now Moses surely was faithful in all God's house as a servant, for a witness of things to be spoken later. But Messiah, as Son, is over God's house—and we are His house, if we hold firm to our boldness and what we are proud to hope. (3:1–6)

Yeshua, even more than anyone else, modeled what it means to be a true and faithful servant of the Lord.

The New Testament portrayal of Jesus as a humble and faithful servant is not just meant to teach us about biblical leadership. It was prophesied that the Messiah had to be like Moses—but more so. Concerning the Messiah, who is the greater Moses (Deut. 18:18), the prophet Isaiah wrote, "Behold, My servant will prosper, He will be high and lifted up and greatly exalted" (Isa. 52:13). What's amazing is that the Hebrew phrase for "servant" (*eved ivri*) has the same numeric value as "Messiah" (*Mashiach*), which is 358. This points to the truth that the Messiah was the ultimate servant and example for us.

Moses and the Messiah modeled the type of leadership all believers should aspire toward. Greatness in the Kingdom comes by serving, not by being served, as Jesus said in Matthew 20: 26–27: "But whoever wants to be great among you shall be your servant, and whoever wants to be first among you shall be your slave." But Jesus was more than just a model of faithful leadership; He is the incarnation of it:

Let this mind be in you which was also in Christ Jesus, who, being in the form of God, did not consider it robbery to be equal with God, but made Himself of no reputation, taking the form of a bondservant, and coming in the likeness of men. . . . He humbled Himself and became obedient to the point of death, even the death of the cross. Therefore God also has highly exalted Him and given Him the name which is above every name. (Phil. 2:5–9 NKJV)

Notice the pattern here. Jesus left His glory in heaven, where He ruled and reigned with the Father, to become a "bondservant" who humbled Himself to death and was then "highly exalted." This is the paradigm for greatness. You will never be highly favored or promoted by the Lord until you humbly become a servant of others.

Messiah Yeshua came to serve, not to be served. If we want to be like Him and hear the words "Well done, good and faithful servant" (Matt. 25:23), then we, like the Messiah, must make God's will our will and humbly serve so that we can be exalted with Him in the messianic Kingdom.

To be a leader for the Lord, you must be humble, faithful, and have a servant spirit. Character and calling are inextricably bound. Calling and charisma are not enough, for charisma without character leads to chaos. In the Kingdom, character is what truly counts. The birth, calling, and character of Moses point not only to why the Lord chose him to lead Israel but also to Jesus being the greater Moses promised in Scripture.

chapter
SEVEN

THE MESSIAH'S AND MOSES' MIRACLES

B uilding anything takes a strong labor force. The bigger the project, the larger the workforce required. Compounding construction efforts during the days of Moses was the absence of heavy machinery to help bear the load. Instead, ancient Egypt was successfully built on the backs of the children of Israel. Not just for a few weeks or a few months but hundreds of years. Because the Israelites were cheap labor that expanded his wealth and empire, Pharaoh wasn't going to let them go.

Further, Pharaoh wasn't going to bend his will to a formerly disgraced and banished prince of Egypt who had an encounter with some unknown God. Words alone were not enough to free Israel from Egypt's clutches, the most dominant superpower of the day. For this reason, God's message—and His messenger—needed to be accompanied by powerful signs that tangibly demonstrated and testified to the believability of God's message.

THE TEN PLAGUES

In Egyptian culture, pharaohs were considered to be part of the cosmological order. According to Egyptian mythology, the greatest spiritual battle was the one that took place between order and chaos. Life and death, sunrise and sunset, and the yearly flooding of the Nile, which made Egypt fertile, were all part of the cosmic rhythm that kept creation from devolving into chaos. Various gods maintained and protected these cycles.

While the gods kept order in the cosmic realm, Pharaoh helped to keep order in the earthly realm. All ten plagues were meant to discredit the false gods of Egypt and Pharaoh's fallacious claim to govern creation as a semi-god. The plagues brought chaos out of order and exposed Pharaoh and the gods of Egypt as powerless before the Lord, the true Creator of heaven and earth.

The ten plagues are also referred to in the Bible as "signs."[1] They were meant to convince all Egypt that the God of Israel existed, that He had a special covenantal relationship with the children of Israel, and that He was the Creator and King of all. Thus, the ten signs were not primarily punitive but redemptive. They were intended to elicit faith among the Hebrews as well as in the hearts of Egyptians so that they would repent and believe in the Lord. The ten signs/plagues are (1) blood, (2) frogs, (3) gnats, (4) flies, (5) death of livestock, (6) boils, (7) hail, (8) locusts, (9) darkness, and (10) death of the firstborn.

The Structure of the Ten Signs

The ten plagues were broken into three sets that demonstrated three spiritual truths to Pharaoh: (1) the Lord exists; (2) His control extends over all creation, from the greatest to the least; and (3) He is all-powerful. The plagues were not random but divinely designed to reflect the character of God as "compassionate and gracious . . . slow to anger" (Ex. 34:6; see also Ps. 145:8). The plagues first affected the environment, then material possessions, and ultimately led to increasing personal harm, culminating in the death of the firstborn when Pharaoh refused to repent. God gave ten opportunities for the Egyptians to have a change of heart, but they refused.

Did God Harden Pharaoh's Heart?

Can we honestly say that the Lord was merciful to Pharaoh and the Egyptians, since the Scripture says, "The LORD hardened Pharaoh's heart"

(Ex. 9:12 NIV)? Pharaoh chose to harden his own heart, after being warned by the Lord (Ex. 7:13, 22; 8:11, 15; 9:34, 35), before God caused Pharaoh's heart to become even more hardened (Ex. 9:12; 10:1, 20, 27; 11:10; 14:4, 8). When God hardened Pharaoh's heart, He was merely strengthening Pharaoh in the way he had decided to go—he would not repent and let the children of Israel go free.

The Lord desires that the wicked repent and not die: "I have no pleasure in the death of the wicked, but that the wicked turn from his way and live" (Ezek. 33:11 NKJV). God, therefore, did not harden Pharaoh's heart in such a way that made repentance impossible; rather, He strengthened his heart (the word "hardened" literally means "to strengthen" in Hebrew) so that Pharaoh would relent not out of pain but out of a sincere heart. In other words, God wanted Pharaoh to release the Hebrews not because his suffering was too great but because he and the Egyptians recognized the error of their ways, were truly remorseful for their sin against the children of Israel, and acknowledged the reality and power of the Almighty.

The Lord never delights in punishing or judging. "The Lord is not slow in keeping His promise, as some consider slowness. Rather, He is being patient toward you—not wanting anyone to perish, but for all to come to repentance" (2 Pet. 3:9).

THE GOSPEL AND MOSES

To truly understand the greatness of Moses and his prophetic significance as a prototype and forerunner of the Messiah, we must begin at the end. The last lines of the last book of the Torah, the Five Books of Moses, say:

> There has not risen again a prophet in Israel like Moses, whom *ADONAI* knew face to face, with all the signs and wonders *ADONAI* sent him to do in the land of Egypt—to Pharaoh, all his servants, and all his land—by the strong hand and great awe that Moses did in the sight of all Israel. (Deut. 34:10–12)

Two distinctions made Moses unique as a prophet. The first is the way in which God spoke to Moses: face-to-face. When God spoke to other prophets, He did not do so directly (Num. 12:6–8).

Moses' ministry began with God speaking with him from the midst of the burning bush. He spent three forty-day periods directly communing with the Lord, as the Lord would talk to Moses regularly in the desert, giving him wisdom and revelation to write the Torah and lead the people. The way the Lord communicated with Moses shows the unique relationship he had with the Lord.

Second, no other prophet in the Hebrew Bible performed as many miracles with such tremendous results as Moses. The miracles demonstrated his unique relationship with God and revealed that he had been sent by Him to be the redeemer of Israel.

Raising a Prophet Like Moses

Before going any further, it's critical to notice how the last lines of Deuteronomy begin: "There has not risen again a prophet in Israel like Moses." Why was the writer concerned that no prophet had yet to arise? What is the deeper meaning behind these words?

This passage refers to one of the most important messianic prophecies found in the entire Torah: "I will raise up a prophet like you for them from among their brothers. I will put My words in his mouth, and he will speak to them all that I command him" (Deut. 18:18). God told the children of Israel that He would raise up a prophet who would be like Moses. Moses was a type—a prototype—of the Messiah. The Messiah would be a prophet like Moses in (1) His unique relationship and communication with God and (2) the signs and wonders He performed.

When Moses died, the Lord buried him, "but no one knows of his burial place to this day" (Deut. 34:6). The phrase "to this day" is key in this passage in Deuteronomy. To what "day" is this verse referring? Some scholars and rabbis believe Moses wrote these words before his death. I believe (as I was taught by one of my mentors and professors, John Sailhamer) these final verses of the Torah were not written by Moses but were added at a later date, most likely by Ezra the scribe after Israel returned from the Babylonian exile, along with a few other editorial comments in the Torah. But, to be clear, 99.9 percent of the Torah was written by Moses.

Deuteronomy 18 and 34, when read together, unlock one of the most important reasons the Torah was written—to point to the prophet like Moses, the second Moses, the Messiah who would bring a greater exodus. How a book ends is one the greatest indicators of its purpose and message. This passage was expressing the people's longing for the promised Messiah like Moses to come.

JOHN, MOSES, AND THE MESSIAH

This Old Testament connection can help us understand not just the primary purpose of the Torah but also the Gospels—especially the book of John.

One of the primary purposes of the Gospel of John is to show that Jesus is the promised prophet greater than Moses. John opened his Gospel with these words: "In the beginning was the Word. The Word was with God, and the Word was God" (John 1:1). John 1:1 begins like Genesis 1:1, which also starts with "in the beginning."

The second part of John 1:1 tells us that the "Word was with God, and the Word was God." In the Greek, the phrase "was with God" is καὶ ὁ Λόγος ἦν πρὸς τὸν Θεόν, which can literally be translated as "was face-to-face with God." A few verses later, John compared Moses and Messiah Yeshua:

Torah was given through Moses; grace and truth came through Yeshua the Messiah. No one has ever seen God; but the one and only God, in the Father's embrace, has made Him known. (John 1:17–18)

God spoke to Moses face-to-face, but Moses was only allowed to see God's back when the Lord caused His glory to pass while Moses was in the cleft of the rock. Yet Jesus was in a face-to-face relationship with the Father from the beginning. John's words make it clear that Jesus is the prophet like Moses who has an even greater and more intimate relationship with the Father.

Three things make the book of John unique when compared to the other three Gospels, called the Synoptic Gospels.* The first is John's high Christology (looking at Jesus as the divine Son of God). There are more explicit statements about Jesus' deity in John than in all the other Gospels combined. A few examples are John 1:1–4, 10:33, and 20:26–29, where Thomas said of Jesus, "My Lord and my God!"

John's Gospel is also unique in its inclusion of Jesus' "I am" statements, which underscores John's high Christology. Seven statements provide the reader with a clear picture of Jesus' unique identity:

1. "I am the bread of life." (6:35, 48)
2. "I am the light of the world." (8:12)
3. "I am the gate." (10:7, 9)
4. "I am the Good Shepherd." (10:11, 14)
5. "I am the resurrection and the life!" (11:25)
6. "I am the way, the truth, and the life!" (14:6)
7. "I am the true vine." (15:1)

These "I am" statements focus on the deity of Jesus and demonstrate that He is the promised prophet of Deuteronomy 18:18, the greater than Moses, who has an even more unique relationship with God the Father. It is no coincidence that John gave us seven statements. Seven is the number of completion and perfection. Yeshua completely and perfectly fulfills the prophecy of Deuteronomy 34.

Remember, the unique signs Moses performed set him apart from all other prophets (Deut. 34:12). Thus, the third uniqueness of the book of John is that it is structured around a set of miracles, some of which are recorded nowhere else in the Gospels. Following is a table that outlines the seven miracles in John's Gospel and how they correlate to the miracles performed by Moses.

---

* Matthew, Mark, and Luke are called the Synoptic Gospels.

	Jesus' Miracles	Moses' Miracles
1.	Changing the water into wine (John 2:1–11)	Changing the Nile into blood (Exodus 4:9)
2.	Healing the nobleman's son (John 4:43–54)	Stopping the plague (Numbers 16:44–50)
3.	Healing the man at the Bethesda pool (John 5:1–15)	Leading the faithful to the Promised Land (Exodus)
4.	Feeding the five thousand (John 6:1–15)	Feeding the people manna (Exodus 16)
5.	Walking on water (John 6:16–21)	Parting the Red Sea (Exodus 14:21)
6.	Healing the man born blind (John 9:1–12)	Bringing darkness to Egypt, the ninth plague (Exodus 10:21–23)
7.	Raising Lazarus from the dead (John 11:1–46)	Killing the firstborn in Egypt, the tenth plague (Exodus 11:4–7)

The Gospel of John is often referred to as the Book of Signs. John's focus on miracles points to Jesus as the greater Moses. As with Moses, the miracles the Messiah performed point to His unique relationship with God.

The Gospel of John not only begins like Genesis but also ends like the last book of the Torah, Deuteronomy:

> *Yeshua* performed many other signs in the presence of the disciples, which are not written in this book. But these things have been written so that you may believe that *Yeshua* is *Mashiach Ben-Elohim* [Messiah, Son of God], and that by believing you may have life in His name. (John 20:30–31)

> There are also many other things that *Yeshua* did. If all of them were to be written one by one, I suppose that not even the world itself will have room for the books being written! (John 21:25)

The Gospel of John, like several of the other Gospels, clearly demonstrates that Jesus is the "One that Moses in the *Torah*, and also the prophets, wrote about" (John 1:45). By understanding Moses better, we gain a deeper and clearer understanding of the person and work of Jesus.

On a practical level it is important to understand that an intimate relationship with the Lord can lead to real spiritual power. The Lord wants to speak to you through His Word, through prayer and worship, and by the Spirit. We are called not only to learn about Moses and the Messiah—and the great miracles they performed—but also to learn from them and imitate them in their relationships with the Lord.

Jesus promised that His sheep will hear His voice and, in regard to His miracles, that we will do "greater things than these" (John 14:12 NIV). Every follower of the Messiah is called to live an extraordinary—not an ordinary—life. Let's not settle for a form of godliness that lacks power (2 Tim. 3:5). I have personally heard God's voice, had encounters with Him, and have even seen miracles in response to prayer. And I desire to see more.

Spiritual encounters and miracles can't be manufactured, but they can be pursued. You can choose to believe and pray in faith for miracles and to hear the Lord. Paul faithfully prayed and performed many miracles, and he told believers, "Be imitators of me" (1 Cor. 4:16). Don't settle for less than God's best. Pursue the Lord's presence and power so that you might be more deeply transformed and boldly proclaim the good news of the Gospel.

TURNING WATER INTO BLOOD

Why was the first plague of turning the Nile to blood brought upon the Egyptians? The Nile River made Egypt a fertile and prosperous nation. Since the Nile was the source of their sustenance, the Egyptians worshiped it as a deity. They personified the Nile as the god to whom they offered sacrifices. The Egyptians also believed that Pharaoh, as a semi-god, was responsible for controlling and maintaining nature's harmony. Therefore,

God chose to show the people of Egypt that their god was powerless. Isaiah 24:21 says, "The LORD will punish on high the host of exalted ones, and on the earth the kings of the earth" (NKJV).

Chapter 8 reveals more about the "blood" (Hebrew, *DaM*) and its numeric value (44). For now, we need to remember that the Egyptians worshiped many gods and deified the Nile River. The value of the Hebrew phrase for "One God" (*El Echad*) is 44. This first miracle and all the subsequent miracles that Moses performed exposed the gods of Egypt as weak, worthless, and unworthy of worship. There are not many gods but only *El Echad*—One God, the God of Israel. God turned the Nile into "blood" (44) to show that there is only "One God" (44). The first miracle taught this lesson to the Egyptians as well as Israel.

Forty-four is also the numeric value of the phrase "the LORD lives" (*YHVH Chai*). This first miracle declared to Pharaoh and to the Egyptians that the God of Israel lives. All the idols of Egypt are dead and powerless, as the psalmist wrote:

> Their futile faith in dead idols and dead works
> can never bring life or meaning to their souls.
> Blind men can only create blind things.
> Those deaf to God can only make a deaf image.
> Dead men can only create dead idols.
> And everyone who trusts in these powerless, dead things
> will be just like what they worship—powerless and dead.
> So trust in the Lord, all his people.
> For he is the only true hero,
> the wrap-around God who is our shield! (Ps. 115:5–9 TPT)

Biblically, blood has both a positive and negative association. On the positive side, blood (*DaM*) is a symbol of life.

Pharaoh and the Egyptians experienced the negative aspect of blood: judgment and death. The first miracle that Moses performed caused all the fish of the Nile to die because the Nile's waters turned to blood.

TURNING WATER INTO WINE

The Torah tells us that one key aspect of Moses was "all the signs and wonders ADONAI sent him to do in the land of Egypt" (Deut. 34:11). It only makes sense that the first sign that Yeshua performed involved the transformation of water into wine at the wedding in Cana (John 2:1–11). Why did He turn the water into wine and not blood? Wine is symbolic of the joy and redemption that the Messiah King will bring about in the messianic age. We read in chapter 4 the messianic promise in Genesis 49:10–12:

> The scepter will not pass from Judah,
>> nor the ruler's staff from between his feet,
>> until he to whom it belongs will come.
> To him will be the obedience of the peoples.
> Binding his foal to the vine,
>> his donkey's colt to the choice vine,
>> he washes his garments in wine,
>> and in the blood of grapes his robe.
> His eyes are darker than wine,
>> and teeth that are whiter than milk.

As the prophet like Moses, Yeshua publicly declared His messiahship by turning the water into wine and not blood because the thief comes to rob, kill, and destroy, but He came that we might have life and have it more abundantly (John 10:10).

THE FINAL PLAGUES BROUGHT FREEDOM

The Egyptians enslaved the children of Israel on physical, spiritual, and emotional levels. God designed the plagues to bring freedom on these three levels. And in the Messiah, we can also experience freedom and transformation. We will focus briefly on the last three plagues and their practical relevance to gain a clearer picture.

Locusts: A Perverted Mind and Corrupted Way of Thinking

The plague of locusts, on an inner emotional level, represents a perverted mind and corrupt ways of thinking. The locusts consumed all the crops and greenery of Egypt. Greenery, in Jewish thought, is associated with Mount Sinai and the Torah. In Jewish tradition, the Lord miraculously transformed the barren desert around Mount Sinai into a green and fertile area. The Lord said to Moses, "Do not let anyone be seen throughout the entire mountain. Even the flocks and herds must not graze in front of that mountain" (Ex. 34:3). To remember this miracle, it is traditional for Jewish people to decorate their homes and synagogues with greenery on the Feast of Pentecost (*Shavuot*).

The Torah is represented by greenery because truth renews the mind. Locusts eating the greenery symbolically represents corrupting our intellect and perverting our minds with false beliefs and lies. Like the locusts, a perverted and corrupt mind can uproot spiritual truth and moral foundations. It can lead to an extreme intellectualism that denies any absolute truth, declares all morals and truth relative, and denies the existence of the one God and His commandments.

How do we defeat the "locusts" of corrupted thinking and find freedom? We must renew our minds with the truth of God's Word. Israel needed physical freedom but also the truth of the Torah given on Mount Sinai. The ten plagues and the Ten Commandments are inextricably bound. Truth transforms. As Jesus said, "You will know the truth, and the truth will set you free" (John 8:32).

The battle is always for the mind. For this reason we are exhorted, "Do not be conformed to this world but be transformed by the renewing of your mind, so that you may discern what is the will of God—what is good and acceptable and perfect" (Rom. 12:2). God wants to free you from lies you have believed as well as all unhealthy and corrupt thoughts. Jesus came to redeem not only your soul but also your mind.

Don't let the locusts devour your thoughts anymore. The Lord said, "I will repay you for the years the locusts have eaten—the great locust and the young locust, the other locusts and the locust swarm" (Joel 2:25 NIV). Stand firm and declare the Lord's promise today.

Darkness: Depression and Sadness

The darkness that was experienced in Egypt during the ninth plague was no ordinary darkness. It was so thick and compact that it not only blinded the Egyptians but also immobilized them, as we read in Exodus 10:23–24. By restricting their ability to move, God punished the Egyptians measure for measure (*midda keneged midda*) by taking away their freedom as they had done to the children of Israel. As they sat confined in the darkness, they physically and psychologically experienced the fear and terror of slavery.

Darkness, in Jewish mystical thought, is associated with depression. Christian mystics associate depression with the dark night of the soul. Deep depression can be heavy and immobilizing, like the ninth plague of darkness. It can make a person feel trapped, causing emotional, mental, relational, and even spiritual paralysis. As Exodus 10:23 states, "Nor could anyone rise from his place."

The plague-of-darkness type of depression (I am not speaking of chemically induced depression) is rooted in a despair that comes from purposelessness. There is nothing worse than losing your purpose—your reason for living. Many of the children of Israel had become so assimilated into Egypt that they lost their reason for being. They forgot God's promises for them. They were *in* the world of Egypt and became *of* it as well. It is so easy for us to lose our purpose; when we do, we lose our passion because there is no passion without purpose.

Darkness and depression can rob us of the love of the Lord and cause us to die in Egypt. Rashi, one of the most esteemed Jewish commentators, articulated a second reason for this plague that underscores this point:

Why did he bring darkness on them? Because there were among the Israelites of that generation evil people who did not wish to leave, and they died out during the three days of darkness so that the Egyptians [would] not see their demise thereby saying, "They are being struck as we are."[2]

Every Israelite who loved Egypt and its material comforts more than the Lord died there during the three days of darkness. The spiritual point being made is that only those who desired to be redeemed from Egypt experienced deliverance.

Depression causes us to feel isolated. It makes us feel like no one is concerned for us or cares about us. And when this occurs, it causes us not to care about others as well. As we see in Exodus 10:23, "They could not see one another." These Israelites felt uncared for, even by the Lord.

Those who died during this plague had lost hope. "Hope deferred makes the heart sick" (Prov. 13:12). Messiah Yeshua came to restore hope. And what has been critical in keeping the people of Israel alive throughout all their centuries of persecution? The exodus from Egypt involved—on a national and personal level—turning the darkness into light. The Israelites had light in their dwellings. Those who came out of Egypt were able to hold on to the hope of redemption. They never lost hope in the future.

Likewise, the Messiah has sustained us. What was true in the days of Moses is true today. Believing with complete faith in the Messiah and longing for the final redemption gives us the hope and joy we need to overcome depression. Joy rooted in hope gives us the strength to defeat the debilitating depression connected to the plague of darkness. Joy breaks every yoke, and the "joy of the LORD is [our] strength" (Neh. 8:10 NIV). We need to ask the Lord to give us the joy that is birthed out of hope, as the apostle Paul prayed, "Now may the God of hope fill you with all joy and peace in believing, that you may abound in hope by the power of the Holy Spirit" (Rom. 15:13 NKJV).

Death of the Firstborn: The Death of Destiny and Identity

The tenth plague was the death of the firstborn. The firstborn son was meant to lead the family after his father's passing, and this was one of the reasons he was given a double portion of the inheritance. The future and destiny of the family depended on the firstborn. Destiny and identity go hand in hand. In fact, identity is destiny. The death of the firstborn, on a psychological level, represented the death of identity and hence a family's destiny. If Israel had stayed any longer in Egypt, God's children would have become so corrupted by the idolatry and immorality of Egypt that they would have been lost forever, according to the rabbis.

There is an important connection between the last three plagues. I believe there is a progression. An unhealthy and corrupt mind naturally leads to depression, which can end up culminating in death on an emotional and relational level, as well as the death of one's identity and destiny, represented by the firstborn.

The only way the children of Israel could avoid the death of the firstborn was by putting the blood of the Passover lamb on the doorposts of their homes. Jesus died, as the greater Passover Lamb, to save you from both physical and spiritual death. But He also died so that you could have a new life, which included a new identity and destiny. Your identity must be rooted not in what you have or what you do but in who you are—a child of the King. In Him, you are a part of God's "royal priesthood" and "holy nation" (1 Pet. 2:9). He has a unique calling on your life, like He had for Moses and the children of Israel. He has set life and death before you. Choose abundant life by knowing your true identity and destiny.

The miracles Moses performed in Egypt were meant to demonstrate God's sovereignty, power, and love. There are many deep truths and practical lessons in the miracles and message of the Passover and the exodus from Egypt, but one of the most important teachings is how Moses and the miracles he performed point directly to the Messiah. Understanding this will provide a better context and a deeper appreciation for the Passover and the miracles that accompanied it.

chapter
EIGHT

THE MESSIAH, OUR PASSOVER

I t's interesting to note that every milestone in Jesus' life occurred on a *chag*, a Jewish holiday. His death was no exception. Jesus died during Passover. He is called the Passover Lamb. Before His death, He dined with His disciples in what is known as the Last Supper. He was observing Passover by having a traditional dinner, called a seder, with his closest friends.

The most famous icon of the Last Supper is a painting by Leonardo da Vinci, which depicts Jesus and his very Western European–looking disciples gathering around a rectangular table with glasses of wine and loaves of fluffy white bread. There is no way such a thing as these leavened loaves sat on Jesus' seder table. Passover is also known as the Feast of Unleavened Bread. The large, flat cracker called *matzah* is the only type of bread eaten during this holiday. Why? The answer reveals a few more mysteries surrounding the Messiah.

THE TENTH PLAGUE: SKIPPING OVER

The year is 1446 BC, and the Hebrews have been oppressed and enslaved by the Egyptians for hundreds of years. God has heard the cries of their hearts, and Moses is His man to set them free. Pharaoh, unwilling to risk an economic downturn for Egypt, refuses to free his slaves. In response, God plagues the Egyptians in ten different ways. But it is only after the tenth plague, the death of the firstborn son in all the Egyptian households, that Pharaoh finally relents and drives Israel out of Egypt.

Passover—*Pesach*, meaning "skip over"—derives its name from the tenth plague. God's angel of death skipped or "passed over" the Hebrew households marked by the lambs' blood on their doorways, sparing their firstborn sons.

Passover is the most important of all the biblical holidays. Israel was birthed as a nation on Passover. In the New Testament, Yeshua's ministry was centered around the Passover. The Last Supper was a Passover Seder, and Yeshua died on Passover as the Lamb of God.

Passover and the Hand of God

On the tenth day of the first month of the Hebrew calendar—referred to as *Aviv*, which means "spring," and later *Nisan*, which means "miracles"—the Lord commanded the children of Israel to set aside a lamb for each household. On the fourteenth of the month, at twilight, the lamb was to be slaughtered and its blood applied to the lintel and two doorposts of the home in which they would eat the first Passover.

In Hebrew, the number fourteen is written with two letters: *yud*, with a numeric value of 10, and *dalat*, which has the value of 4. Their combined value is 14. Combining these two letters also spells the word "hand" (*yad*). God set the fourteenth day of the month as the start of Passover because He wanted Israel to know for all time that He redeemed them out of Egypt "with a mighty hand . . . from the house of slavery, from the hand of Pharaoh" (Deut. 7:8). Like Israel, we must never forget that the hand of our enemies is always powerless before the hand of our God. The fourteenth day stands as an eternal reminder of this truth: "Remember this day, on which you came out from Egypt, out of the house of bondage. For by a strong hand *ADONAI* brought you out from this place" (Ex. 13:3).

The Fourteenth and the Messiah

The Passover prophetically points to the Messiah. God revealed His "mighty hand" of redemption again through Jesus, who revealed the power of

God's hand on the fourteenth day in an even greater way. Jesus' pierced hands point to Him as the One who fulfilled the Passover. It is His hand that saves. Jesus said, "My sheep hear My voice. I know them, and they follow Me. I give them eternal life! They will never perish, and no one will snatch them out of My hand" (John 10:27–28). Notice that He connected sheep with God's saving hand, which connects to what the Lord did at the Passover by means of a lamb.

The Hand of God in History

Fourteen is connected to God's redemptive hand at work in the history of His people. Therefore, it should be no surprise that Israel was declared a nation on May 14, 1948. This miracle could only have occurred by His hand. Arab nations, led by Egypt, invaded Israel, but against all odds the hand (14) of the Lord brought a supernatural deliverance for the modern State of Israel. Israel's rebirth as a nation is referred to in Jewish prayer as the "first fruit of our salvation."[1] It connects back to the Passover and also to a greater future redemption.

The hand of God was seen at the exodus and was made known in a greater way through the death of Jesus at Passover. It will not be fully revealed until the Second Coming, when God fully redeems Israel: "It will also come about in that day that my Lord will again redeem—a second time with His hand—the remnant of His people who remain / from Assyria, from Egypt, from Pathros, from Cush, Elam, Shinar, Hamath, and from the islands of the sea" (Isa. 11:11).

At the Second Coming, the Lord will redeem Israel for a second time with His hand. This second exodus will lead to the salvation of the nations and the establishment of His Kingdom. God's hand is always at work in history. We just need to learn to see it.

THE TENTH PLAGUE: DEATH OF THE FIRSTBORN

As discussed in the previous chapter, the death of the firstborn was the last, and worst, of all the plagues. Based on what the Lord communicated to Moses at the burning bush, it would seem that the last plague was meant to be the first one brought upon the Egyptians: "You are to say to Pharaoh, 'This is what *Adonai* says: "Israel is My son, My firstborn. So I have said to you, Let My son go, that he may serve Me, but you have refused to let him go. Behold, I will slay your son, your firstborn"'" (Ex. 4:22–23).

According to Jewish tradition, the Lord mercifully sent the first nine plagues to offer Pharaoh and the Egyptians ample opportunity to repent before striking them so severely. But Pharaoh ultimately refused to let the Lord's "firstborn" go, so the Lord brought death upon all of Egypt's firstborn sons as divine recompense for all the injustice, oppression, and murderous acts committed against Israel.

To fully understand the magnitude of the tenth plague and the reason for it, we must understand the structure of Egyptian civilization. Egypt was a society built upon the law of primogeniture (firstborn)—the firstborn legally inherited the majority of his family's wealth and succeeded his father as head of the family or ruler of his kingdom. Pharaoh's firstborn held the title *erpa suten sa*—"hereditary crown prince." It was the birthright of the firstborn that gave the son of Pharaoh the right to rule over Egypt and his other siblings. Pharaoh was the firstborn who descended from a firstborn of a firstborn.

The Egyptian firstborn was meant to be the priest, protector, and primary leader of the family. The future of the family lay with the firstborn. The tenth plague struck at the heart of the Egyptians emotionally, economically, culturally, and spiritually.

The Significance of the Firstborn

Biblically, being the firstborn was not enough to be chosen by God to lead His people and receive the blessing of the firstborn. God is no respecter of persons or birth order. The Lord chose Isaac over Abraham's firstborn, Ishmael; Jacob over his firstborn brother, Esau; Judah, the fourth son of Jacob, to be head of the twelve tribes; and David, the youngest of all his brothers, to be king over Israel. The Lord elevated these men to the level of firstborn because of their passion to serve Him and His people.

The Messiah, according to Jewish tradition, would be called "firstborn." He would model for the world what it means to be a true firstborn child of the King. Jesus turned the law of the firstborn on its head, like God did in Egypt—not by lowering our status but by raising everyone's status to the level of firstborn in the Kingdom of God. All who believe in the Lord's Firstborn become a firstborn by becoming part of "the assembly of the firstborn" (Heb. 12:23). All followers of Jesus have an inheritance in heaven and will rule and reign with the Lord in His Kingdom as royal firstborn sons and daughters.

THE PASSOVER RAM LAMB

What is the significance of the slaughtered lamb on the first Passover? Rams were used in the depiction of many Egyptian gods. They were used in temples as sacred animals and were an important religious symbol of fertility, war, and protection. There was even an Egyptian temple dedicated to the ram god.

This is one of the reasons the Lord told Israel to slaughter a *male* lamb—also known as a ram lamb. By offering a ram lamb, Israel was slaughtering the representation of the gods of Egypt, demonstrating their faith in the Lord and their commitment to forsake the idols of Egypt. If the Lord didn't show up, the blood of the ram lamb that marked their homes would mark them for death by the Egyptians. Putting the blood on their doorposts was a bold act of faith that took a lot of *chutzpah*—spiritual audacity.

The Numbers of the Passover Lamb

Exodus 12:5 gives detailed instructions concerning the lamb (*ha-seh*). The numeric value of the letters in *ha-seh* is 310, which is the numeric value of "and make atonement" (Lev. 16:6). This phrase occurs many times in the Torah in relation to the priest offering sacrifices for Israel and is also connected to the Day of Atonement in Leviticus 16:29–30.

The first Passover lamb, *ha-seh* (310), was set aside on the tenth day of the month of *Nisan*, which connects to the tenth day of the seventh month of *Tishrei*, the Day of Atonement (Yom Kippur). The two days are connected: numerically by 10 and 310, and thematically by freedom and redemption.

Passover is known as the "time of our freedom," and on Yom Kippur people are set free, redeemed from their sins through the atonement. On the Day of Atonement in the Year of Jubilee (every seven sabbatical years), the shofar was sounded to declare forgiveness of debt and freedom for slaves.[2]

We see the New Testament connection as Messiah Yeshua entered Jerusalem on Palm Sunday on the tenth of *Nisan*, the same day the lamb (310) was set aside. He died a few days later as the Passover Lamb (310) to make atonement (310) so that we might be set free from sin, from death, and "from evil" (*mei-ra*, 310) in fulfillment of Yom Kippur, the Day of Atonement.

The Requirements for the Passover Lamb

The instructions given for the Passover lamb point to Jesus in significant ways. First, the lamb had to be a year-old male (Ex. 12:5) because the tenth plague was going to strike the firstborn males of Egypt. The blood of the male lamb saved the male firstborns when it was applied to the doorpost. In this regard, the Passover lamb provided a substitute, a life for a life, which demonstrated God's grace and mercy and pointed to Jesus, the greater Passover Lamb.

The Hebrew word for "male" is *zachar*, which has the numeric value of 227. Its value is the same as the Hebrew word for "the firstborn," *habechor* (227).[3]

The Messiah was to be the Lord's Firstborn, according to this messianic prophecy:

> "Also I will set his hand over the sea,
> And his right hand over the rivers.
> He shall cry to Me, 'You are my Father,
> My God, and the rock of my salvation.'
> Also I will make him My firstborn,
> the highest of the kings of the earth." (Ps. 89:25–27 NKJV)

The rabbis connect the Lord's command in Exodus 34:19 to sanctify "every firstborn" as both a reminder of how the Lord spared the firstborn of Israel at the Passover and a prophetic allusion to the Messiah: "I will make the king Messiah a firstborn, as it is stated, I, too, will make him a firstborn, supreme over all the earth's kings (Psalm 89:28)."[4] The New Testament also makes this connection in describing Jesus as the "firstborn of all creation" and "the firstborn from the dead" (Col. 1:15, 18). **The male lamb, offered to save the firstborn of Israel from death, was meant to be a picture of the Messiah—God's firstborn Son.**

The Passover lamb also had to be "without blemish" (Ex. 12:5). The Hebrew word for "without blemish" is *tamim*, which has the numeric value of 490. This is also the numeric value of "Bethlehem" (*Beit Lechem*). The blameless male Passover lamb pointed to Messiah Yeshua, who would be perfect, without any moral or spiritual blemish, and who would be born in Bethlehem. The Hebrew phrase for the words "an unblemished male lamb" adds up to 1022, which is the numeric value of Yeshua in Hebrew when calculated progressively: (1) *yud* = 10; (2) *yud, shin* = 310; (3) *yud, shin, vav* = 316; (4) *yud, shin, vav, ayin* = 386. Added together these equal 1022.

THE SYMBOL OF THE CROSS AND PASSOVER

The Passover lamb was to be slain, and the blood was to be caught in a basin and applied to the top of the door and the doorposts. Only the marked houses were spared from the tenth plague. The sign of the doorposts forms the letter *tav*, which, in ancient Hebrew, was written in the form of a cross. This means that the cross, the symbol of Christianity, was originally a Jewish symbol.

The *tav* was used as both a sign and seal of ownership. *Tav* marked the neck of horses and camels to validate ownership. It made sense that the *tav* was used to mark the homes of the Israelites at the moment of their redemption. The Israelites were owned as slaves by the Egyptians and had little or no freedom, but the Lord was about to redeem His people.

The word "redemption" can literally mean "to buy back." In the book of Ruth, Boaz, who redeemed Ruth, became her kinsman redeemer, her *goel* ("deliverance"). This same word is used of the Lord's redeeming Israel from Egypt. In the New Testament, the word conveys buying a slave from the auction block. It forms the background for many New Testament passages, including 1 Corinthians 6:19–20: "[Believers are] bought with a price."

God used the blood of the Passover lamb, in the form of the letter *tav*, to demonstrate that the Israelites now belonged to Him alone and not to the Egyptians. By the blood of the lamb, the ownership of Israel was being transferred from Pharaoh and the Egyptians to the God of Abraham, Isaac, and Jacob. Israel would once again be free to serve the Lord as His firstborn.

The *tav* as the letter that marked the doors in Egypt makes even more sense when connected with Ezekiel 9:4: "Go throughout the city, through the midst of Jerusalem. Make a **mark** on the foreheads of the people who sigh and moan over all the abominations that are committed in it." The Hebrew word for "mark" here is *tav*. The *tav* was the sign placed upon the foreheads of the faithful—it was the mark for those who were sealed for life.

The letter *tav* is the last letter of the *Aleph-Bet* and symbolizes the end. It points to everything in Israel's history culminating in the cross. Also, the Messiah is the *Alpha* and *Omega*—in Hebrew, the *Aleph* and *Tav*—the First and the Last.

By giving His life as the Passover Lamb, Yeshua sealed our salvation by purchasing back all of creation from slavery to sin, sickness, death, and Satan. The One who redeemed us was the *Aleph* and the *Tav* who declared "It is finished" while dying on a cross in the form of a *tav*. We are sealed by the blood of the Lamb, like Israel in Egypt, and marked with the messianic seal of truth, the *tav* (cross).

CELEBRATING THE PASSOVER

Putting the blood on the doorway of each home was the beginning, not the end, of the Passover. The Passover was to be celebrated by the Hebrews in their homes and in every generation to follow with three elements (Ex. 12:8): (1) the Passover lamb, (2) the unleavened bread (*matzah*), and (3) bitter herbs (*maror*). Other elements were added over time, including four cups of wine. This became known as the Passover Seder ("seder" means "order"), which many Jewish people still celebrate today. All the elements of Passover point to the Messiah, our Passover Lamb.

The Four Cups

Many traditions and elements were added to the Passover Seder over time. The exact order and elements of the Passover in the first century cannot be determined with complete certainty due to the lack of historical records. Passover is structured around four cups of wine, drunk during the seder, that serve as a reminder of the four aspects of the exodus redemption found in Exodus 6:6–7:

- Cup #1: "I will bring you out from under the burdens of the Egyptians."
- Cup #2: "I will deliver you from their bondage."
- Cup #3: "I will redeem you with an outstretched arm and with great judgments."
- Cup #4: "I will take you to Myself as a people."

One of the most detailed accounts comes from the Passover described in the Gospels.

Cup #1: The Cup of Sanctification

Jesus began His Last Seder with the first cup, known as the Cup of Sanctification (*Kiddush*):

And when He had taken a cup and offered the *bracha* [a blessing], He said, "Take this and share it among yourselves. For I tell you that I will never drink of the fruit of the vine from now on, until the kingdom of God comes." (Luke 22:17–18)

The Cup of Sanctification invested the occasion with holiness and spiritual meaning. Not only was the evening being sanctified and set apart for the Lord, but so were Jesus and His disciples.

This is seen in the very next step of the Passover, known as *urchatz*, in which the leader washes his hands before partaking of the seder meal with everyone present. Yeshua, at this point, instead of just washing His hands, washed the feet of the disciples as well (John 13:4–5).

After Israel left Egypt, the Lord instructed the people to build Him a tabernacle, where His presence would dwell and sacrifices of worship would be offered. Aaron and his sons were set aside as priests for the purpose of serving in the tabernacle. At their dedication, their hands and feet were washed. In the same way, Yeshua was setting aside and sanctifying His disciples as priests, according to the order of Melchizedek, for service in the Kingdom. The washing of feet also represented spiritual purification and "regeneration and renewing of the Holy Spirit" (Titus 3:5 NKJV).

Cup #2: The Cup of Reciting

The second cup of the Passover Seder is known as the *Maggid*, the Cup of the Reciting of the Passover story. It is also known as the Cup of Plagues because the ten plagues are told before drinking it. This cup is not mentioned in the Gospel accounts.

Cup #3: The Cup of Redemption

The third cup is consumed after the Passover meal. It is known as the Cup of Redemption and points to the third aspect of deliverance: "I will redeem you" (Ex. 6:6). It also represents the blood of the Passover lamb that was sprinkled three times on the doorposts of the homes in Egypt. This third cup holds significance because Jesus instituted the Lord's Supper with this cup at His Passover Seder:

> And He took a cup; and after giving thanks, He gave to them, saying, "Drink from it, all of you; for this is My blood of the covenant, which is poured out for many for the removal of sins." (Matt. 26:27–28)

Jesus referred to His blood in connection with the Cup of Redemption. The numeric value of "blood" (*DaM)* is 44. This number communicates the deeper meaning of the spiritual and prophetic use of "blood" at the Passover. The first letter, *dalet*, has the value of 4; *mem*, the second letter, equals 40. Not only does "blood" equal 44 but the numeric value of the words "father" (*Av*, 3) and "mother" (*eim*, 41) added together is 44. This is also the value of the words "child" (*yeled*) and "to birth" (*yalad*). Do you see the connection between the use of blood as the means to spare the firstborn sons?

Words and Key Phrases with a Numeric Value of 44

דם	blood
ילד	child
ילד	to birth
אם and אב	mother and father
אל אחד	one God
יהוה חי	the LORD lives
טלה	lamb (1 Samuel 7:9)
יגאל	he will be redeemed (Leviticus 25:54)
גולה	captivity (2 Kings 24:14)
ביבל	in/by Jubilee (Leviticus 25:28)

When these words and phrases are looked at together, the deeper reasoning behind the use of blood in the first and last plagues and in the Lord's Supper is revealed.

Those Egyptians who chose not to repent experienced the death of their firstborn child (remember, "child" equals 44). But those Egyptians who joined Israel in placing the blood (44) of the Passover lamb (44) on the doorposts of their homes were spared, and their firstborn child (44) lived. And the people were delivered out of death and the captivity (44) of Egypt by means of the exodus.

Similarly the Messiah's first miracle (John 2:1–11) involved blood—not real blood but the blood of grapes. He came to bring life (wine), not death (blood) (John 10:10). Messiah Yeshua shed His blood (44) as the lamb (44) to end our exile/captivity (44). The one who believes will be redeemed (44) and enter into the Jubilee (44) of the messianic Kingdom, when

> "The wolf and the **lamb** [*taleh*, 44] will feed together.
> The lion will eat straw like the ox,
>> but dust will be the serpent's food.
> They will not hurt or destroy
>> in all My holy mountain," says *ADONAI*. (Isa. 65:25)

Cup #4: The Cup of Praise

The fourth and last cup of the Passover Seder corresponds to the fourth aspect of redemption: "I will take you to Myself as a people" (Ex. 6:7). This fourth cup is known as the Cup of Praise, for it is drunk in conjunction with the psalms of praise known as *Hallel* (Pss. 113–118). It is also known as the Cup of Acceptance, for after we are redeemed by the body and blood of the Lamb, we are accepted as His children.

Many scholars and messianic rabbis believe that Jesus did not drink the fourth cup because there is no mention of Jesus blessing and drinking the fourth cup. This is underscored by the fact that the fourth cup was drunk after singing the *Hallel*. The Gospels tell us that "after singing the *Hallel*, they went out to the Mount of Olives" (Mark 14:26), with no mention of the fourth cup. It is possible that the Gospel account omitted this detail and other details of Jesus' Passover Seder so as not to detract from the focus on the most important cup, the third cup. Another possibility is that Jesus didn't drink the fourth cup because of the statement He made in Mark 14:25: "Amen, I tell you, I will never again drink of the fruit of the vine, until that day when I drink it anew in the kingdom of God." Maybe Jesus left the fourth cup standing because He was waiting to drink it with all of us in the messianic Kingdom at the marriage supper of the Lamb.

THE PASSOVER LAMB

The Passover lamb in Hebrew is *pesach*. The word "Passover" is derived from this word. At the first Passover, the blood was placed on the doorposts and then the lamb was roasted whole over a fire and eaten before dawn. In later generations, the Passover lamb could only be sacrificed in the Jerusalem temple, and then its meat was eaten with family and friends at the Passover Seder meal. Jesus would have gone to the temple to offer it, then He would have eaten it at the Last Supper with His disciples. This was the most central and sacred element of the Passover meal. In fact, the last piece of solid food to be eaten during the meal was the Passover lamb, for the last thing on one's lips should be the taste of redemption.

Both the blood and the Passover lamb were meant to point to the Messiah. Deeper truths and reasons for the Passover can be discovered by examining its numeric value. "Passover" has the numeric value of 148. This is the same numeric value as *netzach* (נצח), which means "strength" and "victory." The Passover offering (148) gave Israel the divine strength (148) to be victorious (148) over Pharaoh and the gods of Egypt.

Other key words that have the numeric value of 148 are "iniquity" (*ba-avonecha*), "plague" (*maggephah*), "promise" (*epaggelia*), and "children of God" (*benei Elohim*). *Netzach* also can convey the concept of eternity in addition to victory.

What is the connection between all these words that equal 148? The Messiah died at Passover (148) for the iniquity (148) of Israel and the nations so that we might be saved and have victory (148) over the plague (148) of sin and death and experience the promise (148) of eternity (148). For as many as believe in Him become children of God (148). Yeshua, our Passover Lamb, has won the victory so we don't remain stuck. It's time to come out of Egypt, for the one whom the Son sets free is free indeed. The blood, along with the lamb itself, pointed to the Messiah.

The Matzah: The Unleavened Bread

The Passover lamb had to be eaten with unleavened bread, or *matzah*. *Matzah* was such a central aspect to the keeping of the Passover that another name for the feast in Hebrew is the Feast of Unleavened Bread (*Chag HaMatzot*), which we read about in Exodus 34:18: "You are to keep the Feast of *Matzot*. For seven days you are [to] eat *matzot*, as I commanded you, at the time appointed in the month Aviv, for in the month Aviv you came out from Egypt."*

The Passover lamb was eaten on the first night, but *matzah* was eaten for the seven days of the festival. No leavened bread or products are eaten during Passover week.

There is a twofold reason that Jews eat *matzah*. The first is that after the tenth plague, the Egyptians drove the children of Israel out of Egypt quickly out of fear that more Egyptians would die. The Israelites had to leave so hastily that their bread did not have time to rise (leaven). This is why the Lord told them to eat the Passover "with your loins girded, your shoes on your feet and your staff in your hand. You are to eat it in haste" (Ex. 12:11).

---

* *Matzot* is the plural of *matzah*.

The second reason is that the *matzah* reminds Jews of the affliction their ancestors endured as slaves. Even its physical characteristics are reminiscent of oppression, such as the brown stripes running the length of the bread that point to the lashings of the slave drivers upon the enslaved Hebrews.

Matzah is also known as the bread of "freedom and healing" and serves as a reminder of when God redeemed Israel from Egypt "with an outstretched arm" (Ex. 6:6). The *matzah* is pierced, striped, bruised, and broken at the seder. It is meant to point prophetically to the Messiah promised in Isaiah 53:

> Surely he took up our pain
>   and bore our suffering,
> yet we considered him punished by God,
>   stricken by him, and afflicted.
> But he was pierced for our transgressions,
>   he was crushed for our iniquities;
> the punishment that brought us peace was on him,
>   and by his wounds we are healed. (vv. 4–5 NIV)

During the Last Seder, *matzah* was the bread Yeshua lifted, broke, and "gave to the disciples and said, 'Take, eat; this is My body'" (Matt. 26:26). The *matzah's* holes stand for His piercings, and the brown stripes represent His wounds, by which we are healed and set free from bondage to sin. His body was broken in death, like the *matzah*, so that the power of death might be broken and we might find eternal life.

The Bitter Herbs

The Passover was to be eaten with bitter herbs (Ex. 12:8), which represent the bitterness and harshness of slavery. The *maror* at a Passover Seder is usually raw horseradish that is dipped in a second bitter herb known as *charoset*, which is a sweet-tasting mixture of apples, nuts, cinnamon, and wine. It symbolizes the stone mortar used by the Jews for building during their slavery. The *charoset* exemplifies how God can turn what is bitter into something sweet, as Romans 8:28 reminds us: "God causes everything to work together for the good of those who love God and are called according to his purpose for them" (NLT).

On the night Yeshua was betrayed, He revealed His betrayer: "'It is the one to whom I will give this piece of bread when I have dipped it in the dish.' Then, dipping the piece of bread, he gave it to Judas, the son of Simon Iscariot. As soon as Judas took the bread, Satan entered into him" (John 13:26–27 NIV). In addition to the bitterness of slavery, this step represents the bitterness of separation from Yeshua, as exemplified by Judas. In Hebrew, both "bitter herbs" (*maror*) and "death" (*mavet*) share the numeric value of 446. All those who reject Jesus, as did Judas, will experience the bitterness (446) of death (446).

THE TWELVE DISCIPLES AND THE TWELVE TRIBES OF ISRAEL

Why is it significant that Jesus celebrated the Passover with twelve disciples? There were twelve sons born to Jacob, and from them came the twelve tribes of Israel. All twelve tribes left Egypt at the Passover. Yeshua, as the greater than Moses, came to initiate a new spiritual exodus to redeem the lost sheep of the house of Israel and all nations and lead them to the spiritual Promised Land, the Kingdom of God. The twelve disciples symbolize the twelve tribes of Israel. Yeshua, with the third cup, inaugurated the New Covenant found in Jeremiah 31:30–33:

> "Behold, days are coming"
> —it is a declaration of *Adonai*—
> "when I will make a new covenant
> with the house of Israel
> and with the house of Judah—
> not like the covenant
> I made with their fathers
> in the day I took them by the hand

to bring them out of the land of Egypt.

For they broke My covenant,

though I was a husband to them."

it is a declaration of *Adonai.*

"But this is the covenant I will make with the house of Israel
   after those days"

—it is a declaration of *Adonai*—

"I will put My *Torah* within them.

Yes, I will write it on their heart.

I will be their God

and they will be My people. . . .

For I will forgive their iniquity,

their sin I will remember no more."

Jeremiah's prophecy states that the New Covenant must be made and inaugurated with Israel first. The twelve disciples represent the remnant of Israel, the firstfruits of salvation, who one day would lead the salvation of all Israel who will believe in Him at the Second Coming (Rom. 11).

There were twelve tribes of Israel, and each tribe had a leader known as a *nasi*, who was its representative. The twelve apostles were set apart to prophetically represent the heads of the renewed Israel entering into the New Covenant. This connection is seen clearly in the book of Revelation, which says that the New Jerusalem has twelve gates with the twelve names of the twelve tribes, and the wall of the city will have twelve foundations with the names of the twelve apostles (Rev. 21:12–14).

The twelve apostles represent the covenantal promise to the twelve tribes of Israel—that God's chosen people will one day be redeemed and fulfill their destiny to bring salvation to the nations. God never reneges on His commitments; "The gifts and the calling of God are irrevocable" (Rom. 11:29). This is good news for me and you.

Paul communicated this same thinking in Romans 9–11. He ended Romans 8 by saying nothing can separate us from the love of God in Messiah Yeshua. But what about the Jewish people? God has a covenant with them, but they seemed to have been separated and replaced by the church, which was primarily Gentile, non-Jewish in composition. How can anyone be sure that God won't do to them what He seemingly did to Israel?

Paul answered this question in Romans 9–11. In chapter 9, he talked about Israel's past riches and God's covenant with them. In chapter 10, he talked about his unceasing grief because of Israel's present state of unbelief. He said he would gladly give up his salvation for the sake of his Jewish brethren. In Romans 11, he provided several proofs that the Lord is not finished with Israel. The first is that Paul himself, a former persecutor of the Messiah and a Jew, was chosen to bring the Gospel to the nations. A second proof was from Elijah, who, like Paul, was also from the tribe of Benjamin. Elijah believed he was the only Hebrew faithful to God, but the Lord told him there was a remnant of seven thousand who still faithfully believed. The point is that there has always been and always will be, even in the darkest times, a faithful remnant of Jews who follow the Lord. As it was in the days of Elijah, so will it always be, for the Lord is faithful. The twelve disciples, even before Paul, pointed to this promise.

Israel will fulfill its God-given destiny; the twelve disciples are the firstfruits of this promise. These twelve Jewish apostles proclaimed the Gospel—to the Jews first and then to the Gentiles—to bring salvation to the nations. Through the twelve, the Lord caused Israel to fulfill her divine destiny, which goes all the way back to Abraham but is made even clearer by Isaiah: "You will be a light to guide the nations" (Isa. 42:6 NLT). This is ultimately fulfilled by another twelve in the book of Revelation: in the end times, twelve thousand Jews from each of the twelve tribes will be set apart as evangelists to the world (Rev. 7:4–8). And ultimately, as Paul wrote, all Israel will be saved. This is good news for both Gentile and Jew, for if God ultimately keeps His promises to Israel, He will keep His promises to you. The Lord is faithful.

chapter
NINE

THE MESSIAH AND PENTECOST

L ooking for rescue from a merciless situation or an abusive home environment can seem hopeless with no visible way to escape. This physical exile often carries with it a spiritual component. And in the case of the Israelites, God delivered them out of Egypt; then He had to take Egypt out of the Israelites. We discover how this plays out in what happens next.

Many Christians think of Pentecost as a New Testament holiday on which God birthed the church (Acts 2). But Pentecost is a highly anticipated biblical Jewish holiday, first celebrated by Israel fifty days after leaving Egypt (Lev. 23). We cannot appreciate the full spiritual and prophetic significance of what happened on Pentecost in the book of Acts without understanding its historical roots in the Hebrew Bible. To fully grasp the deeper meaning of Jesus' resurrection and ascension, as well as the gift of the Holy Spirit, we must understand Pentecost (*Shavuot*) and the days leading up to it.

On the Passover, God physically redeemed Israel from Egyptian bondage, but Passover was meant to culminate in Pentecost. When God first spoke to Moses at the burning bush, He said: "I will surely be with you. So that will be the sign to you that it is I who have sent you. When you have brought the people out of Egypt: you will worship God on this mountain" (Ex. 3:12). From the beginning, the Lord intended Passover to climax on the first Pentecost, which occurred at Mount Sinai, on the same spot where Moses encountered God in the burning bush.

Passover without Pentecost would not have been complete because the focus of Passover is redemption, and the purpose of redemption is revelation. Without all that revelation brings, we can easily slip into bondage again.

Physical freedom does not mean one is free spiritually and emotionally, which is the greater goal of redemption. We are redeemed, set free, absolved, and saved so that the revelation of who we are in God's divine plan can be made known to us and understood.

PREPARING FOR PENTECOST

The revelation of the Lord at Mount Sinai to Israel—when the Lord spoke the Ten Commandments—occurred fifty days after escaping Egypt. But why did the Lord wait fifty days? Biblically, the number fifty represents freedom. The first connection between fifty and freedom is the Year of Jubilee. Every fiftieth year in the land of Israel, all debts were canceled, slaves were set free, land was returned to the families that had temporarily sold it due to hardship, and all agricultural work was stopped for one year so the people and the land could rest (Lev. 25). At fifty years of age, Levites were released from their service in the tabernacle or temple (Num. 8:25). Numerically, in Hebrew the phrase "in the Jubilee" has the value of 50. And the Torah mentions the exodus event fifty times, for it was the beginning of Israel's freedom.[1]

Holy and Whole

According to Jewish tradition, there is another reason the Lord waited fifty days to give the Ten Commandments and the Torah at Mount Sinai. Before leaving Egypt, Israel sank to a new spiritual low. The rabbis teach that there are fifty levels of spiritual impurity. In Egypt, Israel fell to the forty-ninth level, so God needed fifty days to purify and transform them spiritually and physically.

The children of Israel were in dire need of healing after centuries of abuse in Egypt. They needed to rebuild their relationship with God and renew their relationships with one another. They were physically broken by the abuse of the taskmasters and the relentless severity of the hard work. They were also spiritually broken by the Egyptians' worship of idols. The enslaved people of Israel had broken bodies, minds, hearts, and spirits. It's difficult to fathom that this multidimensional healing from four centuries of horror could happen in only fifty days. Two verses come to my mind: "Nothing will be impossible with God" (Luke 1:37) and "Hope deferred makes the heart sick, but longing fulfilled is a tree of life" (Prov. 13:12). God's miraculous healing of Israel forms the background for the healings that occurred on the day of Pentecost we read about in Acts 2.

WHY TEN?

The children of Israel received the Ten Commandments on Pentecost. As we study this unique holiday, we need to understand these "tablets of stone, written by the finger of God" (Ex. 31:18).

The Ten Commandments are the foundation of the entire Torah and historically became the moral foundation for Jews, Christians, and most of Western civilization built on a Judeo-Christian worldview. Since details matter to God, the fact that the Lord gave the Ten Commandments on Pentecost must be significant.

It is impossible to fully understand the greater purpose and meaning behind the revelation at Sinai and the Ten Commandments without understanding the significance of the number ten. To do this, we must go back to the beginning.

The words "God said" occur ten times in the Creation account in Genesis 1 (vv. 3, 6, 9, 11, 14, 20, 24, 26, 28, 29). By means of these ten utterances, God spoke the world and the universe into existence.[2] Ten is also the number of generations between Adam and Noah and between Noah and Abraham.[3] Ten is connected to Creation, to Noah—a second Adam who entered into a renewed creation after the Flood—and to Abraham, through whom God created the Jewish people.

The Egyptians endured ten plagues before Pharaoh finally freed Israel. It is no coincidence that there were ten plagues in Egypt and ten utterances spoken by God at Creation. Before the Lord first spoke any word at Creation, the world was "chaos and waste" (Gen. 1:2). Through the ten utterances, God brought order, life, and blessing out of chaos.

Pharaoh defiantly chose to disobey God's divine command uttered by the mouth of Moses. Egypt went from a state of order to disorder—a reversal of Creation. God desired to bring order out of chaos, but each time Pharaoh disobeyed God's Word the Egyptians experienced chaos. Instead of light, there was darkness; instead of life, there was death; instead of blessing, there was cursing. The animals no longer feared man but attacked him. The ten plagues were literally an undoing of the ten utterances of Creation.

God's Word is the code for creation on the spiritual level. When the code is broken, a virus enters into the system and nothing runs correctly. Then, when the chaos gets bad enough, the whole system crashes. This is what happened in both Egypt and Eden when man disobeyed God's spoken Word. When the spiritual laws and principles of the Word of God are disobeyed or ignored, even out of ignorance, then chaos ensues. Egypt learned this lesson firsthand. The Scripture devotes so much space to the recounting of the plagues, in part, so that all who read will understand the lesson.

When the Israelites left Egypt, they were literally coming out of chaos, but they themselves were in their own state of chaos. Can you imagine millions of frightened men and women who had been enslaved trying to leave their homes to follow a leader they hardly knew to go to a place they had never been? The chaos is illustrated by their constant grumbling and doubting God; at one point, they were ready to stone Moses and return to Egypt (Ex. 16–17).

On a verbal and structural level, the Ten Commandments (Ex. 20) connect directly to the Creation account. The opening verse of the Bible, Genesis 1:1, in the original Hebrew contains seven words and twenty-eight letters—the same number of words and letters as Exodus 20:1. I believe this was intentional, under the inspiration of the Holy Spirit, to connect the ten of Creation with the ten of the Sinai revelation that resulted in a new creation.

The Ten Commandments are like ten steps to spiritual freedom. They provided the spiritual foundation for Israel's faith, ethics, and religious and civil law. They also serve as the bedrock for building a society that embodies justice and righteousness. That's why many courthouses throughout the United States display them. In Hebrew Scripture, they are called the "Ten Statements," not the "Ten Commandments." This is a significant distinction because the Scripture sets these ten apart from the other 603 commandments found in the Torah. These ten are fundamentally different because they are the foundational principles from which every other commandment in the Five Books of Moses stems.

The ten plagues and the Ten Commandments were intended to help Israel reach its full spiritual potential and ready the Israelites to see the realization of the promises that the Lord made to their forefather Abraham. In Genesis 15, God appeared to Abraham and made a covenant with him in which He promised to give Abraham and his descendants a homeland (Gen. 15:18).

This promise would not be fulfilled until Israel came out of Egypt 430 years later. But when that occurred, God's children permanently removed ten people groups who had been occupying and defiling the Promised Land with murder, sexual immorality, and idolatry for generations. The ten plagues and the Ten Commandments were critical to prepare and empower Israel to defeat and dispose of the ten pagan peoples.

The sum of the numbers of creation (10), redemption (10), and revelation (10) is 30. Creation, revelation, and redemption point to and culminate in the person of Yeshua.

The number thirty can symbolize dedication to a particular task or calling. The Levitical priests began their priestly service at age thirty (Num. 4:3). Joseph was elevated from the prison to the palace at age thirty to serve Pharaoh. King David was thirty years old when he began to rule over Israel (2 Sam. 5:4). And Yeshua was thirty years old when He began His public ministry. As the Creator King, Redeemer, and High Priest, Yeshua brings creation, redemption, and revelation to fulfillment and helps us to experience their fullness in our own lives.

TABLETS OF TWO STONES

Why were the Ten Commandments given to Moses on two tablets? The two tablets correspond to their structure. On the first tablet were written the commandments for the relationship between God and man (*mitzvot bein adam leMakom*). On the second tablet were written the commandments for the relationship between man and man (*mitzvot bein adam lechaveiro*). When Yeshua was asked by a Torah scholar, "Teacher, which is the greatest commandment in the *Torah*?" (Matt. 22:36), He responded with "Love *ADONAI* your God" and "Love your neighbor as yourself" (vv. 37, 39).

Yeshua used the Great Commandment to summarize the two tablets that Moses received from the Lord on Sinai. Love is the ultimate goal of all of God's commandments. But why love above all else? Paul gave us some insight when he wrote, "These three remain—faith, hope, and love. And the greatest of these is love" (1 Cor. 13:13). In the end, when His Kingdom comes, faith and hope will be fulfilled. You only need faith in what you don't see and hope in promises that are not currently fulfilled. "Faith is the substance of things hoped for, the evidence of realities not seen" (Heb. 11:1). But when the Lord comes, our love will not diminish but only increase like the bride who, after a period of separation, finally gets to see her long-awaited groom on their wedding day. Of the three (faith, hope, and love), love is the greatest, for it alone lasts. Love is eternal, for above all "God is love" (1 John 4:8). If we want to fulfill the spirit of the Ten Commandments we must love like Jesus and fulfill the Great Commandment.

The Ten Commandments are seen as both the foundation and the symbol of the Torah in Judaism. The word "Torah" has the numeric value of 611, which seems strange because there are 613 commandments in the Torah. The difference might be that the Torah is not complete without making the two great love commandments the priority and focus. You can try to keep all of God's commandments and even be spiritual, but without love you are just a "clanging cymbal" (1 Cor. 13:1). The heart of Yeshua's teaching is love.

There is great power in love: "Love never fails" (1 Cor. 13:8). "Perfect love drives out fear" (1 John 4:18). "We are more than conquerors through Him who loved us" (Rom. 8:37). And nothing will be able "to separate us from the love of God that is in Messiah *Yeshua* our Lord" (Rom. 8:39). The power of the two tablets and the Great Commandment is love.

Two Sets of Two-Stone Tablets

Moses, after coming down Mount Sinai with the two "tablets of the Testimony" (Ex. 32:15) found Israel committing idolatry by worshiping a golden calf. In righteous indignation, he took the two tablets, which were "the work of God" (v. 16), and "smashed them at the foot of the mountain" (v. 19). Can you imagine the anger and despair Moses felt at that moment? He had been through so much, put up with so much, and sacrificed so much. He must surely have felt that his time on the mountain—his spiritual high point—was the turning point for himself and the children of Israel. But the foolishness of the people shattered his hopeful outlook in an instant.

Surprisingly the Lord said to Moses, "Carve for yourself two tablets of stone like the first ones, and I will write upon them the words that were on the first tablets, which you broke" (Ex. 34:1). The second set of tablets communicated that God was giving Israel a second chance. He was offering them a divine do-over.

DIVINE DO-OVERS

As a third grader I was big and strong for my age, but I was a bit uncoordinated. I remember playing a game of kickball in which the bases were loaded with two outs, and I had the opportunity to score the game-winning run. I kicked the ball with all my strength, but it was caught for what seemed like the final out and end of the game. But, in a moment of inspiration,

I remembered the do-over rule. Every player had one do-over in the game, and I had not used mine—now was the time. This time I didn't fail but scored the winning run. Israel experienced a do-over at Sinai, only on a much greater scale.

God is the God of second chances. The apostle Peter, in the New Testament, experienced this firsthand. He denied the Lord, like Israel, and thought because he had blown it so badly that he might as well go back to his old profession. But the Lord gave him a second chance and restored him as leader of the twelve after asking him three times: "Do you love Me?" (John 21:15–17). God is love, and the two tablets of the Ten Commandments are connected to love. The Lord tangibly demonstrated love when He forgave Israel and Peter. You don't need to live with guilt and shame because you blow it sometimes; you just need to ask the Lord for a second chance. The Lord delights in giving do-overs.

WHOLENESS FROM BROKENNESS

The second set of the Ten Commandments was placed in the ark of the covenant along with the manna and Aaron's rod. But what happened to the first set? Jewish tradition says the broken pieces of the first set were placed in the ark right along with the second set.[4] But why? Most people don't want to keep broken things around, especially when they remind someone of a painful experience or a significant failure.

One beautiful spiritual lesson from this is that brokenness must precede wholeness. Brokenness should make us better, not bitter. Brokenness that results from failures should not depress us but rather develop us. The way to wholeness is through brokenness.

You don't need to feel ashamed of your brokenness or try to hide it. Healing and wholeness come from embracing brokenness and learning from it. Every time the ark of the covenant traveled, the people could hear the rumbling of the broken pieces. This was and is a reminder that wholeness and brokenness can and will coexist until the Messiah returns.

THE TWO SETS OF TWO-STONE
TABLETS AND THE MESSIAH

The two sets of tablets symbolically point to the Messiah. The first set points to the First Coming of the Messiah. Yeshua is the Word that "became flesh and made his dwelling among us" (John 1:14 NIV). He is the living Word who descends from heaven but is smashed, like the two tablets, due to the sin of people. The Messiah's body was broken so we might experience forgiveness of sin and receive a divine do-over. Jesus was broken, like the unleavened bread at the Passover, so we might be made whole. The smashed and shattered tablets point to the world in which we live and, even more so, to the world falling to pieces before Messiah returns.

When the first tablets were smashed, according to tradition, the letters, which had been written supernaturally by the finger of God, ascended back to heaven on the fortieth day, the day Moses descended Sinai. Yeshua, after being broken and rejected for our sins, ascended back to heaven on the fortieth day after His resurrection (Acts 1:1–3). As a result of Israel's idolatry, judgment broke out and three thousand of the children of Israel died. In the book of Acts, three thousand are saved on the day of Pentecost (Acts 2:41). Yeshua's brokenness led to life, not death and judgment.

The second set of tablets points to Jesus' Second Coming, when He will return as the Lion of the tribe of Judah, who will cut off all false gods, cause idolatry like the sin of the golden calf to cease, and defeat all the enemies of God's people. When the Messiah returns as the Son of David, He will also bring salvation, healing, and wholeness to the world by establishing the messianic Kingdom.

The broken tablet pieces point to the Messiah, but they also provide a beautiful picture for you and me. They represent broken dreams, broken promises, and brokenness due to physical ailments, betrayal, rejection, financial ruin, and so on. The Lord wants us to pick up the broken pieces and give them to Jesus, for He is in the business of making the broken whole and turning brokenness into blessing. Bring your brokenness to the One who was broken for you and watch what He can do.

PENTECOST IN THE DAYS OF JESUS

The fifty-day countdown between Passover and Pentecost begins on the second day of Passover, which is also a biblical holiday known as Firstfruits, according to Leviticus 23: "From the day that you brought the omer [a sheaf of grain] of the wave offering, seven complete *Shabbatot* [Sabbaths]. Until the morrow after the seventh *Shabbat* you are to count fifty days" (vv. 15–16).

In the days of the temple, on the second day of Passover, a communal firstfruits meal offering of barley (an *omer*) was waved by the priest. A lamb that was sacrificed as a burnt offering on the altar accompanied this offering. From the time this *omer* offering was brought from the newly harvested barley crop, a seven-week period known as *Sefira* (counting) began, culminating with the holiday of *Shavuot* on the fiftieth day. Until the *omer* was brought and offered in the temple, no one was to eat any new grain that had grown that year. At the conclusion of *Sefira* (the forty-nine-day counting period), two loaves made from the new wheat crop were offered on *Shavuot*.

The counting of the *omer* was meant to cultivate a sense of appreciation and gratitude for the blessings of God. By bringing the *omer* as a firstfruits offering, the children of Israel demonstrated their dependence on God for their sustenance—like their ancestors in the wilderness did—and showed their gratitude to God for it. Trust and thankfulness were two key lessons that the Israelites had to learn if they were going to be blessed by God and enjoy an intimate relationship with Him. Through the daily counting of the *omer*, which Jews still do every day between Passover and Pentecost, we cultivate a belief in God as the ultimate Provider, offer gratitude for His abundant provisions, and literally learn to count our blessings.

JESUS' FIRSTFRUITS AND THE RESURRECTION

Firstfruits (*Yom HaBikkurim*) started on the second day of Passover. It was on this day that the firstfruits offering was given to the Lord as a wave offering. It would be waved before the Lord as a sign of thanksgiving and also with eager expectation, for if you had an abundant early harvest, it was a guarantee that you would have an abundant later harvest. Not only was the firstfruits a sign of the greater harvest to come, but it started the forty-nine-day countdown to Pentecost.

Nothing is random with God. Therefore, it is appropriate that Jesus, who died on Passover, would arise from the dead on Firstfruits as "the firstfruits of those who have fallen asleep" (1 Cor. 15:20).* After He arose, He instructed the disciples, "Do not leave Jerusalem, but wait for the gift my Father promised. . . . For John baptized with water, but in a few days you will be baptized with the Holy Spirit" (Acts 1:4–5 NIV). Jesus' resurrection on Firstfruits (Lev. 23:9–15) started the countdown to Pentecost, when His Father gave the gift of His Spirit (Acts 2:1–4).

PENTECOST TAKE 2: SINAI REVISITED

Suddenly, there was a sound from heaven like the roaring of a mighty windstorm, and it filled the house where they were sitting. Then, what looked like flames or tongues of fire appeared and settled on each of them. And everyone present was filled with the Holy Spirit and began speaking in other languages, as the Holy Spirit gave them this ability.

—*Acts 2:2–4* NLT

The events of Acts 2 seem strange at first glance: the sound of a mighty wind, fiery flaming tongues, and people speaking in foreign languages. When I read this for the first time as a new believer, I was confused—until I began to look at it in light of what happened on the *first* Pentecost when Israel stood at Mount Sinai after coming out of Egypt.

Acts 2 is a reenactment of what happened at Mount Sinai. The windstorm was like the thundering at Sinai when "the whole mountain quaked

---

* Firstfruits is a holiday within the holiday of Passover that begins the forty-nine-day countdown to Pentecost, which is on the fiftieth day.

greatly" (Ex. 19:18). The flames that descended in the Upper Room pointed back to the Lord, who descended in fire upon Mount Sinai. If we look at the ancient Aramaic text, even the most seemingly odd detail, divided tongues of fire over the disciples' heads, also hearkens back to when God uttered the Ten Commandments.

Aramaic became the prominent language for the average Jewish person sometime in the sixth century BC, after the destruction of the first temple and the subsequent exile of the Jewish people to Babylon. So either during or right after the time of Ezra, the Hebrew Bible was translated into Aramaic. *Targum Neofiti*, an ancient Aramaic interpretive paraphrase, describes the revelation at Sinai as follows: "Like torches of fire, a torch of fire to the right and a torch of fire to the left. It flew and winged swiftly in the air of the heavens and came back . . . and returning it became engraved on the tablets of the covenant and all Israel beheld it."[5]

The tongues of fire in Acts 2 are reminiscent of and connect to the divided winged torches of fire that are said to have inscribed the Ten Commandments on the stone tablets. This connection is monumental. God established the Mosaic Covenant with Israel at Sinai, but Israel broke this covenant continually. The Lord graciously and compassionately did not reject or replace Israel; rather, as explained in chapter 8, He promised to make a New Covenant with the nation (Jer. 31:30–33).

On Pentecost, the same day God initiated the Mosaic Covenant, the New Covenant was experienced with similar signs and wonders as a fulfillment of prophecy. Fiery torches wrote the Mosaic Covenant on stone tablets, but the New Covenant was greater because it was indelibly inscribed by the fire of the Spirit on the hearts of all who believe.

GIFTS TO MANKIND

Two of God's greatest gifts were given on Pentecost: the Torah in Exodus 19–20 and the Holy Spirit in Acts 2. In the beginning the Spirit of the Lord was hovering over the face of the deep, which was formless and void. Then

God spoke, and the world came to be (Gen. 1:1–2). Creation came about as the result of God's Word and Spirit. It is for this reason that the Word and Spirit were both given on Pentecost. The greatest and deepest levels of new creation transformation result only from the gifts of the Word and the Spirit. **The Lord must be worshiped in "the Spirit and in truth"** (John 4:24 NIV).

When the Holy Spirit filled the disciples, they were completely transformed. Seven weeks earlier, Peter had denied the Lord three times and, out of fear, had locked himself in the Upper Room with the other disciples. But when the Spirit, the third person of the Godhead, came upon him, Peter boldly proclaimed the Gospel in the Jerusalem temple and three thousand people believed.

The power of God's Word and Spirit completely and forever changed Peter and the other disciples. What the Lord did for them, He wants to do for you. Let the Lord change you through His Word and His Spirit. Every follower of the Messiah is "a new creation. The old things have passed away; behold, all things have become new" (2 Cor. 5:17).

AUTHORITY AND POWER

Most people do not realize how radical the gift of the Holy Spirit was and still is. To understand the gift of the Spirit, one must understand the concept and practice of anointing. In the Hebrew Bible, only priests, kings, and some prophets, such as Elisha, were anointed with specially made olive oil (1 Kings 19:16). This ritual anointing with oil signified that they had been appointed by God to serve in their respective offices.

For many millennia, the Jewish people have awaited the promised coming King and prophet like Moses, known as the Messiah. The title Messiah (*Christ* in Greek) comes from the Hebrew word *Mashiach*, which means "Anointed One." Like all kings of Israel, the Messiah would be anointed ritually with oil, and by the Spirit (Isa. 11:1–2), to lead God's people. The Messiah would be the Lord's anointed Prophet, Priest, and King. These offices all find their fulfillment in Jesus.

This is what makes the gift of the Holy Spirit so incredible. In Acts 2, we see that the Spirit is given not to a few select individuals but to all followers of Messiah Yeshua, the Lord's Anointed One. This means that you have been both appointed and anointed, by the Spirit, with power to serve the Lord.

When I was growing up, I used to love to watch western movies with my grandfather. Every old western town had a sheriff who was often the hero of the story and always wore two things: a badge and a gun. What set him apart from the bad guys was not his gun but his badge. The gun represented power, but even the bad guys had guns. His badge, however, represented rightful authority, true identity, and his mission, which was to serve and protect.

Like the sheriff, in the Kingdom you need a badge and a gun. When a sheriff in the Old West was outnumbered and outmanned, what did he do? He deputized some of the townspeople to be part of his posse for the purpose of maintaining the peace and protecting the town. The giving of the Holy Spirit is a sign that you have been deputized and given a new identity, new power, new authority, and a new purpose to serve in the Lord's posse. Jesus is the ultimate sheriff. "All authority in heaven and on earth" has been given to Him (Matt. 28:18). Time spent in the Word, worship, and prayer is key to activating and increasing in spiritual power and authority.

This is one reason Jesus told the disciples to tarry in prayer and the Word until the day of Pentecost. He said, "You will receive power when the *Ruach ha-Kodesh* [Holy Spirit] has come upon you; and you will be My witnesses in Jerusalem, and through all Judah, and Samaria, and to the end of the earth" (Acts 1:8). As a follower of Jesus, you have been given power and authority to transform the world. The only question is, what will you do with it? Your gun and badge are not meant to be decorative. They are meant to be used for good. What are you waiting for?

The most significant events in the life of Jesus happened on biblical holidays. He died as the Passover Lamb, He rose from the dead on Firstfruits as proof that you will rise, too, as part of the end-time harvest, and He poured out the Spirit on *Shavuot* (Pentecost) so that you might experience new creation transformation and be anointed to change the world.

chapter
TEN

THE MESSIAH IN
THE DESERT

When the word "desert" comes to mind, most people think of a barren, sweltering, uninhabitable, hostile, waterless, sandy, and lifeless place. Spiritually, the desert is often a place of wandering, testing, isolation, dryness, and waiting. All these images contain aspects of truth, but there is much more to the desert—and to wilderness seasons.

I love leading tours of Israel. I relish introducing people to the Promised Land and helping them see it for the first time through Jewish eyes. One of my favorite places to take them is the desert—the Judaean wilderness.

The desert (or wilderness) plays a foundational role in the history and spiritual development of the children of Israel. The majority of the five books of the Torah (from Exodus 15 to Deuteronomy 24) takes place in the desert. One of the most defining events in Israel's desert history was the giving of the Torah. Understanding the desert is key to understanding the Torah, Moses, and Messiah Yeshua.

THE DESERT IS A PLACE OF BIRTHING

When God rescued Israel from Egypt, He had Moses lead the Israelites "by the way of the wilderness to the Sea of Reeds [Red Sea]" (Ex. 13:18).

While the children of Israel were in the desert, Pharaoh changed his mind and attempted to recapture them. Israel seemed to be in a precarious and hopeless situation. The Red Sea was on one side and Pharaoh's advancing army was on the other. But God can make a way where there seems to be no way. He parted the sea and brought Israel through on dry ground. He then closed the waters on the Egyptians. In the desert at the Red Sea, God delivered Israel physically and spiritually.

The name "Egypt" (Hebrew, *Mitzrayim*) comes from the root word *tzar*, which means "a tight or constricted place." Egypt, a place of confinement for the Israelites when Pharaoh enslaved them, can be seen as a womb—a tight place God used to birth Israel. Israel went to Egypt as a family of seventy but grew into a nation of millions by the time of the exodus. God used the confinement of Egypt as a fertile womb in which He supernaturally multiplied the children of Israel.

If Egypt represents the womb, then the parting of the Red Sea characterizes the breaking of water in labor. Passing through the sea is symbolic of a baby passing through the birth canal. Israel came out of the water reborn as a nation of free men and women. God had begun to fulfill His promise to Abraham to make the Israelites numerous "like the sand that is on the seashore" (Gen. 22:17).

God also told Abraham that his descendants would be oppressed for four hundred years and then brought back to inherit the Promised Land. It's no coincidence that Israel wandered the desert for forty years. I believe there is a clear connection between four hundred and forty.

The number forty represents birthing. A full-term pregnancy is forty weeks. Forty in Hebrew is represented by the letter *mem*. The shape of the letter *mem* is said to resemble an open womb. *Mem* also symbolically represents water. The Egyptians' oppression of Israel for four hundred years and Israel's wandering in the desert for forty years are the means by which the Lord spiritually and symbolically birthed Israel as His chosen nation.

This birthing imagery forms the background to the discussion between Jesus and Nicodemus in John 3. Nicodemus, a prominent Pharisee, came secretly to Yeshua at night seeking truth. Yeshua told him, "Unless one is born again, he cannot see the kingdom of God" (v. 3 NKJV).

Nicodemus, confused, responded, "How can a man be born when he is old? Can he enter a second time into his mother's womb and be born?" (v. 4 NKJV).

I understand his confusion. After I finished reciting what I now know to be a form of the sinner's prayer, I was told to raise my hand, for I had just been born again. But I had no idea what that meant. All I knew was Jewish kids don't get born again. And I thought, *I gave my parents enough trouble when I was born once. What will happen if I am born again?* Nevertheless, I felt pressure to raise my hand and praise God even though I was initially hesitant. Being born again seemed like a very un-Jewish thing to do. But, actually, it was the most Jewish thing to do.

Yeshua said to Nicodemus, "You're a teacher of Israel and you do not understand these things?" (John 3:10). How could such a learned and highly prominent religious leader not get what it means to be born again?

We saw how Israel was born twice: (1) as a people in Egypt and (2) as a free nation when the Lord brought Israel through the Red Sea, where, according to Jewish tradition, the Spirit of God fell on the people and they all prophesied. God had to birth Israel physically and spiritually before they could enter the Promised Land, which is symbolic of the heavenly Kingdom of God that was to come.

Sadly, not all of them made it to the Promised Land. The adult generation that escaped Egypt died, with the exception of Joshua and Caleb. The Israelites kept rebelling against God and wanted to crawl back into the womb (Egypt), like babies looking for comfort and security apart from the Lord.

This gives new meaning to Nicodemus's statement "How can a man be born when he is old? Can he enter a second time into his mother's womb and be born?" (John 3:4 NKJV) and ties it back to the exodus. Israel was born four hundred years after Jacob's family moved to Egypt, but God commanded Israel never to enter the womb again. The Lord closed the waters on the Egyptians so there would be no way back. He also closed the waters to wash away Israel's past. This washing away began a process of purification and instilled a new and real sense of freedom. Seeing the drowned Egyptians meant the Israelites did not have to live in fear that their former captors might return to enslave them once again.

Similarly, when we are born again, the Lord makes us new and washes away our past, and we never have to go back to the places that want to confine and enslave us. God birthed Israel physically over four hundred years, which included enslavement in Egypt, and He birthed Israel spiritually over forty years in the desert. We need both Egypt and the wilderness season to be fully birthed into our true identities and destinies.

THE DESERT IS A PLACE OF INTIMACY AND CONNECTION

God could have brought Israel straight to Jerusalem and given His people the Torah in the Promised Land. So why did He choose the desert for the greatest communal revelation in the Bible?

The desert is a place of intimacy and connection. The serene silence and lack of distractions make it a perfect setting for God's new bride to intimately discover her Bridegroom, the Lord. A key aspect of spiritual intimacy is communication. The desert is the place where God first spoke to Moses, so it makes sense that it is the place where the Lord would speak to Israel.

The word for "desert" or "wilderness" in Hebrew is *midbar*. The root of the word *midbar* is *davar*, which means "word" and is also related to *midabber*, meaning "to speak." The desert (*midbar*) is the place where God speaks (*midabber*). This is directly connected to the revelation of the Ten Commandments, which contains the same root *davar* in Deuteronomy 10:4: "the Ten Words [*Asert ha-Devarim*] He had spoken [*dibber*] to you."

The root of the word *midbar* is used to describe another location where the Lord spoke: the Holy of Holies, which is called the *dvir* in 1 Kings 6:5. The word *dvir* can also be translated as "inner sanctuary," which corresponds to the desert. Just as God spoke in the most removed part of the temple, the place where only the high priest was allowed to enter, so the Lord spoke in the desert, a place that is removed from civilization. Don't be discouraged by your wilderness season. The Lord can turn your desert into a *dvir*, a Holy of Holies where He intimately speaks to you.

God revealing His word in the desert also hints to the Messiah, who was baptized in the Judaean wilderness (*midbar*). In the same way that the Lord spoke to Israel in the desert and thus proved that Moses was truly sent by God, the voice of the Lord confirmed Yeshua as the Messiah and the greater than Moses in His wilderness baptism (Matt. 3:16–17).

As we have seen, the root word of "desert" is *davar*, which means "word." In John 1:1, Jesus is called "the Word" (*HaDavar*). In the same way that God revealed His word (*davar*) in the Sinai wilderness, so He revealed Jesus (*HaDavar*) as "the Word became flesh" (John 1:14) in the desert (*midbar*). This connects to the next verses in John 1:15–27 as John testified to *HaDavar* and baptized Jesus in the wilderness.

THE DESERT IS A PLACE OF DEPENDENCE

Dependence is about trust. If Israel was going to be free from years of oppression and dependence on human masters, the nation needed to learn to trust the Lord. Yet the Israelites frequently wanted to stone Moses and return to Egypt because they lacked faith in the Lord. This attitude needed to change if Israel was going to take the Promised Land and start a new life as God's people.

Dependence Is About Direction

The children of Israel had to learn to listen to God as though their lives depended on it. The desert can be a dangerous and unforgiving place, especially for millions of people who lack provisions. The children of Israel had to learn to follow the Lord, like a little child who must learn to follow and take direction from a parent when crossing a busy street. This was a key part of the desert's purpose. Israel was birthed in Egypt but grew to maturity during the forty years in the wilderness, where the Israelites learned the importance of obediently following the Lord. God led them as a cloud of smoke by day and a pillar of fire by night, and they were only to move when they saw the Lord move (Ex. 13:21).

The scarce resources in the wilderness taught Israel to trust God for material needs as well as direction and protection. Israel depended on the Lord for protection from the scorching heat of the day, the cold of the night, and dangerous creatures such as snakes and scorpions. According to Jewish tradition, God's cloud of glory formed a canopy, a tabernacle (*sukkah*), that surrounded the Israelites on all six sides: (1) front, (2) back, (3) right, (4) left, (5) above, and (6) below.

Like the Israelites in the wilderness, we must learn to depend on the Lord for direction, protection, and provision. Trust and dependence come from connection built on clear communication. That is why the root word for "desert" also means "to speak." **Without intimate communication and connection, it is hard to trust God completely for direction**.

Dependence Is About Provision

We need to trust God not only for His direction but also for His provision. Free from Pharaoh, the Israelites murmured. The Lord responded by saying He would "rain bread from heaven"—but only enough for each day, except Friday, when He would provide a double portion of manna so that no one would have to gather it on the Sabbath (Ex. 16:4–5). Through the heavenly manna the Lord would provide sustenance, but it would also serve to test Israel to see if the people would faithfully obey God.

Prophetically the manna points to the Messiah. The correlation between Moses and the Messiah both providing manna is well established in Jewish tradition. "As the former redeemer [Moses] caused manna to descend, as it is stated in Exodus 16:4, so will the latter Redeemer [the Messiah] cause manna to descend."[1] Like Moses, who gave manna to the people, Yeshua on two occasions multiplied food for the multitudes.

In the first miracle of multiplication, Yeshua miraculously fed five thousand men with five loaves of barley bread and two small fish, and there were even leftovers (Matt. 14:13–21). This miracle reminds us of the manna the Lord gave Israel through Moses. It happened in a remote region, reminiscent of the wilderness. Yeshua was ministering in a location where food could not be easily obtained apart from a manna-like miracle. Just as the manna reminded the people that it was the Lord who brought them out of Egypt,

Yeshua performed this miracle near the Passover (John 6:1–4) and made the same connection.

The next day, while teaching in the synagogue at Capernaum, someone asked Yeshua, "What sign do You perform, so that we may see and believe You? . . . Our fathers ate the manna in the wilderness; as it is written, 'Out of heaven He gave them bread to eat'" (John 6:30–31). Yeshua took the opportunity to explain how the heavenly bread that their ancestors ate in the wilderness pointed to Him, the One offering something even greater than manna:

> "For the bread of God is the One coming down from heaven and giving life to the world."
>
> So they said to Him, "Sir, give us this bread from now on!"
>
> *Yeshua* said to them, "I am the bread of life. Whoever comes to Me will never be hungry, and whoever believes in Me will never be thirsty. But I told you that you have seen Me, yet you do not believe." (John 6:33–36)

Instead of graciously receiving "the bread of life" Yeshua offered, those listening in the synagogue grumbled among themselves and against Him just as Israel grumbled both before and after receiving the manna. Yeshua's statement about being "the bread of life" and His subsequent statement about people needing to eat His flesh and drink His blood (vv. 53–55) tested what was in their hearts as the manna in the wilderness tested Israel.

THE MANNA AND THE MYSTERY OF THE MESSIAH'S RESURRECTION

God provided manna from heaven for the first time on the sixteenth of *Iyar*, the second month after leaving Egypt. The last day the children of Israel ate manna was on the morning of the sixteenth of *Nisan*, the second day of

Passover. On this day Israel realized that there was no more manna—from that point on their bread would come from the grain that they would harvest in the Promised Land.

The day the manna ended, the sixteenth of *Nisan*, is the same day of celebrating the Feast of Firstfruits. Yeshua rose from the dead on Sunday the sixteenth. This points to Yeshua as the Bread of Life that brings resurrection. It also points to Yeshua as the fulfillment of everything the manna spoke about. He is **"the hidden manna"** (Rev. 2:17).

WHAT ABOUT THE PROVISION OF WATER?

People in the desert need food, but mostly they need water to survive. After providing manna, the Lord, through Moses, brought forth water from the rock to quench Israel's thirst (Ex. 17:1–6). Like the manna, the water from the rock is also associated with the Messiah in Jewish tradition: "As the former redeemer [Moses] made a well to rise, so will the latter Redeemer [the Messiah] bring up water, as it is stated, And a fountain shall come forth of the house of the Lord, and shall water the valley of Shittim (Joel 4:18)."[2]

Messiah Yeshua as the one greater than Moses offers both the "bread of life" (John 6:35) and the "living water" (7:38). In John 7:37, Jesus went up to Jerusalem to celebrate the Feast of Tabernacles and offered all who believed in Him "living water." But to fully understand this, we need to learn a bit more about the meaning of *Sukkot*, the Feast of Tabernacles, and how it was celebrated in Yeshua's day.

Sukkot celebrates God's provision for the Israelites during their forty years of wandering in the wilderness. One of the primary things that the Lord provided for Israel was water to quench the thirst of the millions who had left Egypt. From where did the water come?

The Jewish sages teach that there was a rock that followed Israel throughout the wilderness wanderings. When water was needed, the leaders of Israel would approach this rock and cry out to the Lord in song, "Spring up, O well!" (Num. 21:17). In response to Israel's prayerful plea for water, this rock burst forth a fountain. Jewish tradition states that streams would flow from this rock and create an oasis of living waters.

After entering the Promised Land, Israel still needed to depend on the Lord for water. If God did not send the early and the latter rain, the crops would not grow, and the people would go hungry. *Sukkot* remembers God's miraculous provision of water and is also the beginning of the rainy season in the land of Israel. For both of these reasons, *Sukkot* was the time that priests led the people in petitioning the Lord for rain.

The "drawing of the water" during the Feast of Tabernacles was one of the most joy-filled celebrations of the year. The sages noted, "One who did not see the Celebration of the Place of the Drawing of the Water, never saw celebration in his life."[3] Every day of the feast at dawn, the priests would lead a large procession with joyous song to draw water out of the spring of Siloam. They would then march back to the temple. Before pouring water on the altar as a libation offering to the Lord, the priests would walk around the altar, and everyone would cry out to the Lord to pour out rain from heaven. This cry was not just for the rain needed to bring forth bountiful crops but also for the Lord to pour out His Spirit upon the people and grant them prophetic inspiration.

On the seventh day of *Sukkot*, they marched around the altar not once but seven times as they cried out even more fervently to the Lord for an outpouring of rain and the Holy Spirit. On this "last and greatest day of the festival, Jesus stood and said in a loud voice, 'Let anyone who is thirsty come to me and drink. Whoever believes in me, as Scripture has said, rivers of living water will flow from within them'" (John 7:37–38 NIV).

Yeshua was communicating to all present that the water their ancestors drank and the spiritual blessing of the Holy Spirit that they were crying out for were to be found only through Him as the Messiah. He was the Rock that followed them, and it was only through Him that they could be filled to overflowing with the living water of the Holy Spirit. This would have astounded the people and caused dismay to many of the leaders present. It's interesting that the Gospel of John talks about the "bread of life" in chapter 6 and the "living water" in chapter 7, which follows the same pattern found in the book of Exodus as Moses gave the bread from heaven in chapter 16 and then the water from the rock in chapter 17. John was demonstrating that Yeshua was the Prophet whom Moses promised in the Torah.

Yeshua is the source of all life and blessing. When we believe in Him, we can experience the transforming and refreshing presence and power of God's Spirit. Messiah Jesus is the greater Moses who offers us "living water" from Himself, the Rock, that will bubble up to eternal life for all who drink.

THE DESERT IS A PLACE OF TESTING

At the end of the Israelites' time in the wilderness, Moses said to them, "Remember how the LORD your God led you all the way in the wilderness these forty years, to humble and test you in order to know what was in your heart, whether or not you would keep his commands" (Deut. 8:2 NIV). The desert is a place where the Lord strengthens His people's faith in Him and dependence on Him through testing. Desert testing is why the Lord brought Moses, Israel, David, Elijah, John the Baptist, the apostle Paul, and others into the wilderness for a season.

Even Jesus had to go into the desert. On the surface this might seem unnecessary since He was the Son of God. Why would He need testing?

The Gospels call Jesus the King of the Jews, and as such He had to fulfill the covenantal promises and prophecies that were given to Israel. A key aspect of redemption, like Jesus' role as the second Adam, is making right that which those who went before Him did wrong. He had to make a repair (*tikkun*) for the sin of Adam, who represents collective humanity, and for Israel, through whom salvation was to come. As part of the redemption process, Jesus had to die for our sin, but He also had to fix the cracks that were created in the spiritual foundation.

Jesus is the second Adam but also the One-Man Israel. The history and destiny of Israel needed to be made right through Him so that He could redeem Israel and ultimately the nations. He needed to relive the foundational moments in Israel's history to bring about a repair (*tikkun*) and redemption for Israel and demonstrate to her and the nations that He is the goal of creation, covenant, revelation, and redemption. In other words, He needed to repeat to redeem and repair.

This in part is why Jesus was taken into the wilderness. Further, He is the greater Moses; He had to begin in the desert like Israel's first redeemer. It is for this reason as well that Yeshua had to go down to Egypt as a child to fulfill the prophecy "out of Egypt I called My son" (Hos. 11:1). Moses and Israel came out of Egypt, so the Messiah had to as well.

After being redeemed, the Israelites, like Moses, also went out to the wilderness to test what was in their hearts. But the generation that came out of Egypt, with the exception of Joshua and Caleb, failed God's test miserably. The next generation inherited the land.

Not even Moses passed the test. He died in the wilderness because, by striking the rock twice for water, instead of only once as the Lord had commanded him, Moses lacked faith (Num. 20:12). Yeshua had to pass the test Israel failed in order to make a repair (*tikkun*) and demonstrate that He is greater than Moses. The details of the Messiah's testing in the wilderness are directly related to Moses' and Israel's testing in the desert.

After being immersed by John the Baptist, Yeshua was led by the Spirit into the wilderness. Hungry from a forty-day fast, Yeshua was tested by the devil, who said, "If You are *Ben-Elohim* [the Son of God], tell this stone to become bread" (Luke 4:3). This test connects to when Israel grumbled by saying, "If only we had died by the hand of *Adonai* in the land of Egypt, when we sat by pots of meat, when we ate bread until we were full. But you have brought us into the wilderness, to kill this entire congregation with hunger" (Ex. 16:3).

Yeshua's first test involved bread; Israel's first failure was not trusting the Lord to meet their physical needs. Yeshua responded to Satan by quoting from Deuteronomy: "Man shall not live by bread alone" (Luke 4:4). God tested the hungry Israelites with manna so they would learn that their survival was not by bread alone "but by every word that comes from the mouth of *Adonai*" (Deut. 8:3). Yeshua passed the test where they failed. The question is, will we? Yeshua's example teaches us to trust the Lord to provide for our spiritual and physical needs.

Next, Satan showed Yeshua all the kingdoms of this world and offered them to Him if He would bow down and worship him. Israel failed this test as well. On several occasions the children of Israel broke the first commandment and committed idolatry in the desert. The first time, they created and worshiped a golden calf (Ex. 32). On another occasion, the Israelites were seduced into worshiping the gods of the Moabites (Num. 25:1–4). God warned Moses before the children of Israel entered the Promised Land that they would break God's covenant by worshiping the foreign gods of the pagan inhabitants of the land (Deut. 31:16).

Yeshua refused to bow down to Satan, and He passed the test that Israel continually failed throughout her history. All of us will be tempted at some time to compromise, to bow down to the idols of this world, in exchange for gold or glory. But, like Yeshua, we must worship the Lord and serve Him only (Deut. 6:13). The Lord hates idolatry—not because He is a jealous narcissist but because He knows the harm it brings to us. Those who worship idols become enslaved to them and become like them. Idols fragment us spiritually, emotionally, mentally, and physically. God freed Israel from Egypt—and prohibited them from returning—so they would not be enslaved by Egypt's idols. In Jesus you have been set free. Don't become a slave to idols; trust and worship Him alone.

Finally, Satan brought Yeshua to the high point of the temple in Jerusalem and told Him to jump to demonstrate that He is the Son of God. This also connects to Moses. At the very end of Moses' life, the Lord took him to the top of Mount Nebo, which is opposite Jericho, close to where the temptation of Jesus would occur. The Lord supernaturally showed Moses the entire land, just as Satan would show Jesus all the kingdoms of the world. The Lord then told Moses, "This is the land that I swore to Abraham, Isaac and Jacob saying, 'I will give it to your seed.' I let you see it with your eyes, but you will not cross over there" (Deut. 34:4). After this vision, Moses died and was buried.

An interesting rabbinic tradition relates to this test: "When king Messiah appears, he will come and stand on the roof of the temple, and make a proclamation to Israel, 'Meek ones, the time of your redemption has come, and if you don't believe me behold my light.'"[4] Satan wanted Yeshua to throw Himself off the temple to demonstrate as a supernatural sign to Israel that He was the promised Messiah.

> The voice [God's] at the baptism declared him to be the Son of God; the voice [Satan] in the wilderness now says, "If you are the Son of God . . ." In the first assault, the devil wants Jesus to perform a miracle in order to meet his physical need; in the second, he wants him to throw himself from the pinnacle of the temple in order to test whether God will keep his promise; in the third, he wants him to obtain what God has promised him (all the kingdoms of the world) by the devil's way, avoiding the cross altogether.[5]

We cannot avoid the cross of the Messiah. We can overcome the testing times by seeking the redemptive power of the cross, by studying God's Word so we can bring it to mind when we're tempted, and by believing that God will keep His promises.

THE DESERT IS A PLACE OF TRANSFORMATION

Desert experiences change a person. The desert forces you to come to the end of yourself. It's when that end comes that God can begin to transform you. The Lord used the desert to transform the Israelites and prepare them for the Promised Land.

The desert is also linked to the future promise of transformation and renewal. The Lord promised Israel, through the prophets, that one day the desert would bloom: "For ADONAI will comfort Zion. . . . He will make her wilderness like Eden, her desert like the garden of ADONAI" (Isa. 51:3). The land of Israel became a desert wasteland due to Israel's disobedience and exile, but the Lord would restore and make it like Eden.

The people of Israel would one day say, "This land that was a wasteland has become like the garden of Eden. The waste, desolate and ruined cities are fortified and inhabited" (Ezek. 36:35). Israel was still a desert in 1867 when Mark Twain visited the land and described it as a "desolate country . . . given over wholly to weeds . . . a desolation . . . hardly a tree or a shrub anywhere. . . . We never saw a human being on the whole route."[6]

Significant change came in 1948 when Israel became a state. Today the Lord has caused the desert to bloom. Israel is an agricultural miracle—currently, its desert produces approximately 60 percent of its vegetables and more for export. Israel is an agricultural powerhouse with one of the world's highest rates of crops per acre. Prophecy has been fulfilled in our day. By God's grace the desert blooms again.

THE DESERT IS A PLACE OF RENEWAL AND REDEMPTION

The prophet Hosea prophesied about Israel's renewal in the desert:

> "So then, I Myself will entice her,
> I will bring her into the wilderness
>   and speak to her heart.
> I will give her back her vineyards from there
> and make the valley of Achor a door of hope.
> She will respond there—
>   as in the days of her youth,
>   as in the day she came up out of the land of Egypt."
>   (Hos. 2:16–17)

The Lord will return Israel to the desert before the final redemption to renew His relationship with her. The Lord will also use the desert at that time to protect her from Satan the dragon, according to the book of Revelation:

> Then the woman fled into the wilderness, where she has a place prepared by God so they might take care of her for 1,260 days.

But the woman was given two wings of the great eagle, so that she might fly away from the presence of the serpent into the wilderness, to the place where she is taken care of—for a time, times, and half a time. (Rev. 12:6, 14)

As it was in the beginning, so will it be in the end. Jesus, the King of the Jews and One-Man Israel, overcame Satan in the wilderness—a prophetic act that makes it possible for Israel to be redeemed at the end of days. They overcome, along with all who have believed in Him, because Jesus not only relives and embodies Israel's history but is the forerunner who breaks open and makes possible salvation for Israel and the nations.

THE DESERT IS A PLACE TO BIRTH NEW BEGINNINGS

Israel spent a total of forty years in the desert, but they wandered as punishment for their unbelief for thirty-eight years (Deut. 2:14). This is significant because it ties into an often-overlooked detail that is vital to understand the healing Jesus performed at the pool of Bethesda.

After this there was a **Jewish feast**, and *Yeshua* went up to Jerusalem. Now in Jerusalem there is a pool by the sheep gate, called Bethzatha in Aramaic, which has five porches.

Now a certain man had been an invalid there for **thirty-eight years**. Seeing him lying there and knowing he had been that way a long time, *Yeshua* said to him, "Do you want to get well?"

The invalid answered Him, "Sir, I have nobody to put me into the pool when the water is stirred up. While I'm trying to get in, somebody else steps down before me!"

Yeshua tells him, "Get up! Pick up your mat and walk!"

Immediately, the man was healed! He took up his mat and started walking around. Now that day was *Shabbat*. (John 5:1–2, 5–9)

The number of years this man was an invalid connects to the number of years Israel wandered in the wilderness due to their unbelief. Thirty-eight is the numeric value of "his heart" (Hebrew, *libo*). By asking the man if he wanted to be made well, Yeshua was testing him to see what was in his heart (38).

The generation of adults that came out of Egypt had such a slave and victim mentality that they kept testing God and died in the wilderness. Yeshua did not want that to happen to this man. Part of the reason John recorded this miracle was to demonstrate that this victim mentality does not have to happen to us. There is hope—if we choose to believe and have faith in the greater than Moses, Messiah Jesus. Yeshua healed this man to a new normal. God's creative and healing power began to flow through this man, and he walked—immediately.

You don't have to die in the desert. You don't need to spend the next thirty-eight years in your desert waiting for a miracle. **The desert was intended not to be the end but rather a place that births you into a new beginning. I encourage you to declare, "I don't have to live in the desert wilderness. I can get up and follow Yeshua!"**

chapter ELEVEN

THE MESSIAH IN THE LOVE STORY OF RUTH AND BOAZ

The love story of Ruth and Boaz is one of the sweetest stories in both secular and sacred history. A Jewish family, living in Bethlehem during the time of the judges (1200–1020 BC), faced severe famine. Naomi, her husband, Elimelech, and their two sons fled for their lives with no food and no home. After a little while they decided to settle in Moab.

Elimelech's choice to bring his family to Moab during a time of famine seems strange since the Moabites were known for their lack of hospitality and deep enmity toward the Hebrew people. In quick succession we read about the death of Naomi's husband, then the deaths of her two sons who had married Moabite women. The text seems to imply that these three men died prematurely due to God's displeasure with them.

Grief-stricken, Naomi, an impoverished widow, now faced the daunting question: "How will I survive?" She instructed her two Moabite daughters-in-law, Orpah and Ruth, to return to their "mother's house" (Ruth 1:8). Orpah decided to return. But Ruth heard the cry of her mother-in-law, and she lovingly and courageously laid down her life in response. Ruth pledged unswerving loyalty to Naomi in Ruth 1:16–17:

"Entreat me not to leave you,
Or to turn back from following after you;
For wherever you go, I will go;
And wherever you lodge, I will lodge;
Your people shall be my people,
And your God, my God.
Where you die, I will die,
And there will I be buried.
The LORD do so to me, and more also,
If anything but death parts you and me." (NKJV)

YOUR GOD MY GOD

Returning to Bethlehem, Ruth and Naomi were in a seemingly hopeless state until God sent Boaz, their kinsman redeemer.[1] Exhausted physically and emotionally from the journey—and no doubt hungry—Ruth asked Naomi to let her glean in the fields of Bethlehem. According to the Torah, the corners of the field could not be harvested by its owner, and any forgotten sheaves of grain in the field could not be gathered but had to be left for the poor, widows, orphans, and foreigners (Lev. 19:9). Knowing this command, Ruth set out and randomly chose a field to glean. This decision, made out of extreme desperation, took courage, since it could be dangerous for a poor, young, unmarried foreigner like Ruth to glean in a stranger's field.

But by God's grace, the field belonged to Boaz, a wealthy, godly, older man, who just happened to be closely related to Ruth's mother-in-law, Naomi. Boaz took notice of Ruth, she found favor in his eyes, and he protected and provided for her while she was in his fields.

Naomi and Ruth were destitute until Ruth met and married Boaz. When Ruth united with Boaz in a covenantal relationship, she received the full inheritance—she went from merely surviving from the scraps to thriving. But to really appreciate the story of Ruth and Boaz, we need to first unlock their ancestry, which is critical for understanding the lineage of King David and the promised Son of David, Yeshua.

Backstory on Moab

Ruth was a Moabite. Why is this significant? Friendship between Israel and Moab was prohibited, as the Torah makes clear:

> No Ammonite or Moabite is to enter the community of *Adonai*—even to the tenth generation none belonging to them is to enter the community of *Adonai* forever—because they did not meet you with bread and water on the way when you came out from Egypt, and because they hired against you Balaam . . . to curse you. But *Adonai* your God refused to listen to Balaam, and *Adonai* your God turned the curse into a blessing for you because He loves you. You are never to seek their *shalom* or welfare all your days. (Deut. 23:4–7)

Ruth, a Moabite, married Boaz, an Israelite, creating a mixed marriage. Did Boaz break God's commandment by marrying her? No, not according to Jewish tradition. Jewish law holds that a Jewish man could marry a Moabite or Ammonite woman, though it was discouraged and the union would be severely frowned upon because Moabites had a long history in the Bible of sexual promiscuity and idolatry. On the other hand, mixed marriages between a Moabite or Ammonite man and a Jewish woman were strictly forbidden under Jewish law. Clearly, Ruth made a huge sacrifice and took a big risk by following destitute Naomi back to the land of Israel, knowing that there was little chance of her remarriage as a widow and foreigner from a despised people. But love for the Lord and for Naomi made the risk of rejection and living in poverty worth it.

The union of Ruth and Boaz can't be fully appreciated, or its messianic significance understood, without knowing the history of Moab. **The coming together of Ruth and Boaz is the reuniting of Abraham and Lot.** It's amazing how God is so specific in handpicking each and every one of our genealogies.

BLESSED TO BE A BLESSING

In Genesis 12, God spoke to Abraham: "Get going out from your land" (v. 1). Abraham took a great step of faith and left his homeland with Sarah and his nephew Lot. God promised Abraham that He would bless those who blessed him and curse those who cursed him (v. 3). God richly blessed Abraham, and all that his fingers touched prospered. Lot flourished because God's blessing of Abraham spilled over into his life. As long as Lot stayed close to Abraham and blessed him, he was blessed in fulfillment of God's promise to "bless those who bless [Abraham]" (Gen. 12:3) and his seed, the Jewish people.

Cursed

God kept His word. Abraham and Lot prospered to the point that the land could not sustain them both, so Abraham and Lot separated. Abraham ascended and dwelled in the Promised Land. Lot decided to live in Sodom, which, before the Lord destroyed it, looked like "*ADONAI's* garden, like the land of Egypt" (Gen. 13:10). When Lot separated from his uncle Abraham, he removed himself from the abundance of God's provision.

Lot split from Abraham on his journey to Sodom and Gomorrah, and judgment ensued. In the destruction of Sodom, Lot lost everything. His daughters thought the world had ended and that they were the only ones left. They took matters into their own hands: they got their father intoxicated so they could become impregnated by him. Their sin gave birth to two nations: Ammon and Moab. Ruth descended from Moab, a name that literally means "from my father." It's astonishing to realize that by the time of the exodus, Moab had become Israel's bitter enemy.

Lot and his family were only saved because of Abraham. Even their wealth came as the result of the Abrahamic blessing. But Lot's descendants became like the people of Sodom and Gomorrah—immoral and inhospitable, refusing to help the Israelites during their wilderness wanderings. The king of Moab even hired Balaam to curse Israel and, when that didn't work, hatched a plan to seduce the men of Israel into committing sexual immorality and idolatry with Moabite women.

There is an interesting connection here with Lot's name. His name can either come from the Hebrew root word meaning "fragrant" or from the Aramaic verb *lut*, which means, "to curse." Lot was meant to emit blessing like a fragrant flower but became a curse when he and his family became morally and spiritually corrupted by Sodom. This contamination not only impacted Lot and his daughters but their descendants as well. Instead of being fragrant, like a garden blessed by the Lord, Lot and his daughters became a curse to themselves, to the land, and to Abraham's seed, without whom they would not have existed. God will truly bless those who bless Israel and curse those who curse them.

THE RESTORATION OF ABRAHAM AND LOT

Ruth's commitment not to separate from Naomi and her God is seen as a *tikkun*—a repair or correction—for Lot's decision to separate from Abraham and live in Sodom. Her kindness to Naomi brought about both God's and Boaz's favor, which resulted in Boaz's marriage to her and the redemption of her deceased husband's ancestral land so their family inheritance would not be lost. Ruth and Boaz's marriage was a restoration of the relationship between Lot and Abraham. But why does this matter?

It Takes Two, Both Gentile and Jew

The reason that the story of the Gentile Ruth the Moabite and Hebrew Boaz from Judah is significant enough to be included in the Bible is that their relationship laid the foundation for the lineage of King David and ultimately the Messiah. There are four women cited in the genealogy of Yeshua: (1) Tamar, (2) Rahab, (3) Ruth, and (4) Bathsheba. Why only these four women? They are definitely not the most prominent or noteworthy. God chose these women because they were all Gentiles who played key roles in building the line of Judah and lineage of the Messiah through the house of David. In the same way it took both Gentiles and Jews to birth the line of Jesus, it takes Gentiles and Jews to birth the Kingdom of God.

On *Shavuot* Jews read the book of Ruth for two reasons: (1) the story of Ruth and Boaz took place at Pentecost, which is harvesttime; and (2) the book is read to honor King David's birthday, which, according to Jewish tradition, was on *Shavuot*.[2] In both the Hebrew Bible and the New Testament, one of the major themes of *Shavuot* is unity. Neither the Torah at Mount Sinai (Ex. 19:8) nor the Holy Spirit in Acts 2 are given until the people are unified in "one accord" (Acts 2:1 NKJV), like one man with one heart. God's presence, power, and provision are always proportional to the unity of God's people.

One Man with One Heart

When Jew and Gentile unite in Jesus, we become an unstoppable force for salvation, transformation, and revival. This is seen in what is known as Jesus' Farewell or High Priestly Prayer:

> I pray not on behalf of **these** only, but also for **those** who believe in Me through their message, that **they all may be one**. Just as You, Father, are in Me and I am in You, so also may they be one in Us, so the world may believe that You sent Me. The glory that You have given to Me I have given to them, that they may be one just as We are one—I in them and You in Me—that they may be **perfected in unity**, so that the **world may know that You sent Me** and loved them as You loved Me. (John 17:20–23)

It is only when "these" and "those" unify as one that the body of the Messiah will be "perfected in unity" and the world will finally realize that God sent Jesus. In this passage, "these" refers to the Jewish disciples of Jesus, and "those" refers to the nations who could believe as a result of the Great Commission. When Jew and Gentile unite, as did Boaz and Ruth, the body of the Messiah will grow to healthy maturity. Only when we become one in Jesus will the world be won to the Lord. The Enemy has tried to keep Boaz and Ruth, Jews and Gentiles, from coming into covenantal relationship and walking together because he knows that when that happens, we will become an unstoppable force for transformation and revival in the world.

I believe the modern-day Ruths are Gentile Christians who represent the believing remnant of the nations. And the modern-day Boaz is the believing remnant of Israel that follows Yeshua. When the church walks in covenantal relationship with the messianic Jewish community, she is greatly blessed.

Like Boaz, the messianic Jewish community cannot fulfill its destiny without the Gentile Ruth, the Christian church; without her the messianic community remains childless, like Boaz without Ruth. But when the two come together, they help birth Kingdom revival, like Ruth and Boaz birthed Obed, the grandfather of David.

Jew and Gentile have always needed each other. Now more than ever, Ruth and Boaz must unite. When they do, we will see the power of unity released to bring forth the transformation of Israel and the nations, the renewal of all things, and the restoration of heaven and earth. When the fusion of Ruth and Boaz occurs, we will witness God's power and presence in unprecedented ways.

God wants us to be like one man with one heart, not just praying, "Your kingdom come" but living and modeling it "on earth as it is in heaven" (Matt. 6:10). The picture the Scripture paints is clear: the Kingdom is Jew and Gentile together in the Messiah, worshiping and serving the Lord together. We see this in verses such as Zechariah 14:16, where all the nations of the world will join with Israel in the new Jerusalem at the Feast of Tabernacles/*Sukkot* to worship Jesus.

ALLUSIONS TO THE MESSIAH IN THE BOOK OF RUTH

Everything in Scripture was written for the sake of the Messiah. The book of Ruth is no exception. It provides not only the backstory for the birth of King David but also many deeper revelations and allusions to the Messiah.

One of the seemingly subtle but deeply significant allusions to the person and work of the Messiah is found in Ruth 2:14:

At mealtime Boaz said to her, "Come over here and eat some bread and dip your piece ["small morsel" in Hebrew] into the wine vinegar." So she sat beside the harvesters and he held out to her roasted grain. She ate until she was full, and some was still left.

Boaz's dialogue with Ruth seems very wordy given the fact that Ruth was a foreign woman whom he had just met. The amount of detail also seems to be a bit too mundane and even uncharacteristic of Boaz. Would Boaz, after being so generous to Ruth, really just offer her a tiny morsel of bread? Something deeper must be implied. Rabbinic commentators see Boaz's words to Ruth as prophetic allusions to important events that would occur in the life of her future descendants.

"Come Over Here"

The first way that commentators prophetically interpret Boaz's statements is by connecting them to King David:

"When it was time to eat, Boaz said to her, 'Come over here (*halom*).'" . . . R. Elazar said: [By using the word *halom* he gave her a prophetically inspired hint], telling her in effect: The royal house of David will descend from you. [Ruth was the great-grandmother of David.] . . . *Halom* is also used in reference to David, for it says, "Then King David came and sat before God, and he said, 'What am I O Lord God, and what is my family, that You have brought me *halom*, to this point (2 Sam. 7:18)." [*Halom* thus refers to both Ruth and David.][3]

King David was a type and shadow of the Messiah. The events in his life were meant to point to the Messiah, the ultimate Son of David. Thus, the life of Jesus would mirror the life of David in many important ways. This connection is powerfully seen by the way the rabbis connect Ruth 2:14 as speaking prophetically both about King David and the Messiah.

When Boaz said to Ruth, "Come over here," he was actually alluding, on a prophetic level, to Ruth's future descendant, King Messiah, who would establish the messianic Kingdom. The phrase "coming near" is important in Jewish thought. It has been interpreted by the rabbis as "come/draw near to the Kingdom."[4] The foundation of Old Testament worship was the offering of sacrifices. The Hebrew word for "sacrifice" is *korban*, which is derived from the Hebrew root *karav*, meaning "to draw near." Sin creates separation, but a sacrifice draws one near to the Lord. The Messiah, Jesus from a New Testament perspective, would offer His life as a sacrifice (*korban*) to draw us close (*merkarev*) to the Lord. This was the primary mission of Jesus and His ministry—to draw near and cause us to come closer to God:

> But now in Messiah *Yeshua*, you who once were far off have **been brought near** by the blood of the Messiah. . . . And He came and proclaimed *shalom* to you who were far away and *shalom* to **those who were near**. (Eph. 2:13, 17)

> On the last and greatest day of the Feast, *Yeshua* stood up and cried out loudly, "If anyone is thirsty, let him **come to Me** and drink." (John 7:37)[5]

Concerning Jesus, even the rabbis in the Talmud say He was "near to the Kingdom."[6] Ruth and the Messiah who descended from her would both "come near to the Kingdom"[7] and draw others near as well.

"Eat Some Bread"

Boaz's invitation for Ruth to "eat some bread" (Ruth 2:14) alludes to "bread in the kingdom" (Luke 14:15). The Messiah, like Moses, would provide bread from heaven and would actually be "the bread of life" (John 6:35). The rabbis connect bread and kingship on the basis of 1 Kings 4:22 (NIV), which associates the royal provisions of Solomon with bread. The total amount of flour and meal mentioned (90) is the numeric value of both "bread" (*lechem*) and "king" (*melech*) in Hebrew. In the Lord's Prayer that Jesus taught His disciples, the messianic Kingdom is significantly connected with bread: "Your **kingdom** come. . . . Give us this day our **daily bread**" (Matt. 6:10–11).

"Dip Your Piece into the Wine Vinegar"

After telling Ruth to "come over here," Boaz told her, "Dip your piece into the wine vinegar" (Ruth 2:14). This points to the suffering of the Messiah:

> He was pierced because of our transgressions,
> crushed because of our iniquities.
> The chastisement for our *shalom* was upon Him,
> and by His stripes we are healed. (Isa. 53:5)

Amazingly, the rabbis interpreted Isaiah 53 as referring to the Messiah, which some later rabbis and Jewish scholars deny.

Boaz's request connects back to two key events in the life of Jesus. The first was the Last Supper, when Jesus spoke about the one who would betray Him: "He it is, to whom I shall give a sop, when I have dipped it. And when he had dipped the sop, he gave it to Judas Iscariot, the son of Simon" (John 13:26 KJV). Both the original Greek text of John 13:26 and the Greek translation of Ruth 2:14 use the same word—*psomion*, which refers to food soaked in liquid before being eaten. Ruth's dipping her morsel in the sop, which the rabbis connect to the suffering of the Messiah in Isaiah 53, was partially fulfilled when Jesus dipped the sop and gave it to Judas. Judas's betrayal of Yeshua for thirty pieces of silver would directly lead to the Messiah's suffering and affliction on the cross.

Ruth's dipping her "piece into the vinegar [*sop*]" also alludes to the Messiah's death on the cross:

> After this, Jesus knowing that all things were now accomplished, **that the scripture might be fulfilled**, saith, I thirst.
>
> Now there was set a vessel full of **vinegar**: and they filled a spunge with **vinegar**, and put it upon hyssop, and put it to his mouth.
>
> When Jesus therefore had received the vinegar, he said, It is finished. (John 19:28–30 KJV)

What Scripture was Jesus seeking to fulfill when He said, "I thirst"? Jesus, the Son of David, was fulfilling Psalm 69:22, a psalm of David, which says, "For my thirst they gave me vinegar to drink." The Hebrew word for "vinegar" is *hometz* and is the same word used in Ruth 2:14 for the sop of vinegar in which Ruth dipped her bread, which clearly connects to Yeshua drinking vinegar on the cross.

The Greek word for "vinegar" is *oxos* and has the numeric value of 400. The Hebrew letter *tav*, written in the form of a cross, also equals 400, as well as the words "unto glory" from this passage: "For it was fitting for Him . . . in bringing many sons **to glory**, to perfect the originator of their salvation through sufferings" (Heb. 2:10 NASB). The Messiah tasted the vinegar (400) of affliction both at the Last Supper, the start of His suffering, and on the cross (400), which ended His suffering, so that we might be brought to glory (400) as God's children.

"She Sat Beside the Harvesters"

Ruth 2:14 continues with the phrase "she sat beside the harvesters." This verse alludes to the kingship being taken from the Messiah for a time. But the key question is when.

According to the rabbis, this will occur during the end-times battle between the Messiah and Gog, the king of Magog, as the prophet Zechariah described in Zechariah 14:2. I don't agree with the interpretation of the rabbis. I believe that kingship was taken when the majority of the leaders of the Jewish people rejected Jesus as the Messiah. This is substantiated by Isaiah 53:3–5:

> He was despised and rejected by men,
> a man of sorrows . . .
> One from whom people hide their faces. . . .
> Surely He has borne our griefs
>   and carried our pains.
> Yet we esteemed Him . . .
>   . . . afflicted.
> But He was pierced because of our transgressions.

This connects the idea of the Messiah's affliction, which the rabbis connect to Ruth's dipping in the vinegar, to the Messiah's rejection.

This rejection of the Messiah will lead to Him being hidden for a season, as Esther Rabbah expounded: "Just as the first redeemer, so too the final redeemer, the Messiah. Just as the first redeemer [Moses] appeared and was concealed from them . . . so too the final redeemer will appear [to the Jewish people] and will be concealed from them for a time."[8] Moses was concealed twice, just as the Messiah was. Moses and the Messiah were both concealed at their births when they were safely hidden from homicidal rulers. Moses was concealed a second time after he struck the Egyptian taskmaster dead while trying to save his Hebrew brothers. Stephen, commenting on this in the book of Acts, said, "He [Moses] was assuming that his brothers understood that by his hand God was delivering them, but they did not understand" (7:25).

Moses had to flee Egypt and was hidden for forty years due to being rejected by the children of Israel. In the same way, the Messiah was rejected and had to be concealed like Moses until the day Israel's final redemption comes.

"He Held Out to Her Roasted Grain"

The kingdom of David, as a political earthly domain centered in Israel, in some real sense was taken from the Messiah Yeshua. But the good news is that it will be restored, which is the meaning of "he held out to her roasted grain" (Ruth 2:14). David's kingship was renewed: "He will strike the land with the rod of His mouth" (Isa. 11:4). As it was with David, so must it be with the Messiah.

POINTING FORWARD

A key part of Ruth and Boaz's beautiful love story is its conclusion. Ruth's marriage to Boaz points to the greatest fulfillment of grace and the truth of the Messiah. Boaz shows Ruth incredible grace, protection, and provision.

Likewise, the Messiah, when we trust fully in Him, gives us a vast amount of grace, protection, and provision. The key is looking forward, not backward, to the promises of Messiah and to what He can do in your life.

Ruth is a perfect example of someone who wasn't everything the world thinks is ideal. Ruth was destitute. She was a widow. She was a foreigner who came from a people group hated by the local community. But Ruth's unwavering loyalty and trust opened the door not only for Gentiles to be part of the line of Yeshua but for anyone willing to set aside what they did in the past and come to Yeshua, the Messiah. Ruth opened the door for anyone who thinks they fall short of what the Messiah is looking for. This means you.

Pastor Jon Courson wrote:

Ruth was washed, anointed, and clothed with new raiment just like we have been washed in the blood of the Lamb, anointed by the Holy Spirit, and robed in His righteousness. She's washed. She's anointed. She's robed. She's amazed.[9]

Ruth, the foreign widow, was amazed. You will be amazed as well when you let Yeshua have the reins of your life. You and Yeshua, like Ruth and Boaz, can travel together in a glorious story. God doesn't give up on His people.

chapter
TWELVE

THE MESSIAH, SON OF DAVID

In this book we've taken a biblical journey from Creation to King David. On our journey we've uncovered many mysteries of the Messiah. We've looked back at the Old Testament and connected it with the New Testament to find the flow of events from Creation to today that reveal the Messiah.

One of the primary themes of the entire Hebrew Bible is the coming of the Messiah, who is first mentioned as the Seed of the woman (Gen. 3:15). The Torah and the Prophets were written to provide clear details, insights, and hidden clues that would help solve the mystery of the Messiah. As we have seen, the Messiah would have to be from the seed of Abraham, from Isaac and not Ishmael, from Jacob and not Esau, and from the tribe of Judah and not any of the others. And of all the families in Judah, the Messiah would come from the lineage of David according to the promise that was made by the Lord through Nathan the prophet:

> "Moreover, *ADONAI* declares to you that *ADONAI* will make a house for you. When your days are done and you sleep with your fathers, I will raise up your **seed** . . . and I will establish his kingdom. . . . and I will establish his **royal throne forever**. I will be **a father** to him, and he will be **a son** to Me. . . . So your house and your kingship will be secure forever before you; your **throne** will be **established forever**." (2 Sam. 7:11–14, 16)

The Messiah would be both prophetically and literally the "Son of David." Only a biological heir of David could reign on the throne of David. Based on this, one of the primary titles given to the promised messianic King was "Son of David," which is applied many times to Jesus in the New Testament.

Just as the Messiah would be the greater than Moses, so the Messiah would be the greater than David. David's life and lineage provide insight and revelation into the person and work of the Messiah. The promised "Son of David" would be so much more than just a biological descendant of David's lineage.

THE MYSTERY OF THE MISSING LETTER
VAV AND THE GENEALOGY OF DAVID

As described in the previous chapter, the primary purpose of the book of Ruth is revealed in the genealogy listed in its closing verses. The promised Messiah, the Seed of the woman, would come from not just *any* family in Judah but from the line of Ruth and Boaz. This genealogy connects David's ancestry to Perez, the firstborn son of Judah, and provides deep insights into the Messiah.

The genealogy of Perez, which reaches its climax in the birth of David, begins in Hebrew with the word *toledot*, which can be translated as either "generations" or "genealogy" (Ruth 4:18). The Hebrew spelling of this word communicates mysterious truths about the work of the Messiah. But to understand this, we must go all the way back to the story of Creation.

The first time the word *toledot* (תולדות) is used is Genesis 2:4: "These are the genealogical records of the heavens and the earth when they were created." The Hebrew word תולדות is written with two *vav*s (ו). The next usage of the word *toledot* is found in Genesis 5:1: "This is the Book of the Genealogies of Adam." The word *toledot* is written defectively here because it is missing one of its letters: תולדת. The first *vav* is present, but the second *vav* is missing. In fact, every other time the Hebrew Bible uses the word *toledot* from this point forward, with the exception of one place, as we will see, it is always written defectively, missing either the first or second *vav*.

What is the meaning of this mystery? As revealed in chapter 1, the first place the letter *vav* occurs is in Genesis 1:1: "In the beginning God created the heavens **and** [ו] the earth." Thus *vav* is the letter that connects "heavens" and "earth." When Adam and Eve sinned in Eden, the connection between heaven and earth was broken. Therefore, the *vav* is missing in every genealogy going forward as a reminder of the disconnection of heaven and earth, the physical and spiritual, that occurred as a result of the Fall.

When would the *vav* be restored? When the promised messianic Seed of the woman came. The only other time after Genesis 2:4 that the word *toledot* is written in its full form is when we read, "These are the generations [*toledot* / תולדות] of Perez" (Ruth 4:18). The restoration of the missing *vav* alludes to the promised messianic Seed of the woman, who would defeat the serpent, coming through the line of Judah, through David, who was born of the line of Ruth and Boaz.

Ultimately it's through the Son of David that the Messiah would come and restore (like the restored *vav* in *toledot*) the connection between heaven and earth. The mystery of the missing *vav* points to the fact that when the Messiah would come, He would remove the defect caused by the Fall, restoring the fullness of God's blessing for all humanity, symbolized by the word "generations" written in its full form.

This directly connects to Matthew 1:1: "The book of the genealogy [*toledot*] of Yeshua" the Messiah, Son of David (*Ben-David*). The first book of the New Testament deliberately uses the same phrase used throughout the Torah and in the book of Ruth to bear witness that Yeshua is the promised messianic Seed of David.

The number six and multiples of six are central to the book of Ruth:

1. Boaz gave Ruth six measures of grain (Ruth 3:15).
2. In Hebrew the names Boaz and Ruth both have three letters, totaling six when added together.
3. Ruth 1 uses the verb "return" six times in speaking of Naomi's return to Bethlehem (vv. 6, 7, 10, 21, 22, 22).

4. Ruth 1 uses the verb "return" six times in speaking of returning to Moab (vv. 8, 11, 12, 15, 15, 16).

5. In Ruth 2, the Hebrew word for "glean" is used twelve times (6 x 2).

6. Boaz's name appears eighteen times (6 x 3)—not counting the use of Boaz's name in the genealogy—and Ruth's name appears twelve times (6 x 2).

This culminates in the restoration of the second *vav*, whose value is 6. For the promised Messiah from the seed of David would come, the One who would restore all that was lost in Eden.

DAVID: GOD'S ANOINTED

God, after rejecting King Saul for his disobedience and continued lack of trust, told the prophet Samuel to travel to Bethlehem to secretly anoint one of Jesse's sons as the next king. Seven of Jesse's sons presented themselves to Samuel, but the prophet chose none of them. Somewhat reluctantly, Jesse called his youngest son, David, who was out in the fields. Upon David's arrival, the Lord said to the prophet Samuel, "Arise, anoint him, for this is the one" (1 Sam. 16:12). So Samuel anointed David with holy oil, and the Spirt of the Lord came strongly upon David to empower and testify that he truly was the Lord's anointed.

The Lord chose David over his brothers because "*ADONAI* looks into the heart" (1 Sam. 16:7), and David was truly a man after God's own heart (1 Sam. 13:14). But what made David such a man? What can we learn from his life to help us follow after God's heart?

DAVID: THE BELOVED LOVER

In Hebrew, David's name has three consonants: *dalet, vav, dalet* (דוד). The middle letter of David's name is the *vav*—the letter of connection. David

was a man after God's own heart because he sought a deeper, more intimate connection with the Lord. We see this in the meaning of David's
name: "beloved." It is used in connection to lovers, as in "I am my beloved's
[Hebrew, *dodi*] and my beloved [Hebrew, *dodi*] is mine" (Song 6:3). King
David was a lover of God.

In the same way the book of Ruth is connected to the Hebrew letter
vav and the number six, so is David. The *vav* at the center of David's name
alludes to the fact that seeking deeper spiritual and relational connection
was part of his nature. And what was at the heart of David's intimate connection with the Lord? It was God's Word, the heart of which is the Torah.
In the sixth word of the Torah is a *vav*. It serves as the connecting force
between the letters and also binds together heaven and earth. There is no
deep connection to the Lord without a deep understanding of the Word of
God—both Old and New Testaments.

The Torah, which was meant to help restore the connection between
heaven and earth, was given on the sixth of *Sivan*, which is Pentecost—the
day on which King David was born and died in Jewish tradition. It makes
perfect sense that David is associated with Pentecost because he pursued a deep
connection with God through his love of and meditation on the Word—which
we read so much about in the Psalms. One commentator observed:

> Our rabbis tell us that David was the greatest Torah scholar of his
> generation. He was the man to whom the most complicated legal
> questions were brought. This king pushed away sleep and personal
> physical enjoyment and rose each night at midnight to pray privately
> to G-d and then to study His Torah. When he was needed at court or
> in some meeting, we are told that King David would start out with the
> best of intentions, but instead his feet would carry him to the place of
> his first love: the hall of Torah study.[1]

In the Old Testament, Pentecost is the day the Torah came, but in
the New Testament, Pentecost is the day the Holy Spirit was given. The
Holy Spirit, like the Word, is foundational for intimate connection with the

Lord. The Holy Spirit spiritually baptizes us into the Messiah (John 3:5) and illuminates God's Word to know Jesus better (Eph. 1:17–20). One of the signs of being filled with the Holy Spirit is "speaking to one another in psalms, hymns, and spiritual songs, singing and making music in your heart to the Lord" (Eph. 5:19).

The intimate bond that the Spirit creates occurs through both the Word and worship. David was a man not only of the Word but also of the Spirit. David was inspired by the Holy Spirit to write most of the psalms in the book of Psalms, the worship hymnal of Israel,[2] and prophetically spoke of the Messiah in many of them.[3] Jesus, like David, arose early in the morning to worship and pray, and He called His disciples to worship "in the Spirit and in truth" as He did (John 4:24 NIV). To settle for the Spirit or the Word, as many believers do, is to miss out on a fuller connection to the Lord. If we want to seek after God's own heart, we must become individuals who constantly pursue deeper connection with God by means of the Word and the Spirit. Both David and Jesus embodied this, and therefore both are associated with Pentecost.

Jesus relied on prayer and worship to overcome testing and trials. Before Jesus was arrested in the Garden of Gethsemane, He asked His disciples to join Him in praying, but they fell asleep three times. Perhaps if Peter had stood with Him in prayer the three times he was asked, he would have had the spiritual courage needed to not deny Jesus three times.

David, a man of passionate worship and prayer, spent much of his days in the field as a shepherd, and later with his warriors, worshiping the Lord and writing psalms of praise. David, one of the greatest warriors in Israel's history, was courageous; he did not fear the lion, the bear, or even the giant Goliath. What made him such a great warrior was that he was such a great worshiper.

We see in Psalm 78:70–72 that David's ability to shepherd his father's sheep is one of the primary reasons the Lord selected him to become the royal shepherd of Israel. A beautiful story in Jewish tradition connected to these verses says David would let the small nursing ewes graze first on the tender tips of the grass. Then he would let the more mature sheep eat the center portion, and only then would he bring the strong rams to consume the tougher roots. Upon seeing this, the Holy One said, "He who knows how to look after sheep, each according to its own capacity, is to look after My sheep—Israel."[4]

The Lord also called Moses to lead God's people while he was shepherding his father-in-law's sheep in the wilderness (Ex. 3:1). Moses, like David, was chosen because of the compassionate manner in which he tended the sheep. The *Midrash* says that while Moses was tending the sheep, one of them ran away. Moses left the entire flock, pursued the single sheep that strayed, and found him drinking from a pool of water. Instead of being angry or disciplining the runaway sheep with his shepherd's rod, Moses said to it, "I did not know you ran away because you were thirsty. You are so exhausted!" Then he picked up the little sheep, placed it upon his shoulder, and walked back to the flock. The Holy One, Blessed be He, said, "Since you tend the sheep of human beings with such overwhelming love—by your life, I swear you shall be the shepherd of My sheep, Israel."[5]

God's choice of David and Moses, two compassionate shepherds, forms the New Testament background for Jesus' statement "I am the Good Shepherd" (John 10:11). Jesus is the Good Shepherd who, like Moses, leaves the ninety-nine to go after the one. He is also the "the great Shepherd of the sheep by the blood of an everlasting covenant" (Heb. 13:20). It is on account of this that Jesus says, "The reason my Father loves me is that I lay down my life" (John 10:17 NIV).

There is no shepherd, not even Moses or David, who can compare to Messiah. He provides, protects, guides, knows every member of His flock, personally speaks to them, and even lays down His life for the sheep (John 10). Jesus' statement "I am the Good Shepherd" points to Him as the fulfillment of prophecy:

So I will set up One Shepherd over them, **My servant David**—He will tend them, He will feed them Himself and be their shepherd. (Ezek. 34:23)

"And you, Bethlehem, land of Judah,
      are by no means least among the rulers of Judah;

For out of you will come a ruler

who will **shepherd My people Israel**."

(Matt. 2:6; see Mic. 5:1–3)

The Messiah was the royal Shepherd and, like David, was born in Bethlehem. Jesus came to fulfill all that was spoken concerning Him in the Torah and the Prophets.

Every believer must follow in the footsteps of Moses, David, Jesus, and the apostles by becoming shepherds. When Yeshua restored Peter in John 21, He asked him three times, "Do you love Me?" Many say Jesus asked Peter three times because Peter denied the Lord three times. In addition, I believe He asked three times because it connects to the greatest commandment—to love God with (1) all your heart, (2) all your soul, and (3) all your strength (Deut. 6:5). Jesus was asking Peter if he was willing to love Him completely.

But how was Peter going to put his love into action practically? Jesus made it clear with three statements: (1) "Feed My lambs!"; (2) "Take care of My sheep!"; (3) "Feed My sheep!" (John 21:15–17). Peter's love for the Lord would be demonstrated by his lovingly shepherding God's flock.

Yeshua called Peter to follow in the footsteps of the Good Shepherd even to the point of laying down his life for the sheep:

"When you grow old, you will stretch out your hands, and someone else will dress you and carry you where you do not want to go." Now this He said to indicate by what kind of death Peter was going to glorify God. And after this, *Yeshua* said to him, "Follow Me!" (John 21:18–19)

At one point in my ministry, I felt like I was being treated unkindly by some people I was ministering to. The pressure was so bad I questioned if I wanted to be in ministry any longer. During a time of prayer, the Lord spoke to me and said, "Jason, I said to Peter, 'If you love Me, feed My sheep.' I didn't say if the sheep were nice and friendly. I said, 'If you love Me, feed my sheep and tend My flock.'" I realized the only healthy motivation for serving the Lord was loving Him, not people's response.

Every believer—not just those in full-time ministry—has been anointed by God for spiritual service. You have been called and empowered to minister compassionately to the people God has placed in your life. You are called to shepherd your family as a mother or father, your neighbors, your coworkers, and whoever else the Lord allows you to lead. Until believers take this seriously, we will not rightly impact the world. Like Peter and Jesus, we are called to shepherd people into the Kingdom.

THE HEBREW NASA

A key biblical term for leadership is *nasi*, which in the Bible is usually translated as "prince" or "chieftain." This term was applied to the leader of each of the twelve tribes of Israel during their wilderness wanderings. In modern Hebrew, the president of Israel is called the *nasi*. The promised Son of David, the Messiah, will be both Shepherd and Prince (*Nasi*) over Israel (Ezek. 34:23–24).

The word *nasi* comes from the Hebrew root *nasa*, which literally means "to lift up." When the Lord tells Moses to take a census of the children of Israel, he is told to *nasa*—"[lift up the heads] of all the community of [Israel]" (Num. 1:2). The reason the term *nasi* is used for Israel's leaders is because the princes of Israel were meant to serve the people selflessly and lift them up. Historically, kings and princes took more than they gave and, for the most part, elevated themselves by stepping on the backs of those below them to build their wealth and their empire. This was not to be the case with godly leaders; a true *nasi* is one who leads by elevating others. David and the Messiah both lived, led, and embodied the true heart of a *nasi*.

The word *nasi* can also mean "to bear" as in bearing a burden: "Thus says *ADONAI*, 'Guard your souls! Carry no burden on the day of *Shabbat*'" (Jer. 17:21). Leaders are meant to have broad shoulders that carry the weight of other people's burdens. Jesus was a burden bearer: "Come to Me, all who are weary and burdened, and I will give you rest" (Matt. 11:28). His words and actions testified that He was fulfilling the prophetic promise that the Messiah would be both Shepherd and Prince (*Nasi*) of Israel (Ezek. 34:23–24).

We are called to emulate Yeshua. We are called not to be a burden but to bear burdens like our Redeemer. This is at the heart of what it practically means to fulfill the love commandment. Paul wrote, "Bear one another's burdens, and in this way you fulfill the *Torah* of Messiah" (Gal. 6:2). We are called to bless others and to demonstrate God's love by helping to lighten other people's loads.

The Hebrew word *nasa* also means "to forgive," as in "The LORD, the LORD God, merciful and gracious, longsuffering, and abounding in goodness and truth . . . forgiving [*Nosei*, from the root *nasa*] iniquity and transgression and sin" (Ex. 34:6–7 NKJV). The Messiah is the *Nasi*, the messianic Prince, who comes as the *nosei avon*—forgiver of iniquity.

The numeric value of *nasi* sheds deeper insight into the person and work of the Messiah. *Nasi* in Hebrew equals 361. In Greek, 361 is the mathematical value of "flesh" (*sarx*), "lamb" (*amnos*), and "from the heart" (*ek kardias*). Yeshua the *Nasi* (361) "became flesh" (361, John 1:14), lived and led from the heart (361), and died as the Lamb (361, John 1:29) to bear (*nasi*) our sin and become the forgiver of our iniquity (*nosei avon*) so we might be lifted up (*nasa*) with Him.

All the above ties together the mission of the Messiah as the *Nasi* with His place of birth. The Messiah was born in Bethlehem to fulfill the prophecy in Micah 5:1–4. King David was born there, so the Messiah as the Son of David also had to be born there.

Bethlehem (in Hebrew *Beit Lechem*, "House of Bread") has the numeric value of 490. It should come as no surprise that 490 also links to forgiveness. Peter came to Jesus and asked, "'Lord, how often shall my brother sin against me, and I forgive him? Up to seven times?' Jesus said to him, 'I do not say to you, up to seven times, but up to seventy times seven [which equals 490]'" (Matt. 18:21–22 NKJV).

Peter thought he was being very spiritual by his willingness to forgive up to seven times. Jesus' response to forgive someone up to 490 times must have been quite a shock. Jesus never wasted a word. So the number of times He instructed us to forgive must have some deeper significance.

The number 490 is also the numeric value of the biblical Hebrew word *tamim*, which means "complete," "perfect," or "finished." A person who can't forgive will always live an imperfect and incomplete life that lacks a true understanding of the "finished" gracious work of the cross. The Hebrew phrase "Let your heart . . . be perfect" (1 Kings 8:61 KJV) also has the value of 490. Forgiving helps to make us complete and is key to perfecting our hearts.

But there are even deeper connections. The words "nativity" (*moladati*) and "Bethlehem" both individually add up to 490. This makes perfect sense since Jesus was born so that we might be forgiven. Forgiveness is associated with bread in the Lord's Prayer: "Give us this day our daily bread. And forgive us our debts as we also have forgiven our debtors" (Matt. 6:11–12).

We celebrate this forgiveness by partaking of the broken bread of Communion. Jesus said, "This is My body, given for you. Do this in memory of Me" (Luke 22:19). Just as a person can't live without their daily bread, an individual can't survive spiritually and relationally without forgiveness. Just as Jesus—the One who was born in the House of Bread and who is the Bread of Life—died so we might partake of the bread of forgiveness, we need to extend this bread to others.

FOURTEEN AND DAVID

The name David in Hebrew has the numeric value of 14. Fourteen is associated with royalty because, in the Bible, gold is associated with kingship. The Hebrew word for "gold," *zahav* (זהב), adds up to 14.

All of this connects directly to the Messiah as the royal Son of David. Matthew's Gospel opens with "the genealogy of Jesus the Messiah the son of David" (NIV). This genealogy is divided into three sets of fourteen generations: (1) from Abraham to David, (2) from David until the Babylonian exile, and (3) from the Babylonian exile until the Messiah (Matt. 1:17). Every generation pointed to and found its fulfillment in Jesus.

Matthew broke his genealogy into three sets because he was spelling David's name three times. In Hebrew, when you say something three times, it means the maximum; for example, "Holy, holy, holy" (Rev. 4:8) means "the

most holy." By using three sets of fourteen, Matthew was communicating
that the Messiah was the ultimate King of kings and Son of David. This
also relates to the wise men who brought three gifts to Jesus, one of which
was gold, linking Him to being the King of Israel and tying back to David
since both have a value of 14.

The number fourteen is the number of redemption and salvation.
God redeemed Israel from Egypt on the fourteenth day of the first month
(Ex. 12:6, 18). Every year the Passover is celebrated on the fourteenth day of
the first month of the Hebrew calendar. In the book of Esther, God saved
the Jewish people from the genocidal hand of Haman on the fourteenth day
of the last month of the Hebrew calendar. Thus the Jewish year begins and
ends with God redeeming His people on the fourteenth.

In Hebrew the number fourteen is written with the letters *yud* and *dalet*,
which spells *yad* (יד), meaning "hand." Fourteen is the number of the hand.
God redeemed Israel from Egypt with a "mighty hand [*yad hazakah*] and
an outstretched arm [*zeroa ne-tu-yah*]" (Deut. 26:8). It was God's hand (14)
that redeemed Israel out of Egypt on the fourteenth of *Nisan* and the Jewish
people from the hand of Haman on the fourteenth day of *Adar*. Fourteen is
also the number of bones in the human hand. The modern State of Israel
was also birthed on the fourteenth—May 14, 1948.

Yeshua is connected to the fourteenth because He is the "mighty hand
and . . . outstretched arm" of God who brings about a greater redemption
than the exodus and superior deliverance than the one that occurred through
Moses, David, and Esther. Speaking of the future messianic Redeemer, the
prophet Isaiah said, "To whom is the arm of ADONAI revealed?" (Isa. 53:1),
and "I looked, but there was no one to help. . . . So My own arm won victory
for Me" (Isa. 63:5). The hand and the arm of God are no longer hidden, but
the mystery has been revealed in the person of Jesus.

There is also an interesting connection between the number fourteen
and the incarnation in the Bible. John 1:14 says, "And the Word became
flesh and tabernacled among us." Isaiah 7:14 says, "Behold, the virgin will
conceive. When she is giving birth to a son, she will call his name Immanuel
[God with us]." In all fairness, there were no chapters and verses in the

original Hebrew and Greek manuscripts, but this seems to be more than just coincidence. God knows the end from the beginning. Jesus is the royal Son of David (14), the revealed hand (14) of God who became incarnate to bring about a greater Passover (on the fourteenth day). Redemptions, royalty, and incarnation—all connected to the number fourteen—all find their fullness and fulfillment in Jesus, the Son of David.

DAVID THE EIGHTH SON

The numbers 8 and 888 reveal some additionally profound mysteries and connections between David and Jesus, the Son of David. David is the eighth son of Jesse. To understand the significance of this, we must understand a bit more about the number eight in the Bible.

Eight is the number of covenant. God commanded through Abraham, and again through Moses, that every male Jewish child must be circumcised as a sign of the covenant on the eighth day. Seven is the number of the completion of the natural world, but eight is the number of the supernatural that causes one to rise above the natural order of things.

Eight is also the number of new beginnings. Thus, as we saw in the introduction, eight is associated with the messianic age. When the Messiah comes, the world will experience a new beginning—literally a "new heaven and a new earth" (Rev. 21:1)—and humanity will finally transcend the Fall and be restored to our supernatural state when we receive our glorified bodies.

This all connects to Jesus, the supernatural Son of David (the eighth son of Jesse), who rose from the dead on the eighth day. The Messiah died on Friday, which is the sixth day of the Hebrew week, rested as God did on the seventh day after finishing the work of redemption, and rose on the eighth day, which was also the first day of the week. His resurrection caused the supernatural (8) to be made manifest in the natural (7). An eight turned on its side is the symbol of infinity. With the resurrection of the greater David, infinity and eternity broke into time and space.

The genealogy of David at the end of the book of Ruth begins with "These are the generations" (4:18). The values of these words add up to 888. This is mind-blowing since Jesus (Greek, Ιησούς) adds up to 888, which relates to Matthew 1:16. This numeric connection speaks directly to the fact that Jesus fulfilled the genealogy of Ruth.

What's also amazing is that 888 is found in connection with several messianic prophecies in the book of Isaiah. In Isaiah 9:6, 888 is the numeric value of the phrase in Hebrew "His name will be called Wonderful, Counselor, Mighty God, Everlasting Father" (NKJV).* But there is an even deeper connection. Encoded in every seventh Hebrew letter of the verse, there seems to be a mathematical reference that the words are actually pointing to Jesus:

> For unto us a Child is born,
> Unto us a Son is given;
> And the government will be upon His shoulder.
> And His name will be called
> Wonderful, Counselor, Mighty God,
> Everlasting Father, Prince of Peace. (Isa. 9:6 NKJV)

The sum of every seventh Hebrew letter in Isaiah 9:6 equals 888.

כי־ילד ילד־לנו בן נתן־לנו ותהי המשרה על־שכמו
ויקרא שמו פלא יועץ אל גבור אביעד שר־שלום
$$30+50+400+5+6+6+90+1+300 = 888$$

This sum total also ties back to King David's genealogy. This can be no coincidence. What makes this even more plausible is that the number 888 occurs in the following verses from Isaiah 52–53, which is the longest and most significant messianic prophecy about the suffering and death of the Messiah:

---

* To make the spiritual connection, the word "Everlasting" is not included in this count.

salvation of our God (52:10)	ישועת אלהינו
He . . . carried our pains. Yet we esteemed Him stricken. (53:4)	ומכאבינו סבלם ואנחנו חשבנהו נגוע
Like a lamb led to the slaughter, like a sheep before its shearers (53:7)	כשה לטבח יובל וכרחל לפני גזזיה
and none of his generation protested his being cut off (53:8 CJB)	דורו מי ישוחח כי נגזר

In the same way the book of Revelation uses 666 in reference to the Antichrist, the book of Isaiah seems to use 888 as a hidden calculation encoded in the Hebrew text that points to the person and work of the Messiah.

The difference between the number of the antichrist and Jesus is 222—the value of the *bechor* ("firstborn"), one of the titles of the Messiah. "He is the image of the invisible God, the firstborn of all creation" (Col. 1:15). The number 222 connects to Jesus as the second person of the Godhead and the ultimate Son—two to the maximum. "The voice of God" also equals 222, which points to the way Jesus, as the messianic Son of David, will defeat the Antichrist and all the enemies of God: "With the breath of His lips He will slay the wicked" (Isa. 11:4) and "From His mouth comes a sharp sword" (Rev. 19:15; see also Rev. 1:16). All Jesus has to do is speak, and His voice overpowers those who are hostile to Him. This is seen when He spoke to those who came to arrest Him in the Garden of Gethsemane: "So when *Yeshua* said to them, 'I am,' they drew back and fell to the ground" (John 18:6).

As we've noted, the day that Jesus rose from the dead is simultaneously the third and the eighth day. Jesus performed His miracle of turning water into wine on the third day to point to His future resurrection and the abundant blessing that would result from it. The phrase "on the third day" (Greek, *he hemera he trite*) totals 888 (John 2:1).

The prophet Malachi, speaking of the appearance of the Messiah, wrote:

"Suddenly He will come . . .
—the Lord whom you seek—
and the Messenger of the covenant . . .
But who can endure the day of His coming?
Or who can stand when He appears? . . .
For I am *ADONAI*. I do not change." (Mal. 3:1–2, 6)

The words "I am *ADONAI*. I do not change" total 888. Thus 888 alludes to the divine and unchanging nature of Jesus, the firstborn Son. Only the One who does not change can effect eternal change and transform us.

THE KING FOREVER

There's one more mystery I want to show you.

After King David brought the ark of the covenant back to Jerusalem, he placed it in the tabernacle. He appointed three men to direct worship and praise: Asaph, Heman, and Ethan (1 Chron. 15:7). Many scholars believe this is the same Ethan who wrote Psalm 89, a beautiful psalm mostly committed to praise and deep prayer:

"I also will set him as firstborn—
the highest of the kings of earth.
I will maintain My love for him forever,
and My covenant with him will be firm.
His seed I will establish forever,
and his throne as the days of heaven.

I will not violate My covenant,
nor alter what My lips have uttered.
Once for all I have sworn by My holiness
—surely I will not lie to David—
his descendants will endure forever,

and his throne as the sun before Me,
and as the moon, established forever,
and a trustworthy witness in the sky." *Selah* (vv. 28–30, 35–38)

By His grace, God chose David to be king of Israel. David was tested in his battle against Israel's enemy Goliath. He was faithful over a few things, and the Lord promoted him to greater things. David was a beloved lover of God. He was a leader (*nasi*) who expanded Israel's territory and strength. He was the eighth son of Jesse, but the Lord made David His firstborn, the son of honor who received the greatest inheritance.

But Ethan was not only writing about King David in these verses. He was describing the King of kings, Jesus Messiah.

- Jesus is the firstborn, the honored Son of God who received the greatest inheritance.
- David was "the highest of the kings of earth" (v. 28). Jesus is the King of kings (Rev. 17:14; 19:16).
- David was promised a dynasty, a throne that would last forever. That promise is fulfilled in Yeshua—our Messiah.

Charles Spurgeon wrote:

In our Lord Jesus the dynasty of David remains on the throne. Jesus has never abdicated, nor gone into banishment. He reigns and must reign so long as the sun continues to shine upon the earth. A seed and a throne are the two great promises of the covenant, and they are as important to us as to our Lord Jesus himself; for we are the seed who must endure forever, and we are protected and ennobled by that King whose royalties are to last forever.[6]

Today we need to step back and realize our Messiah has never and will never break His promises to us.

THERE'S ALWAYS MORE

As we come to the end of this particular journey together, I want to be sure you know that there is still so much more hidden treasure waiting to be discovered. Uncovering the mysteries of the Messiah, the divine connections God has woven throughout Scripture, is a lifetime adventure that will never disappoint. To mine God's Word for yourself and find the countless treasures between Genesis and Revelation will be an adventure far greater than anything you've ever experienced.

And while there is tremendous mystery inherent in the search itself, our Messiah sits at God's right hand and prays for us. And our Messiah is coming again. There's no mystery about what I'm writing. We need to rejoice as Ethan wrote:

> I will sing of the love of *ADONAI* forever.
> To all generations I will make known Your faithfulness with
>   my mouth.
> For I said, "Let your lovingkindness be built up forever!
> The heavens—let Your faithfulness be made firm there!"
>   (Ps. 89:2–3)

We can sing because of God's faithfulness and for sending us His own Son, Jesus. We can declare the revealed mysteries of the Messiah to anyone who will listen. We can experience God's lovingkindness because He gave us His Son, the Messiah, and His seed is established forever—from creation to today and eternity.

Shalom berakhah ve-tov lecha. Peace, blessing, and good to you.

ACKNOWLEDGMENTS

This book is the result of an amazing team of people. Their sacrificial efforts and unrelenting faith made this book possible. Without each of their unique contributions, this would be just a dream. I want to thank and express my great gratitude and deep appreciation to them:

Mom and Dad—it is not possible to have more loving, supportive, and generous parents. You are the best! I thank God for you. I would not be who I am and able to do what I do without you! I could never thank you enough. I love you.

Avi and Judah—I love you both so much! I believe in you and know you will do great things to make a difference in the world. Thank you for being so patient and understanding during the long days of writing. It's such a joy to be your dad.

The Fusion Board, Wendy, Kevin, Helena, Leslie, Don, and Dane— thank you for your wisdom, support, and friendship throughout the years. I treasure each of you, and I am so grateful for friendship. The best is yet to come!

Ted Squires—your wisdom, council, years of experience in publishing, encouragement, and friendship have been a huge blessing! You are one of the most selfless, faithful, and kingdom-minded men I have ever met. A true role model.

Wayne Hastings—I do not know what I would have done without your incredible support in helping to shape and edit this book. Thanks for being the friend who stuck closer than a brother in this whole process. Your wisdom, scholarship, and passion for the Word is such a huge inspiration! I thank God for all you do for the Fusion Team.

Alicia Barmore—thank you for your friendship and faithful service throughout the years. I appreciate all you have done for me personally and for Fusion. You believed in the vision from early on and have stayed the course. It's time to possess the promises!

Drew Nicolello—you have added so much in such a short period of time. Your ability to combine high levels of creativity with strategy is unique and special. I thank God and Dane for introducing us!

John Leniart, my dear brother who led me to Yeshua—I am so thankful for you and how you allowed God to use you in my life. I will never forget, "Who is this Isaiah 53?"

Debbie Wickwire and the W Publishing Team—thank you for believing in this project and for your tireless effort. You do such incredible and important work. You make it look easy and do it with so much joy unto the Lord. You made the birthing of this book not only possible but a lot easier and more enjoyable. Thank you from the bottom of my heart!

APPENDIX

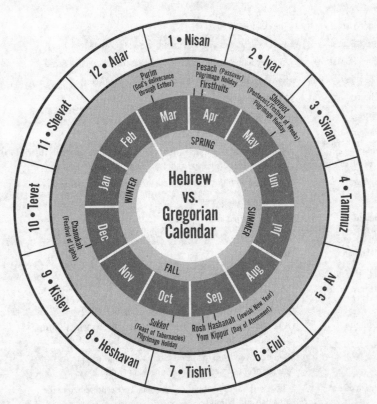

The circular chart shows the Hebrew vs. Gregorian Calendar.

Outer ring (Hebrew months):
1 • Nisan
2 • Iyar
3 • Sivan
4 • Tammuz
5 • Av
6 • Elul
7 • Tishri
8 • Heshavan
9 • Kislev
10 • Tevet
11 • Shevat
12 • Adar

Inner rings (Gregorian months and seasons):
Mar, Apr, May, Jun, Jul, Aug, Sep, Oct, Nov, Dec, Jan, Feb
SPRING, SUMMER, FALL, WINTER

Center: Hebrew vs. Gregorian Calendar

Holiday markers:
Purim (God's deliverance through Esther)
Pesach (Passover) Pilgrimage Holiday
Firstfruits
Shavuot (Pentecost / Festival of Weeks) Pilgrimage Holiday
Sukkot (Feast of Tabernacles) Pilgrimage Holiday
Rosh Hashanah (Jewish New Year)
Yom Kippur (Day of Atonement)
Chanukah (Festival of Lights)

There are two aspects of the Jewish calendar. The civil calendar is the official calendar of kings, childbirth, and contracts, reflected by the numbers on this chart. The religious calendar is used for the dates of feasts and festivals. Tishri is the first civil calendar month, and Nisan is the first month on the religious calendar.

Glossary of Hebrew Terms

Word	Definition
Abba	Father
Adonai	Divine name of God translated as "Lord"
Aleph	The first letter of the Hebrew alphabet
Amen	Hebrew word meaning "so it is" or "let it be"
Bar Mitzvah	Son of the Divine Law or son of the commandment; event occurs for boys at the age of thirteen
Ben-Elohim	Son of God
Benei Elohim	Children of God
Bnei-Yisrael	The children of Israel
Brit Chadashah	The books of the New Testament, the New Covenant
Chag HaMatzot	Another name for the Passover, the Feast of Unleavened Bread
Chanukah	Jewish eight-day winter celebration also called "Festival of Lights"
Chesed	Mercy, kindness
El Shaddai	God Almighty
Elohim	Yahweh (YHVH), the God of Israel
Firstfruits (Yom HaBikkurim)	Firstborn child or animal or first parts of any crop, which, in Hebrew thought, were considered as holy and belonging to the Lord
Gemara	Combined with the Mishna, these texts make up the Talmud
Goel	Close kinsman; redeemer
Golah	Exile, or carried away
Hallel	Praise
Halakhah	Jewish law
Hanukkah	Feast of Dedication
Hebrew Bible	The Old Testament
Israel	The name given to Jacob and his descendants meaning "strive with God"
Jeduthun	A Levitical musician who oversaw music in the temple (1 Chron. 25:1–6; 2 Chron. 5:12)
Jew	Name derived from the Jacob's son, Judah, and used to identify God's chosen people descended from Abraham (Jews)
Jewish Sages	The Jewish sages ("rabbis" = "teachers") are represented in the Mishnah and Talmud
Kohen gadol	The High Priest
Kohen/kohanim	Priest(s)
Kosher	Proper or fit; relates to foods that conform to Jewish law

Word	Definition
Maccabees	Central characters of Chanukah, a band of Jewish fighters who liberated Israel from occupation by Syrian Greeks
Machalatle'anot	Stringed instruments
Matzah/matzot	Unleavened bread(s)
Messiah/Moshiach	Anointed One
Metzora	Leper
Midrash	Ancient Jewish commentaries, with stories and parables as the primary teaching method
Mishnah	A foundational Jewish collection of oral traditions and written Bible commentaries (AD 200)
Parashat	A weekly Shabbat reading
Pasach	Passover
Pentecost/Shavuot	The fiftieth day after the second day of the Passover, also called the Feast of Weeks because it was observed for seven weeks, celebrates the giving of the Torah at Mt. Sinai and the Holy Spirit in Acts 2
Purim	Celebrates the salvation of the Jews in the ancient Persian Empire recorded in the book of Esther
Rabbi	Teacher
Rosh Hashana	Beginning of the Jewish civil year
Ruach	Spirit, wind, breath
Ruach Elohim	The Spirit of God
Ruach HaKodesh	God's Holy Spirit
Seder	Order
Shabbat	Sabbath rest
Shalom	Completeness, soundness, welfare, peace
Shema Yisrael	Hear O Israel
Shofar	A ram's horn used to sound alarms in spiritual warfare and celebrations
Sukkot	Feast of Tabernacles celebrated in the fall
Talmud	Writings that set forth the beliefs and practices of Judaism from both written and oral traditions
Tanakh	The Hebrew Bible and the textual source of the Christian Old Testament
Tav	The last letter of the Hebrew alphabet
Torah	The first five books of the Bible, also called the Pentateuch (the law)
Yehovah	Name for God formed by adding the vowels of the Hebrew word Adonai to the consonants of the Hebrew divine name YHVH
Yeshua	Jesus
Yom Kippur	The Day of Atonement

Hebrew Alphanumeric Chart

Letter	Name	Value	Letter	Name	Value
א	Aleph	1	ל	Lamed	30
ב	Bet	2	מ	Mem	40
ג	Gimel	3	נ	Num	50
ד	Dalet	4	ס	Samekh	60
ה	Hei	5	ע	Ayin	70
ו	Vav	6	פ	Peh	80
ז	Zayin	7	צ	Tsadee	90
ח	Cheit	8	ק	Qof	100
ט	Tet	9	ר	Resh	200
י	Yod	10	ש	Shin	300
כ	Kaf	20	ת	Tav	400

NOTES

The Adventure Begins

1. Here's how the Hebrew numeric system works: the first ten Hebrew letters increase in value by a factor of one (*aleph* is 1, *bet* is 2, and so on). The next ten Hebrew letters increase in value by a factor of ten (*kaf* is 20, *lamed* is 30, and so on). The final Hebrew letters increase in value by a factor of one hundred (*kof* is 100, *reish* is 200, and so on) through the final letter, *tav*, with a value of 400.

2. Stringed instruments (Ps. 4:1), wind instruments (Ps. 5:1), Gittite lyre (Ps. 8:1), *machalatle' anot* (Ps. 88:1, Hebrew version), Yedu Sun (Ps. 39:1), lyre and harp (Ps. 33:2), and the eight voices of the singers.

3. "Ancient Jewish Coins: Hasmonean/Macabbean Coins (135–37 BCE)," Jewish Virtual Library, accessed August 17, 2020, https://www.jewishvirtuallibrary .org/hasmonean-macabbean-coins.

4. Lois Tverberg, "Can We Use Jewish Sources to Study Jesus?" *Our Rabbi Jesus: Insights from Lois Tverberg* (blog), November 28, 2012, https://ourrabbijesus .com/articles/can-we-use-jewish-sources-to-study-jesus.

Chapter 1: The Job Description of the Messiah

1. Raphael Patai, *The Messiah Texts: Jewish Legends of Three Thousand Years* (Detroit: Wayne State University Press, 1979), 21. Original note found in Lamentations Rabbah 1:51, quoted in Raphael Patai, *The Messiah Texts* (Detroit: Wayne State University Press, 1998), 36.

2. For more information on this, see Asher Intrater, "Secret Prophecy of the Name of Yeshua," Revive Israel, May 11, 2017, http://tribe.reviveisrael.org/secret -prophecy-of-the-name-of-yeshua.

3. Midrash Mishle, quoted in Raphael Patai, *The Messiah Texts* (Detroit: Wayne State University Press, 1998), 22.

4. Targum Jonathan on Isaiah 53. Found in *The Fifty-Third Chapter of Isaiah According to Jewish Interpreters*, trans. S. R. Driver and A. Neubauer (Oxford and London: James Parker and Co., 1877), 5.

5. Rabbi Mosheh Kohen Ibn Crispin, quoted in Adolf Neubauer and Samuel Rolles Driver, *The Fifty-Third Chapter of Isaiah According to the Jewish Interpreters*, vol. 2 (Brooklyn: KTAV Publishing House, 1969), 99–114.

Chapter 2: The Messiah of Creation: Adam and Eve

1. Jacob ben Asher, *Perush 'al ha-Torah* [*Perush Ba'al ha-Ṭurim: 'al ha-Torah*], *Baal HaTurim Chumash: The Torah with the Baal HaTurim's Classic Commentary*, translated, annotated, and elucidated by Avie Gold, initial translation of the Baal HaTurim by Eliyahu Touger, 4 vols. (Brooklyn: Mesorah Publications, 1999–2003), 2 (s.v. *Bereishis*).

2. Babylonian Talmud, Sanhedrin 98b, quoted in Edith Wyschogrod, *Emmanuel Levinas: The Problem of Ethical Metaphysics* (Berlin, Germany: Springer Netherlands, 2012), 185.

3. John H. Sailhamer, *Genesis*, vol. 1 of *The Expositor's Bible Commentary*, rev. ed., ed. Tremper Longman III and David E. Garland (Grand Rapids: Zondervan Academic, 2017), e-book edition.

4. The William Davidson Talmud, Bava Batra 16a, Sefaria, accessed May 29, 2020, https://www.sefaria.org/Bava_Batra.16a.8?lang=bi.

5. J. W. Etheridge, *The Targums of Onkelos and Jonathan Ben Uzziel on the Pentateuch; with the Fragments of the Jerusalem Targum from the Chaldee* (New York: KATV Publishing House, 1968), 166n8. This Targum is commonly referred to as the Targum of Jonathan Ben Uzziel.

Chapter 3: The Messiah Promised to the Patriarchs: Abraham, Isaac, and Jacob

1. Edward Bridge, "Patriarchs," in *The Lexham Bible Dictionary*, ed. John D. Barry et al. (Bellingham, WA: Lexham Press, 2016).

2. Mishnah, Pirkei Avot 5:2–3, trans. Sefaria community, Sefaria, accessed August 31, 2020, https://www.sefaria.org/Pirkei_Avot.5.2?ven=Sefaria _Community_Translation&lang=bi.

3. These types of covenantal agreements were contractual in nature and, like the suzerain-vassal treaties of the ancient Near East, were commonly made between individuals, tribes, and nations.

4. Babylonian Talmud, Yevamot 64b, in *The Wiley Blackwell Companion to Religion and Materiality*, ed. Vasudha Narayanan (New York: John Wiley and Sons, 2020), 76.

5. Babylonian Talmud, Rosh Hashanah 11a.

6. "Rashi on Genesis 25:19," in *Pentateuch with Rashi's Commentary*, trans. Abraham Silbermann and Morris Rosenbaum (Berkeley, CA: The University of California Press, 1929), 118.

7. The Passover holiday—which calls to remembrance the Israelites' exodus out of Egypt—is foundational to every part of Jewish life. In many ways, it is also foundational to all of Jewish spirituality and much of Jewish practice. Passover, or *Pesach* in Hebrew, literally means to "skip over," referring to the angel of death who skipped or "passed over" the Jewish households marked by the lambs' blood on their doorways. The seder is a ritual feast commemorating the Exodus from Egypt and falls in late March or April of the Jewish calendar.

8. When it comes to understanding some aspects of the rabbinical tradition that may seem fanciful, the point is not to necessarily agree literally but to make the correlation because it ties into a Jewish understanding of Messiah.

9. "Rashi on Genesis 22:5," trans. Rabbi Kalman Moore, in *Chumash and Rashi's Commentary with Integrated Translation and Explanatory Notes*, trans. Rabbi Binyamin S. Moore (Nanuet, NY: Feldheim Publishers, 2002), 216.

10. Beresheit Rabba 56:3, in Samuel Zinner, *The Gospel of Thomas* (London: The Matheson Trust, 2011), 136.

11. Jacob Nuesner, *Mekhilta Attributed to Rabbi Ishmael*, vol. 9, *A Theological Commentary to the Midrash* (Lanham, MD: University Press of America, 2001), 19.

12. "The Passover Lamb," Sar Shalom, April 7, 2016, https://rabbiyeshua.com/articles-by-kehilat/item/10-passover-lamb.

13. Pirkei DeRabbi Eliezer 31:10, trans. Gerald Friedlander (London: n.p., 1916), Sefaria, accessed August 1, 2020, https://www.sefaria.org/Pirkei_DeRabbi_Eliezer.31?lang=bi.

14. Pirkei DeRabbi Eliezer 31:13.

15. *Baal Haturim Chumash*, vol. 1, *Bereishis* (Brooklyn: Mesorah Publications, 1999), 253.

16. Pesikta Rabbati 37, Sefaria, accessed August 2, 2020, https://www.sefaria.org/Pesikta_Rabbati.37?lang=bi; Genesis 1:4, Sefaria, accessed August 2, 2020, https://www.sefaria.org/Genesis.1?lang=bi&aliyot=0.

17. Lamentations Rabbah 1:51, quoted in Raphael Patai, *The Messiah Texts* (Detroit: Wayne State University Press, 1998), 22.

18. Rev. W. Robertson Nicoll, *The Sermon Bible: 1 Peter–Revelation* (New York: Funk & Wagnalls Company, 1900), 365.

19. John Sailhamer, *The Pentateuch as Narrative: A Biblical-Theological Commentary* (Grand Rapids: Zondervan, 1992), 87.

Chapter 4: The Messiah, Son of Joseph and Judah

1. Obadiah ben Jacob Sforno, *Commentary on the Torah* (Brooklyn: Mesorah Publications, 1997), 198.

2. Sforno, *Sforno Commentary on Genesis*, Gen. 37:3, trans. Sefaria community, Sefaria, accessed August 2, 2020, https://www.sefaria.org/Sforno_on_Genesis.37.3?lang=bi.

3. "The first temple was destroyed because the Jewish people transgressed the three cardinal sins of idol worship, murder, and sexual immorality. However, during the second temple period the Jews engaged in Torah study and fulfilled the commandments! For what sin was it destroyed? For the sin of groundless hatred, i.e., hatred that is not a response to another's evil actions." Mordechai Becher, *Gateway to Judaism: The What, How, and Why of Jewish Life* (Brooklyn: Shaar Press, 2005), 241.

4. Bereishit Rabbah 84:8, trans. Sefaria community, Sefaria, accessed August 2, 2020, https://www.sefaria.org/Bereishit_Rabbah.84.8?ven=Sefaria_Community_Translation&lang=bi.

5. *Anamenov* in Greek.

6. Book of Jubilees 34:23–25, in *Apocrypha*, trans. R. H. Charles (London: n.p., 1917), Sefaria, accessed August 2, 2020, https://www.sefaria.org/Book_of_Jubilees.34.23-25?lang=bi.

7. "A demonic figure to whom the sin-laden scapegoat was sent on the Day of Atonement (Lev. 16:8, 10, 26). The Hebrew word has been traditionally understood as a phrase meaning 'the goat that escapes,' giving us the word 'scapegoat.'" Paul J. Achtemeier, *Harper's Bible Dictionary* (New York: Harper & Row, 1985), s.v. "Azazel," Logos Bible Software Edition.

8. The William Davidson Talmud, Shevuot 2b, Sefaria, accessed August 17, 2020, https://www.sefaria.org/Shevuot.2b?lang=bi.

9. *Midrash of Rabbi Alshich on the Torah*, trans. Eliyahu Munk (Brooklyn: Lammbda Publishers, 2000), 686.

10. The William Davidson Talmud, Yoma 39b, Sefaria, accessed August 2, 2020, https://www.sefaria.org/Yoma.39b?lang=bi.

11. A compulsory marriage of a widow to a brother of her deceased husband, with the purpose of creating offspring who carry on the name of the deceased brother.

12. *Midrash Rabbah: Sefer Bereishis, Genesis*, vol. 4, *Vayeishev-VaYechi*, Kleinman Edition (Brooklyn: Mesorah Publications, 2011), 85:1.

13. "In the Bible, the word *shalom* is most commonly used to refer to a *state of affairs*, one of well-being, tranquility, prosperity, and security, circumstances unblemished by any sort of defect. *Shalom* is a blessing, a manifestation of divine grace." Dr. Aviezer Ravitzky, "Shalom: Peace in Hebrew," in *Contemporary Jewish Religious Thought: Original Essays on Critical Concepts, Movements, and Beliefs*, ed. Arthur A. Cohen and Paul Mendes-Flohr (New York: Scribner, 1987), My Jewish Learning, https://www.myjewishlearning.com/article/shalom/.

14. In Targum Onkelos Genesis (Brooklyn: Metsudah Publications, 2009), Chapter 49, Sefaria, accessed August 2, 2020, https://www.sefaria.org/Onkelos_Genesis .49?lang=bi.

15. The Targum of Jonathan ben Uzziel, trans. J. W. Etheridge (London: Longman, 1862), Genesis 49, Sefaria, accessed August 18, 2020, https://www.sefaria.org /Targum_Jonathan_on_Genesis.49?lang=bi.

16. I am greatly indebted to Dr. Michael Rydelnik for first opening my eyes to aspects of this understanding.

17. The William Davidson Talmud, Shabbat 15a, Sefaria, accessed August 18, 2020, https://www.sefaria.org/Shabbat.15a?lang=bi.

18. Babylonian Talmud, Sanhedrin 4, 37a, in M. M. LeMann, *Jesus Before the Sanhedrim*, trans. Julius Magath (Nashville: Southern Methodist Publishing House, 1886), 28–30, emphasis in original.

19. Pirkei de-Rabbi Eliezer, *Pirkê de Rabbi Eliezer (The Chapters of Rabbi Eliezer, the Great): According to the Text of the Manuscript Belonging to Abraham Epstein of Vienna*, trans. Gerald Friedlander, 4th ed. (New York: Sepher-Hermon Press, 1981), 141.

20. The weekly celebration of Shabbat is the first holiday mentioned in the Bible. This word means "to rest" in Hebrew. It marks the weekly Sabbath, starting at sundown on Friday and ending at sundown on Saturday. God rested on the seventh day, so we do as He did. Rest from work is mandatory, allowing time to gather with family and recount your blessings. This rest also enables us to remember Him as Creator and Redeemer and thank Him for this life as well as eternal life. Shabbat can be looked upon as a weekly Passover in that we remember our redemption.

Chapter 5: The Messiah Revealed in Moses: His Good Birth

1. J. Paul Nyquist, *Prepare: Living Your Faith in an Increasingly Hostile Culture* (Chicago: Moody Press, 2015), chap. 4, e-book edition.

2. The William Davidson Talmud, Sotah 12b, Sefaria, accessed August 2, 2020, https://www.sefaria.org/Sotah.12b?lang=bi.

3. The William Davidson Talmud, Megillah 14a: 14, Sefaria, accessed August 2, 2020, https://www.sefaria.org/Megillah.14a.14?ven=William_Davidson _Edition_-_English&lang=bi.

4. Dr. Arnold G. Fruchtenbaum, "Christology: The Doctrine of Messiah," Ariel Ministries, accessed May 29, 2020, http://www.messianicassociation.org /ezine45-af-christology-messianic.htm.

Chapter 6: The Messiah, Greater Than Moses: His Divine Calling

1. Midrash Tanchuma, Shemot 14, Sefaria, accessed August 3, 2020, https://www .sefaria.org/Midrash_Tanchuma%2C_Shemot.14.4?lang=bi&with=all&lang2=en.

2. Exodus 28:1–43 and 39:1–31 provide detailed explanations of what God wanted priests to wear. There is no mention of shoes.

3. "Rashi on Gen. 44:18," in the *Pentateuch with Rashi's Commentary*, trans. M. Rosenbaum and A. M. Silbermann, Sefaria, accessed August 3, 2020, https://www.sefaria.org/Rashi_on_Genesis.44.18?lang=bi.

4. The William Davidson Talmud, Sanhedrin 98b, Sefaria, accessed August 3, 2020, https://www.sefaria.org/Sanhedrin.98b.14?lang=bi&with=all&lang2=en.

Chapter 7: The Messiah's and Moses' Miracles

1. See various references to "signs" in Exodus 4, 7, and 10.

2. *The Metsudah Chumash/Rashi: Shemot*, trans. Avrohom Davis (Ann Arbor, MI: University of Michigan Press, 1991), 105; Exodus 10:22.

Chapter 8: The Messiah, Our Passover

1. *The Koren Siddur: A Hebrew/English Prayerbook*, trans. Chief Rabbi Jonathan Sacks (New Milford, CT: Koren Publishers Jerusalem, 2009), 988.

2. There are many explicit Bible references to the shofar (a ram's horn), not just the Rosh Hashanah commandment. The shofar was blown at the giving of the Ten Commandments, the beginning of the Jubilee year, and by warriors in battle and musicians in the temple.

3. As mentioned earlier, the numerical value of the word "firstborn" (*bechor*) is 222. But "*the* firstborn," which has the definite article (*ha* in Hebrew), equals 227. *Bechor* (222) + *ha* (5) equals 227.

4. *Midrash Rabbah: Sefer Shemot, Genesis*, vol. 1, *Shemos-Beshalach*, Kleinman Edition (Brooklyn: Mesorah Publications, 2013), 19:7.

Chapter 9: The Messiah and Pentecost

1. *The Zohar*, Shemot 85b, trans. Harry Sperling and Maurice Simon, 5 vols. (London: Soncino Press, 1984), 3.258.

2. Pirkei Avot, *Mishnah Yomit by Dr. Joshua Kulp*, 5:1, Sefaria, accessed August 3, 2020, https://www.sefaria.org/Pirkei_Avot.5.1?ven=Mishnah_Yomit_by_Dr._Joshua_Kulp&lang=bi.

3. Pirket Avot, *Mishnah Yomit by Dr. Joshua Kulp*, 5:2–3, Sefaria, accessed August 3, 2020, https://www.sefaria.org/Pirkei_Avot.5.1?ven=Mishnah_Yomit_by_Dr._Joshua_Kulp&lang=bi.

4. The William Davidson Talmud, Bava Batra 14b, Sefaria, accessed August 3, 2020, https://www.sefaria.org/Bava_Batra.14b?lang=bi.

5. Martin McNamara, Kevin Cathcart, and Michael Maher, eds., *Targum Neofiti 1: Exodus*, vol.2, *The Aramaic Bible: The Targums*, trans. Martin McNamara, and *Targum Pseudo-Jonathan: Exodus*, trans. Michael Mahe (Wilmington, DE: Michael Glazier, 1994), 84.

Chapter 10: The Messiah in the Desert

1. Midrash Kohelet Rabbah 1:9:1, in the *Jerusalem Anthology*, trans. Rabbi Mike Feuer, Sefaria, accessed August 18, 2020, https://www.sefaria.org/Kohelet _Rabbah.1.9.1?lang=bi&with=all&lang2=en.
2. Midrash Kohelet Rabbah 1:9:1, Sefaria.
3. The William Davidson Talmud, Sukkah 51b, Sefaria, accessed August 18, 2020, https://www.sefaria.org/Sukkah.51b?lang=bi.
4. *The Book of Legends: The First Complete Translation of Sefer Ha-Aggadah*, trans. Hayim Nahman Bialik and Yehoshua Hana Ravnitzky (New York: Shocken Books, 1992), 396–97.
5. Iain D. Campbell, *Opening Up Matthew's Gospel*, Opening Up Commentary (Leominster, MA: Day One Publications, 2008), 36.
6. Mark Twain, *The Innocents Abroad, or The New Pilgrims' Progress* (Hartford, CT: American Publishing Company, 1879), 216–53.

Chapter 11: The Messiah in the Love Story of Ruth and Boaz

1. "Male relative who, according to various laws found in the Pentateuch, had the privilege or responsibility to act for a relative who was in trouble, danger, or need of vindication." *Baker's Evangelical Dictionary of Biblical Theology* (Grand Rapids, MI: Baker, 1996), Logos Software Edition.
2. *New World Encyclopedia*, s.v. "Shavuot," accessed August 18, 2020, https://www.newworldencyclopedia.org/entry/Shavuot.
3. Rabbi Yaakov Ibn Chaviv, *Ein Yaakov: The Ethical and Inspirational Teachings of the Talmud*, trans. Avraham Yaakov Finkel (Lanham, MD: Rowman and Littlefield Publishers, 1999), 110.
4. *Midrash Rabbah: The Five Megillos, Ruth*, vol. 1, Kleinman Edition (Brooklyn: Mesorah Publications, 2013), 49:1.
5. See also Mark 10:14; 12:34.
6. Bernhard Pick, "The Personality of Jesus in the Talmud," *The Monist* 20, no. 1 (January 1910): 29. Babylonian Talmud, Sanhedrin 43a.
7. *Midrash Rabbah: The Five Megillos*, Rabbah 49:1.
8. *Midrash Rabbah: The Five Megillos*, Rabbah 49:2.
9. Jon Courson, *Jon Courson's Application Commentary: Old Testament*, vol. 1 (Nashville, TN: Thomas Nelson, 2005), 820.

Chapter 12: The Messiah, Son of David

1. "Psalms (Tehilim)," Torah.org, https://torah.org/learning/basics-primer-torah -psalms/.
2. Many Psalms are used in Jewish liturgy. For example, Psalms 113–118 make up the *Hallel*, which is recited on various Jewish holidays. Seven psalms form the core of the *Kabbalat Shabbat* (Friday night service).

3. See, for example, Psalms 18:49; 22:11, 15–16; 27:12.

4. Hayim Nahman Bialik and Yehoshua Hana Ravnitzky, eds., *The Book of Legends, Sefer Ha-Aggadah*, trans. William G. Braude (New York: Schocken Books, 1992), 117.

5. Exodus Rabba 2:2 on Exodus 3:1, Sefaria, accessed August 4, 2020, https://www.sefaria.org/Shemot_Rabbah.2?lang=bi.

6. Charles H. Spurgeon, *Treasury of David*, Pubic Domain, e-Sword Bible Software edition.

ABOUT THE AUTHOR

RABBI JASON SOBEL is the founder of Fusion Global. This ministry seeks to bring people into the full inheritance of the faith by connecting treasures of the Old and the New. Rabbi Jason's voice is authentic, being raised in a Jewish home, and qualified by years of diligent academic work. His voice is prophetic—touched by the life of the Spirit. He has a radical testimony of his supernatural encounter with Yeshua-Jesus. This moment awakened him to his calling and destiny.

Rabbi Jason received his rabbinic ordination from the UMJC (Union of Messianic Jewish Congregations) in 2005. He has a BA in Jewish Studies (Moody) and an MA in Intercultural Studies (Southeastern Seminary). He is a sought-after speaker and has made multiple appearances on national television, including the Trinity Broadcasting Network, the Daystar Network, and the *Dr. Oz Show*. Rabbi Jason is the author of *Breakthrough: Living a Life That Overflows* and *Aligning with God's Appointed Times*; he is also the coauthor of the *New York Times* bestseller *The Rock, the Road, and the Rabbi* with Kathie Lee Gifford.

You can learn more at

Rabbisobel.com or fusionglobal.org

JOURNEY WITH ME, RABBI JASON SOBEL, TO THE HOLY LAND ISRAEL

TEXT:
"TOURS" to 33777

VISIT:
ROCKROADRABBITOURS.COM

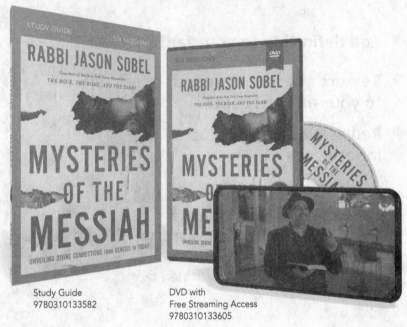